Life is an Audible

Life is an Audible

≈

The Jimmy Murray Story

by

Steve McWilliams
&
Jimmy Murray

HARROWOOD BOOKS

NEWTOWN SQUARE, PA

FIRST PRINTING: APRIL, 2019

10 9 8 7 6 5 4 3 2 1

LIBRARY OF CONGRESS CATALOGING-IN-PUBLICATION DATA

Names: McWilliams, Steve (Stephen Thomas), 1954- | Murray, Jimmy (Football manager) author.

Title: Life is an audible : the Jimmy Murray story / by Steve McWilliams, Jimmy Murray.

Description: Newtown Square, PA : Harrowood Books, [2018] | Includes bibliographical references and index.

Identifiers: LCCN 2018040844 | ISBN 9780915180639 (hardcover : alk. paper)

Subjects: LCSH: Murray, Jimmy (Football manager) | Football managers--United States--Biography. | Philadelphia Eagles (Football team)--History.

Classification: LCC GV939.M87 M49 2018 | DDC 796.332092 [B] --dc23

LC record available at https://lccn.loc.gov/2018040844

HARROWOOD BOOKS
NEWTOWN SQUARE, PA 19073-2297
610•353•5585
WWW.HARROWOOD.COM

PRINTED IN THE UNITED STATES OF AMERICA

I dedicate this book to my Family,
my Faith, and my Friends
AND for all of the great people in my life
who don't appear on these printed pages
but have had such a great impact on me.

CONTENTS

ILLUSTRATIONS

Foreword

by Ray Didinger

The night before the NFC Championship game, Jim Murray was in a TV studio in Philadelphia, sitting across from Tex Schramm, general manager of the Dallas Cowboys. In a matter of hours, their teams would meet at Veterans Stadium with the winner earning a ticket to Super Bowl XV.

The Eagles were underdogs even though they were playing at home. The Cowboys had dominated the Eagles for years. As the TV show was winding down, the host asked Murray, the Eagles general manager, what a win would mean for the long-suffering Philadelphia fans.

"Well, when we win tomorrow," Murray began.

He said it with a smile but he said it firmly, purposefully.

"When we win tomorrow...

That was the Philly in Jim Murray talking. That was the kid from 49th and Wyalusing, the kid who grew up in what he called "the Irish ghetto" of West Philadelphia. He called out the Dallas Cowboys and their general manager right there on live TV. It was bold but like most things in Jim's life, it came true.

The Eagles defeated the Cowboys, 20-7, on a frigid afternoon in South Philadelphia. When the game ended, Jim celebrated with the coaches and players but his thoughts, as always, were with the fans.

"It has been 20 years since the Eagles gave this city a championship," he said, referring to the 1960 team with Chuck Bednarik and Norm Van Brocklin that upset Vince Lombardi's Green Bay Packers for the title. "There are no words to describe how good this will make people feel. It's a beautiful thing."

Jim Murray talks like that, like a Hallmark card, all openness and warmth. He talks about growing up in a West Philadelphia row house as if it were Camelot with a front porch. He talks about hls Sundays spent in the East stands at Franklin Field cheering for the Eagles. His roots are deep and lasting.

He went away for awhile—working for a minor league baseball team in Atlanta then running a restaurant in Malibu—but he always knew he would come back to Philadelphia. When he joined the Eagles front office in 1969, it was with the idea that one day he would give the old gang from the upper deck something to cheer about. He did exactly that, helping coach Dick Vermeil construct the team that won the NFC title.

But Jim did more than win football games; he helped in the creation of the Eagles Fly for Leukemia charity and in the process took philanthropy to another level as co-founder of the Ronald McDonald House which started as one house in West Philadelphia and now boasts more than 360 facilities around the world providing housing for families with children undergoing treatment for various forms of cancer. Jim calls it "the power of sport for good."

"You don't forget your roots, you don't forget where you grew up," he said. "Where I grew up, we never locked our doors. The neighbors were there with the chicken soup and Irish stew, whatever you needed. People looked out for each other and that's what the Ronald McDonald House does.

"It's like a neighborhood under one roof. It's people pulling together. When you see what these families go through, it touches your heart. It's a place where hope and love are all that matter. This is the house that love built."

People often told Jim that his life was like a book. Well, now it is a book, a funny, fascinating and inspiring tale of a kid who followed an unlikely path from serving Mass at West Catholic High School to shaking hands with Pope John Paul II at the Vatican. Jim's story is about football, yes, but it is about so much more.

Acknowledgments

First and foremost, I need to thank my wonderful and blessed wife, Dianne, who has been with me through the good and the bad. How did I get so lucky to be married to such a wonderful person?

My children Karin, Amy, Jimmy, Brian, and John Paul…you've provided me with all the joy possible in this life. I thank each one of you.

To my parents, though in heaven, I pray that you know how grateful I am for all that you did to make me the person I grew into.

I want to acknowledge every person who was in some shape or form involved in the formation of the Ronald McDonald Houses, nationally and worldwide. Thank you to all of the house founders, those who built and staffed these miraculous places, and the millions of volunteers who help create miracles everyday.

Thanks for all of the thousands of families who have stayed in the houses and been touched by the idea of neighbors helping neighbors in a time of need. I've met so many brave and courageous people in the Ronald McDonald House journey and I have personally been enriched by meeting you and experiencing the profound love you demonstrate for your children and your families.

A shout out to all of the people in the world of sports who helped a naïve, little Philly kid go from street urchin to an NFL executive. How lucky can a guy get to meet great coaches, players, and employees and say you were part of professional sports.

To Don Tuckerman and Ed Rensi, who were there at the beginning of the Ronald journey. Great ideas only happen when great people respond to them.

To my biographer and writing partner Steve McWilliams...I feel like you've been living with me for...it's not possible...six years! I've driven you crazy and you revised the manuscript so many times that you threatened to have me committed. Steve, you've been a pal, a partner, a listening post and a true scholar. God Bless You.

To my Publisher, Paul Nigel Harris of Harrowood Books. You have proven to be a gift from God...you've had the patience of Job and the publishing skills to edit our manuscript and photos and then create this book which is a testament to your professionalism, stiff Brit upper-lip, and caring. "Press on Regardless" said your Dad...you did!

Lastly, to Dr. Audrey Evans, a humble Welsh doctor who changed the world with her vision, compassion, and commitment to the well-being of children.

If you should be mentioned here and you're not, Forgive Me. I could fill another book with thank you's but my memory and space prohibit anything other than a huge thank you for coming into my life.

Love,
Jimmy

Introduction

by Dick Vermeil

If this title is going to connect properly with any author planning to utilize it, it will be this guy, Mr. Jim Murray. Now why do I say this? Because Jim's daily routine and leadership responsibilities within his job description were not defined by the normal disciplines assigned to his title: General Manager of the Philadelphia Eagles. This guy worked in a very unique NFL huddle (office) 24 hours a day and very seldom came up to the line of scrimmage and went with the call he made in the huddle (in his office). No. He had to be flexible! He had to call an audible!

I first met Jim in early January 1976 when he and Leonard Tose, the owner of the Philadelphia Eagles, flew out to Southern California with the intent to hire a young UCLA football coach whose team they had just watched upset the number one team in the country, the Ohio State Buckeyes, coached by the legendary Woody Hayes. This quick decision following the ball game to fly out to Southern California and hire this coach they had never met was an audible made within minutes after the National TV broadcast. Leonard Tose impulsively makes the decision he is going out there and hire this guy, then assigns Jim Murray to get it organized so they can fly out to Beverly Hills and execute this plan! Consequently, Jim moves into his audible mode, calls all the right plays on the run to fulfill Mr. Tose's request, and here I am still living in Pennsylvania. Not a typically used process to hire an NFL Head Coach even in those days. Lucky for me!

What I didn't realize at the time is that this was Leonard Tose's way of doing things—act impulsively, assign Jimmy Murray the responsibilities, then sit back and support almost everything Jim was doing to get it done. Leonard was very passionate about "his" Eagles and equally compassionate about "their" fans, therefore I don't believe he ever said no to Jim in a request for financial support, even when it made the banks mad. I know for a fact that Jim had to push the envelope a number of times just to keep the locker room doors open. I'll never forget when local bank leaders showed up at training camp to define all the can-do's, cannot-do's to me as I sat there in my August training camp office—a very different experience for a young NFL head coach as well as for a young NFL administrator. Of course, I dropped the bank problems in Jimmy's lap and moved on to coach my football team. I can't even imagine how many audibles Jim called within this time period, from solving football administration problems, draft and contract negotiation situations, as well as overseeing the day-to-day routines that had to be attended to just to keep the team moving forward. Everyday may not have been a crisis solving day for us, but I do believe there were things going on that Jim would never allow me to get involved in —he didn't want me to be distracted by things that didn't make a difference in winning and losing. I would handle the football problems that were much more defined than the problems Jim would

be confronted with most of the time. I could define, delegate, organize a plan, attack a problem and, for the most part, get it done.
Not so easy for Jimmy. He often had to call an audible to confront
the new situation he was faced with as he walked into his office to
start his day.

Leonard Tose's own personality and ego had to be managed, nour-
ished and directed in a way that would slow the process of self-destruction down. Jimmy could do that, and I believe, after developing
a very personal friendship with Leonard, I could help as well. There
were times when Jim needed my help and I was close enough to at
least take some pressure off of Jim. When it came to Leonard's gambling problems there was nothing I could do, and not a lot Jimmy
could do either, but Jim was in there battling in an environment
that he had never really been exposed to in his Philly Irish Catholic
days. Working with lawyers, fighting with lawyers, working with
casinos, fighting casinos—but Jim hung tough. Maybe the toughest
time period in Jim's career in the NFL was when Leonard turned
on Jim, accusing him of many things that never really happened.
Someone always has to take the blame! I learned a lot in watching
Jim fight through the emotional pain created by someone you have
dedicated your integrity, professional career and loyal friendship to,
and who then turns on you and attempts to tear you down to cover
up their own personal shortcomings. Leonard did this to Jim, so I'm
curious to read how Jim handles this within the pages of this book.
Knowing Jim like I do, he will take the high road. This is one of the
many things Jimmy taught me: "Never carry a grudge." If anyone
ever had a good reason to fight back negatively, Jim certainly did.
I've often said to Jim, "you should have been the general manager

for the Pope!" And I meant it! Jim can bless, forgive and say a prayer for anyone. No qualifications needed. Just be human!

With all this said, or because of what has been said, our organization under Leonard Tose, Jim Murray, my staff and I were able to take one of the losingest NFL franchises at that time and win an NFC Championship in 1980, lose a Super Bowl two weeks later, then come back to make the playoffs in 1981. That is hard to do even today. We did not have a first- or second- or third-round pick in 1976 and 1977, and no first- or second-round pick in 1978. I sincerely believe if we would have had these draft choice opportunities, we would have won Super Bowl XV and gone back to compete for Super Bowl XVI. I bring these points up, not to make excuses for losing, but to emphasize what a great job Leonard and Jimmy did, irrespective of not doing things like some of the other very successful NFL teams were doing it at that time. Yes, Jim called a lot of audibles, but you know something—a winning percentage of them worked.

The other thing that Jim and Leonard Tose introduced me to was the community, the Philly fans, their passion, intensity and their loyalty. There may not be another city in the NFL that can match it. Part of the credit for this intensely loyal fan base can be directly given to Leonard Tose and Jimmy Murray. When it came to charity involvement, all the people needed to do was ask Leonard for help, and he would assign Jim to do everything they could do to make a significant contribution. Leonard always said, "there are givers and there are takers—far better to be a giver." Which he was—even at times when he didn't have the money to give. The whole Ronald

McDonald House story that originated here in Philadelphia in 1974, would not be what it is today without Leonard Tose's initial financial support and Jim Murray's emotional leadership. Without these two men, I don't think there would be 366 Ronald McDonald Houses in 42 countries, serving families in need. The underlying mechanics producing these positive results are no different than those the two of them used to rebuild the Eagles and later keep them here in town. Leonard providing the money, Jim calling the audibles! It is amazing how much you can accomplish if no one cares who gets the credit.

As I finish up this Introduction, there is one other topic I hope Jim Murray comments on before he pens his last page, that being the ALMOST sale of the Eagles franchise to Arizona. I have my thoughts, in that I was still communicating with Leonard Tose at that time, but I was not in the real "know" of what was going on. I believe Jimmy knows a lot more than has ever been written. With my limited insight, I still believe that Leonard Tose backed out on the sale when it came down to signing the agreements to let the team move to Arizona. He just could not do it! He cared more about the Eagles and their fans than the money he was about to receive. This one time, he did not hand it off to Jim Murray and ask him to call the audibles needed to get the job done. I also believe if it had ever come to this, it would have been the first time Jim would not do as instructed.

Enjoy the Read.

Preface

In 1981, while acting as the General Manager of the Philadelphia Eagles professional football team, I sat in a box with an impressive group of celebrities of the day. Among them were Phyllis George, the former Miss America turned sportscaster, James Michener, noted Pulitzer Prize winning author, and John Cardinal Krol, the Archbishop of Philadelphia. We, the Eagles, played the Oakland Raiders that year in Super Bowl XV, and to our collective disappointment, we lost. A woman, whom I didn't know, and an avid Eagles fan to boot, came up to the Cardinal after we lost. With attitude, she snapped at the Cardinal, "What happened? God didn't answer our prayers and I prayed very hard for us to win." Cardinal Krol, who was direct TV before there was "DirectTV," didn't miss a beat responding, "God always answers our prayers but sometimes he answers, *NO!!!*"

All of my life, God has answered my prayers. Sometimes with a yes, and sometimes as Cardinal Krol suggested, with a no. But I've always received an answer when I listened. I've been blessed in my life to have met thousands and thousands of great people, and I've been doubly blessed, by working in the world of sports. And if that's not enough, I received one of the biggest blessings I could have ever imagined, when I became one of the founders of the now famous Ronald McDonald House. The Ronald McDonald House is the miracle that has helped millions of ill children throughout the world. What never ceases to amaze me is how God has used me throughout my life. In everything that I've ever done, I see His purpose. Does that sound a bit egotistical or maybe downright crazy? But, at each step along my life's path, it feels as though God knew exactly what I needed. Then, He provided me with the necessary ingredients not only for my happiness, but for the good of others around me. At a young age, I became an altar boy and it changed my life. As a teen, I tried to become a priest and it changed my life. I married my wonderful wife Dianne, and it changed my life. I love sports and it changed my life. We had children and they changed my life. I had grandchildren and grandparenting changed my life. You see, I'm one of those crazy people who believes, there are no accidents in life. You'll find this theme repeated in this book.

Throughout my journey, many good people, some very famous (I'll name drop often before this book is through, I promise I will!) and some, not famous at all. So many fascinating people's paths have intersected mine. Some you will recognize immediately and some you'll only know by picking up this book. If you keep score, you might be surprised at the ones you don't know or have never heard of, outperforming the ones you do know. If I composed a report card, the humble people I've met have been the most influential in my life. One thing I've learned with certainty is that all of these people, famous and not so famous, came into my life for a reason. Some to help, some to test, some to love me, some to cause me pain, but always with a lesson to offer me. I repeat, there is a reason for everything and everyone. "There is a time for every purpose under heaven." I'm Irish. So what does that mean? The Irish perception of the world is unique. Traditionally, the Irish, and the Irish who surrounded me, didn't dwell on sadness or expect everything in life to be roses. My Irish parents and their parents and their parents' parents, possessed and passed on to me a deep faith in God. Like old farmers in the fields, they believed. At noon, they stopped, prayed, and just believed. No reason, no pay off. They simply held a plain, simple belief in the goodness of God's plan. I too, am a farmer of sorts. When I consider my past 80+ years, I see it analogous to working the fields. I've been in all of the fields, fertile and barren. My good fortune has allowed me to traverse a big portion of the planet. And like every other human being, the tough part of my journey came discovering my purpose. We all struggle with this, don't we? Isn't the search for meaning in our lives the thing which makes us human? Certainly dogs and cats are not asking themselves, "Who am I?" or "What does God want me to do?" Who knows? Maybe there are a few introspective house pets I've overlooked. But many of us— and I'm talking about us crazy believers—want to have an answer to the question, "How do we get back to God?"

I'm writing this book because of the great life given to me. Because of my good fortune and the positions I held, I still get called to speak frequently in public. I'm a waterfall of one liners, and as an Irishman, I love hearing and telling a good story. For many years, people have cajoled, encouraged, and challenged me to write a book about my experiences. As I mentioned earlier, I was one of the original founders of the Ronald McDonald House (RMH), an amazing charity dedicated to helping children and their families struggling with illness. Being involved in the Ronald McDonald House from its inception is one of the great sports stories of all time. Though it has never been covered on sports television, the launching and subsequent success of the RMH movement, represents to me the very best of what life is about. It's the best of what America is about and it is what all of the immigrants that came to this country wanted, an opportunity to dream. Martin Luther King's great speech, "I Have A Dream," is alive and well, and living in our hearts. My involvement in the RMH taught me with crystal clear clarity that sometimes, life is cut short for no sensible reason. Sometimes, we don't get to live the dreams we love or hope for. Sometimes we're forced to learn to live another dream that we didn't plan for. Sometimes, we have to find a new dream. And sometimes, we can lose our ability to dream, imagine, and hope. To use a football metaphor, there are some days when life sacks us and throws us on our backs with the force of a 300-pound lineman. I've been sacked plenty. Yet, there were so many days when God let me throw the perfect spiral to win the Super Bowl. I know the joy of making the team and the hurt of being cut. This is at the core of my purpose for writing this book. To write a book, I think that you need one of two things. One either has to think they have something to say or have done something so significant that their actions have proved that they do have something to say. I hope through my stories and experiences that I give you at least a few laughs and some great stories. Most importantly, I pray I give you some substantial food for thought. Without ego, I hope I might have something to say. Hopefully after 80+ years on this planet, I've picked up a few things. I pray too, that what I say helps you connect with the goodness that lives inside all of us.

On the surface, things in our lives don't always feel connected. Yet in the great mosaic of God's plan, we are all painters. All of us get to put the brush to the canvas of our life. You and I may not be Michelangelo, but while we're painting, we often don't have a clue about what we're doing, God helps us paint. If you trust, if you listen, you'll paint the portrait of what God wants in your life. This is a true story of how I allowed God to help me paint. And the biggest part of my painting is the Ronald McDonald House. I'm the most unlikely candidate to begin such a magnificent story. I wasn't born with extraordinary gifts but one day God tapped me on the shoulder and spoke to me through a total stranger. From that day forward, I painted. And today, I still paint. Because the painting doesn't stop until the day God calls us home.

I'll share this and many stories with you over the course of several chapters. But please don't just read this book. Pray this book. Catholic, Jew, Protestant, Buddhist, Hindu, Muslim, Atheist? Read on! I promise, there's something in this book for you. And what is the worst-case scenario? You'll laugh! I promise, you will laugh. At least, you'll chuckle as I do when I recognize the foibles and the greatness that lives in each of us. My sincere wish is that this book brings a flicker of hope to all who struggle with this thing we call life. Of all the virtues that exist, hope is what we need the most! Read on!

*And for those who question my credibility...yes...
James Michener was an Eagles fan!!!*

CHAPTER 1

An Unexpected Turn

*"There are no accidents... there is only
some purpose that we haven't yet understood."*

– DEEPAK CHOPRA

I will begin by repeating my favorite theme. There are no accidents in life! I'm sure that you've heard that before. It's not particularly profound. But the experiences that I am about to relay to you were profound and proved...there are no accidents in life! I'll start this book by describing one of the most significant events that happened in my life. Yes, meeting my wife Dianne is the most significant. (You think I'm stupid?) But another event altered my life in the most unexpected and remarkable way. Aside from my marriage and the birth of my children, my work with the worldwide Ronald McDonald Houses has been the most important part of my earthly journey. Sometimes in my life, God has tapped me on the shoulder and gently suggested that I take a certain path. But on this occasion, God smacked me in the face and then He led me down a road that I never imagined.

In 1971, I was the Director of Public Relations for the Philadelphia Eagles of the National Football League. I'll tell you later about how I came to work for the Eagles but for now, you only need to know that I held a relatively low level job with an NFL team. You see sometimes God chooses little people to carry out His big plans. Our tight end at the time was a handsome, Hollywood-type. Fred Hill was named All-American as a player for USC and we drafted him that same year. Soon after graduation, he married his high school sweetheart, the beautiful Fran Hill. Fred was a good player but not a great player. I hope he'll forgive me—but Fred, that was the scouting report! He was big, strong, and became the starting tight end for our team. That year was a great year for the Hills. With an NFL starting position, a professional contract to play football, what else could anyone want? However, things quickly changed when the Hills received the absolute worst news that young parents could receive. Their precious daughter, Kim, was diagnosed with leukemia. Keep in mind that in the 1970s the cure rate for childhood leukemia was extremely low. It was nowhere near today's rate. At that time, parents routinely faced the worst possible outcome. From this ultimate parental horror, one of Fred's neighbors, Stan Lane, came forth with an idea of hosting a team fashion show to raise some money for Kim Hill's treatment. Stan's efforts took the name "Eagles Fly For Leukemia." In hindsight, everyone was so excited about the idea that we failed to check out the grammatical error in the phrase, "Eagles Fly FOR Leukemia." Fortunately, everyone focused on the charitable nature of the venture and not the grammatical incorrectness.

I'm fairly sure no one wanted a charity "FOR Leukemia" but absolutely everyone's heart was in the right place.

Our owner, Leonard Tose, an extremely generous man, decided that the Philadelphia Eagles would support the first fundraiser of this new but fledgling effort. Stan and some friends decided to host a fashion show in South Jersey with the Eagles' players as models. There was a furrier involved and I vividly remember several huge linemen walking down the runway in fur coats. It had the look of a parade of Sasquatches. The event turned out to be a huge success, a sellout. The Eagles' brass, Tose, General Manager Pete Retzlaff, Coach Eddie Khayat, put their full weight behind the evening. At this time, I was only the lowly PR guy. I stood in the back, out of the way, in this very fancy venue with lots of beautiful people. I watched a great evening where everyone was happy, and we felt very good about ourselves because we were raising money for a good cause and for one of our own players. Stan Lane and his friends, along with the Eagles' wives, hit a fundraising home run and their efforts weren't wasted on Leonard Tose. Here's a side note of advice on event planning. If you want an event to be a success, get the wives to run it. I hope that doesn't smack of sexism but I find women to be smarter and better organized than men. Leonard loved big shows and he especially loved when everyone around him was happy. Sometime during the event, he summoned me over to his table.

He whispered in my ear, "Why don't you do your homework here and maybe we'll make this our team charity?"

Great idea, right? Leonard had many great ideas and then he would quickly lateral them to me. I was his executioner, so to speak. We were opening Veterans' Stadium that season and things within the organization were hectic. I wanted to help with the team's charity work but I wasn't sure I could give it my full attention. Let me give a more thorough description of Leonard Tose in a later chapter but for now just know that with Leonard came larger than life expectations with any idea he brainstormed. There's an old adage, "Success has many fathers, but bad ideas you own all by yourself." Once Leonard put his name on this charity, he looked at me and said, "You had better not screw things up!" He then instructed me to, "Go talk with some people and see how we can get involved!" That was my charge. Basically, he wanted me to go out on the streets, find out who needs money, then come back and find that money. AND by the way, make sure the Eagles look good doing so.

Both Fred Hill and Stan Lane mentioned the name of a pediatric oncologist at St. Christopher's Hospital for Children, located in North Philadelphia. St. Christopher's was the hospital where Kim Hill was being treated. I learned the name of her hematologist, Dr. Laurie Naiman. I flunked biology three times and I couldn't even pronounce hematologist, never mind finding one. And then, with that science background, I had to hold a conversation with one. (Laurie was a him with a deep voice and believe me, I spent some time looking for a her). St. Christopher's Hospital, an old, run-down building in disrepair, looked like a Depression-era tenement. While trying to find Dr. Naiman's office, I felt a bit anxious. After being commissioned by Leonard for my first big assignment, surely I had better come back to the office with a firm scouting report. I was still in my trial phase with the organization so I couldn't afford not to represent him well. One part of me was nervous and the other part of me felt like John Beresford Tipton. Few people remember the old 1960's television character from the show "The Millionaire." Each week on this show, "The Millionaire," a reclusive billionaire like Howard Hughes, decided on a worthy recipient of his million-dollar gift. John Beresford Tipton, who represented the millionaire, walked around awarding a million dollars to deserving people who were down on their luck. While waiting to speak with Dr. Naiman, I slipped into a meditation room just off the main corridor. I pray when I'm uneasy. It relaxes me and if I listen, God usually gives instructions like, "just go with it and have faith." It was a small, quiet, non-denominational room where families sat in quiet time. Absent were crosses, statues, bibles or Korans. I sat there and said a small prayer. I told God that I was scared and unsure of my mission. In all my conversations with God, I ask him to lead me to the place where I can do his work. Then I left the prayer room and walked upstairs to see Dr. Naiman. So began a chain of events that altered the course of my life… forever.

I walked into Dr. Naiman's office with my normal, chirpy, Irish attitude. Some people might call it my *schtick* but I fancy myself with the ability to put a smile on everyone's face. My first words were, "Hello Doc, I'm Jimmy Murray from the Philadelphia Eagles and I'm here to help. Through the Hill family we've identified St. Christopher's as our potential charity and you're our man, so what do you need?" Much to my surprise, he didn't match my top-of-the-morning enthusiasm. He pondered a long moment and then he said, in an almost somber tone, "Look at this place, it's falling down."

He pointed to cracked ceilings and peeling paint. I waited for him to give me a dollar amount...a price tag that I could take back to Leonard. I asked again, "what kind of contribution do you think makes sense?" He paused again. Then he said something that to this day remains one of the most unselfish and profound things that was ever spoken to me.

"Yes for sure, we need a lot. We need everything. But you know, there's someone with a greater need and I think you should go speak with her."

Talking to myself, I asked, *"Hey, wait a minute! I came up here to see if the Eagles could help out and now you're sending me away?"*

"There's a doctor down in South Philly...18th and Bainbridge... Children's Hospital...a wonderful oncologist...Dr. Audrey Evans. They're a little short and could really use some help. Go see her."

I stood drop-jaw stunned. I came bearing gifts and this guy sent me off to a competitor. In retrospect, Dr. J. Lawrence Naiman acted as selflessly as a human being can.

"Sure we need the money but..."

☙❧

How many times has that happened in the history of mankind? Someone is offered money and they give the gift away to someone in more need? Never happened in my life! I'm sure that his Board of Trustees would never forgive him if they had heard our conversation. It was an overpowering moment of deep human kindness. It was his wonderful attitude of "We're in this together to help children fight cancer," and the purity of his intentions that nailed me to the wall. I went back to the meditation room on the way out because I had to let God know I was paying attention. I sat in the room thinking to myself there was something bigger at work... something transcendent. I looked out a window and I saw a young teenage girl leaving the hospital with a baby. Something came over me. Looking at this girl made me reflect on the cruel irony of someone leaving with a new baby while I was there because of a couple fighting to help their baby.

I said to God, "Alright, you convinced me. I know you're working through me here and I'm going to ride the wave."

Next, I cruised right down to South Philly to see this prim and proper Welsh doctor, Audrey E. Evans, MD.

Again, I entered her office and gave the same effervescent greeting that I gave Dr. Naiman. "Hi, Doc! I'm Jimmy Murray, Philadelphia Eagles."

She barely looked up from her desk and said, "Yes? What can I do for you?"

Clearly she wasn't impressed.

Next I said, "Philadelphia Eagles, football team? NFL?"

"Who are they?"

"We're a football team. Admittedly, not a very good one but we're real big in the city."

"I don't know anything about that stuff," she said with disinterest.

"But we're on television every Sunday."

"I don't own a television."

Now I had two strikes against me and she had me on the ropes. I was reeling from the consecutive left jabs that she was landing. She had all the warmth of a nun about to crack your knuckles with a ruler. That was until the moment I said the magic words: "Doc, we have money."

Well, if she was one of the Seven Dwarfs, she wouldn't be Bashful. Then she proceeded to throw a list of demands at me longer than the Articles of Confederation. I couldn't turn off her spigot. Eventually she slowed to catch a breath. Sensing I was over my head, I suggested, "Why don't I take you to see our owner, my boss, Leonard Tose?" And I did just that.

❧

Before we met Leonard, I had to orient Dr. Evans to the subtleties of speaking with Leonard Tose.

"If we're to pitch your list, you have to be very specific, so pitch specific."

I promised Dr. Evans that I would "oil him up" before our meeting. I also warned her,

"He's got attention issues and he only listens in 20-second sound bites."

This, of course, preceded the 20-second sound bite and this was well before anyone every heard the initials "ADD." Eventually, Leonard became the poster boy for all disorders related to no attention.

She explained to me that she wanted money for these things she called "Life Islands." Life Islands were sterile environments where they had to put children who were going through chemotherapy. Good! That's easy, I thought. I can explain that quickly and Leonard will grasp that right away.

The meeting between Leonard and Dr. Evans was arranged and I escorted her to the Eagles' offices. We began the meeting by exchanging mild pleasantries. It was clear Dr. Evans wasn't one for small talk. She didn't care about football and worse, she didn't know or care about the celebrity of Leonard Tose. I began the meeting in a nervous stammering sort of way. I gave a stumbled summary of Dr. Evans career and research interest. Leonard, quickly losing focus, cut me off immediately. True to form, Leonard's attention didn't even last the full 20 seconds.

He said, "How much?

"$50,000," she said.

"How many rooms?

"Two."

"How much for the whole floor?"

"One million."

Without batting a eye, Leonard said, "Alright the Eagles pledge one million dollars and Jimmy Murray is in charge of getting it."

Immediately I reached for a pair of rosaries. What? I'm getting the money? What had I done to deserve such a fate? And just for some deeper context for those of you who weren't around in 1971, one million dollars was like what ten million is today. It was a tall, tall order. What was I supposed to do now? What's my next move? Actually what is your first move when you have to find a million dollars? Call John Beresford Tipton? In truth, I was not as frightened at the task of raising a million dollars as I'm pretending I was. Yes, a million dollar pledge was a big deal. But, at the risk of tooting my own horn, I've always had a knack for marketing. I can't say I'm gifted but I am proud of my small creative gifts.

The first thing that I did was I asked myself, "Who are we playing next?" We were scheduled to play the San Francisco 49ers in California. Both teams had poor records. It never mattered what our record was, we still drew a great television audience. Then I said to myself, "Maybe we can put a phone number at the bottom of the viewers' television screen at halftime?" I was laying the rails for future PBS fundraisers. In a small way you can thank me for those fundraising drives that interrupt your television viewing. The idea that I had was that we would advertise the need and then have people call in and give us a donation for Children's Hospital. We had a

captive audience and good ratings. I salivated with that combination. Raising this money was going to be a breeze! It was the good
old days before cell phones and computers. Telephone operation was
the sole monopoly of one company, Bell Telephone. Ma Bell was as
impenetrable as the Vatican but I knew people who knew people on
the inside. I contacted a few friends who promised me that they
could deliver 50 phones and install them at Eagles headquarters.
The day of reckoning approached. I had Stan Lane and his friends,
the players' wives, volunteers and the custodial staff report to our
offices. Everyone sat around this huge table shaped like a football. I
was in San Francisco with the team but I had a great set up. I even
hired a first class caterer knowing that if you want the best from
people, you better feed them. I was feeling that by the time we got
home, we'd have fifty thousand without breaking a sweat. But like
I say, God has a sense of humor. In the first half of the game, the
49ers shellacked the Eagles to the tune of 28-0. The phone number
flashed at halftime but the only calls the volunteers received back
in Philly were from the angry South Philly bookies. Anyone with
money on the Eagles was losing on the spread. I called Philly. "Murr,
these people calling are really pissed! You gotta do something!" The
wind completely died down. My sails went completely flat. Next, I
said, "Kill the phones, eat the food," and then I hung up. A new problem immediately surfaced. What to tell Leonard?

On the plane ride home, Leonard as usual was sitting in first class,
while I was in steerage. In fact, I should have let them pack me
away with the luggage.

"Get Jimmy Murray up here," Leonard bellowed.

I gingerly walk toward the front of the plane.

"How much did YOU raise with YOUR brilliant promotion?"

"$18.00."

"You got what?" he barked.

"Hey but the volunteers were happy, they had a good time, you know God has a…"

He screamed loud enough for the control tower to hear, "Don't give me that God crap!"

Leonard then proceeded to earn a Guinness Book of Records entry for the number of times someone dropped the "F-bomb" in a single sentence. At this point, I thought that he was going to fire me at 30,000 feet. It would be a completely new "Mile High" club. But his demeanor suddenly changed because—and I know this to be true— God was feeling my pain. He saw my worried, sweat-covered brow then quickly interceded.

Then Leonard said, "I hear you're having a party for the opening of Veterans' Stadium. I'll invite MY friends to YOUR party. Make the tickets $500 per couple." Leonard had lots of rich friends.

I protested, "Hey, that'll eliminates my friends."

Leonard downed a few more Gatorades (code for straight scotch) and called me up again.

"Make it a $1,000 per couple."

I said, "That eliminates my whole neighborhood."

The next week we held the party. It was getting close to Christmas and we were fortunate to get some great publicity from my friends at the local radio station, WIP.

Sheepishly, I asked Leonard, "Can we do a phone-a-thon from the station?" I still thought the phone pledging idea was brilliant. It was Christmas time, and people, even the South Philly gamblers, would be in better moods than they were at the halftime of the 49er's massacre. I had the players dress up in their jerseys and they schmoozed Leonard's friends like Fred Astaire dancing with Ginger Rodgers. Smoother than Japanese silk. It was perfection. At the end of the night, we tallied $88,000. At the last moment Leonard threw a few more bucks in the till which gave us $125,000 down payment on the million dollar pledge. I was jumping up and down like we won the NFL championship. I would keep my job and probably get a week off. Bursting with pride, I set out to hand over a large check to Dr. Evans.

The next day, I called Dr. Evans and asked her to meet me at the Blue Line. The Blue Line was a bar in the old Spectrum, which was the home of the Philadelphia Flyers and the 76ers. I had her check in my pocket and I most definitely felt like "The Millionaire." We sat down and I couldn't contain enthusiasm. I blurted out, "I've got a check for $125,000!"

Without missing a single beat, Dr. Evans shot back, "You know what else I need?"

You know what else I need? Doc, are you kidding? Couldn't we at least do a quick celebratory dance around the bar? Maybe toast a shot? We're in for a mil! What else could you possibly need? Her next words were the most powerful pitch ever spoken to me.

"Jimmy, do you have any idea what happens when parents get the diagnosis that their child has cancer? They don't hear what I say. I've just changed their lives and their family's lives forever. It destroys everyone. All of the other kids, now, no longer will have their parents' attention. There's a 75% divorce rate among parents who have to deal with or bury a cancer victim. Wouldn't it be nice if we could put all of these families with the same problem together in one place? They all have the same problem and they could support one another because they're the only ones who understand what it really feels like. They could talk, support and discuss chemo, radiation, hair loss, and just be there for one another. We need something like a YMCA."

At the moment, I did what I do best, open mouth insert foot.

I delivered a counter pitch. "Doc, where are you? You're in Philly! We're talking neighborhood here! We're all about the neighborhood. What you need is a house!" Like the house I grew up in on Brooklyn Street where everyone was family. It didn't matter, everyone on the block related or unrelated, chipped in when someone was down. When Mom got sick, ten people were there with chicken soup.

"Then get us a house!" she commanded me like Patton to an aide-de-camp! Okay, I'll get you a house! Under my breath I murmured,

"Where do I get you a house?" We left the bar, she with the check in hand, and I with an entirely new mountain to climb. Dr. Audrey Evans shared her mountain with me. She was climbing it in her work to help families with cancer. It became a mountain that I willingly agreed to climb with her.

A fashion show with Leonard...he passes to me...I follow the Hills to Saint Christopher's Hospital and I discover my life's work. From that moment on, my passion in life became the cause of helping children and parents deal with the worst diagnosis of all. I begin this book with this story only because I'd like to make the point that it almost didn't happen. If just one person is absent for just a split second, an entirely different story gets written. But the stars lined up perfectly. All of the players came together in this drama and each spoke their words on cue. Most importantly, it was no accident. I'm convinced and I believe with all of my heart that it's part of grand design. God puts us together so that we may help one another in the way He intended. I'll come back later to more tales of my McDonald's story. For the moment, the only thing you need to know is that the most important work of my life seems a mere accident. Unintentional? I think not!

CHAPTER 2

My Roots

"Your life is the dash between two events, birth–death."

– JIM MURRAY

The dash is our life. 1938– to the present. That little dash! See it? That's my dash. It stands between birth and death. The dash goes by too quickly. Think about it! Isn't that amazing? All of the years, all of the moments, represented by a tiny dash! One of the important activities in my life is attending funerals. I am fascinated by funerals. You can call me morbid if you like but I'm no longer getting up there in years. I've arrived! One of the consequences or benefits of living longer, depending on your mood, is that you have the opportunity to attend a lot of funerals. It's important I believe, to attend funerals. First, by attending I give my condolences, which is I think, the one time in life we can really be present to others. As Barbra Streisand said, "People who need people are the luckiest people in the world." I like to add to this that we're the luckiest when we realize that others need us, and then we respond with kindness. Second, I'm standing, I'm breathing, and I'm going to luncheon afterwards. So, I'm grateful that God grants me some more time on this earth to share with those I love so dearly. Sometimes, I stand in a cemetery and I gaze upon all of the gravestones. I see a name, I see the dates the person lived, and then I'll focus on the dash. Everyone who has ever lived on earth has a dash. The dash for each of us is packed with the happy moments, the sad, the triumphant, the tragic, a mixture of them all. Each dash is unique and I believe, part of God's mysterious plan for each of us. I think it's very important for us to reflect on and appreciate the dash. Another of my themes throughout this book is my gratitude for my dash.

My dash began on June 5, 1938, in Philadelphia, Pennsylvania. Actually, the dash was preceded by the marriage of my parents, James Murray and Mary Kelly. They met at a skating rink in a place called Woodside Park which, sadly, no longer exists. I never learned all the details of their courtship but they eventually took a great leap of faith and married with only fifteen dollars to their names. That alone tells you how much times have changed. Do you know anyone today that would make a life time commitment with only fifteen dollars? The only knowledge I have of the details is that they entered marriage totallly committed to one another with few requisites other than generously giving to one another. It was a time long ago when you married because you loved another person, and you gladly wanted to share in the ups and downs of life. Sounds simple, doesn't it? It is! My Dad was young, actually just a couple of years out of Roman Catholic High School, which is in the heart of center city Philadelphia. Leaving high school, he quickly went to work at the University of Pennsylvania. It turned into the only job he ever had. Dad worked in the Dining Services department and eventually he worked his way up to an administrative position. Mom had the very unglamorous, but oh so important job of having children. Today she would be called a "stay at home mom." Again, this was a very different time. Today, my mother would be frowned upon for such a decision but that was the world we lived in. My Mother, like so many mothers, was the postcard picture of love and sacrifice. I was an extremely fortunate son to be born to Mary and Jim. They had five children in rapid succession. Eleven months after me, came my Irish twin sister, Janie. My brother, Franny was born in 1940 shortly before World War II broke out and sister, Catherine or "Kay Kay" came home to us in 1942. Another sister, Mary, died at birth and that memory stays with me even today.

We lived on a tiny, narrow block called Brooklyn Street. It was so narrow that you could reach across the street with a broomstick and poke a neighbor in the belly. I still remember every family in every house on the street. Outside of our row house was a step that we shared with my grandfather, "Pop-Pop" Kelly, who lived right next door. If you were raised in Philadelphia or any other north-eastern cities, you're probably familiar with the steps. The shared step between row houses was the central location for all neighbor-hood activity. Gossip, bragging, life lessons, stories, all happened on the step. In those days, people, working class people, never trav-eled far from their surroundings because they were poor. They spent their spare time in the neighborhood, and on a warm summer night, we'd play stickball in the street and the adults would trade joys and sorrows on the steps outside their homes. Across the street lived my Aunt Peggy and Uncle Bill. Next to them was Mom-Mom Bittner, a wonderfully warm woman, who wasn't my real grandmother...but I called her "Mom-Mom." Next to her were Aunt Mae and Uncle Bob. Uncles Bill and Bob were old navy guys and the kind of characters that every kid remembers from their childhood. The day when they arrived home from serving in World War II seems like yesterday. They brought back treasures from around the world. To us kids, who never got off the street, it was a jaw-dropping time when they would hand us some artifact that they picked up in Italy or Germany. Aunt Mae was the first woman I ever smelled. Can you imagine? Isn't it funny how certain things get etched in your brain? The scent of Aunt Mae's perfume still floats in my memory. Everyday she dressed as if she was going to the prom. In addition to smelling good, Aunt Mae worked at a theater downtown taking tickets and when she left the house, you swore she had a date with Sinatra. My sister Catherine was named after my Aunt Catherine or 'Aunt Taddy," as we called her. She was married to my Uncle Jim, who was one of the funniest men I have ever met. He was quick and very witty. I'd like to think that I took a lot of my act from him. His mother and father were divorced, which was unheard of at that time. They called Uncle Jim, the "Bobby Breen of Woonsocket, Rhode Island." Bobby Breen was a popular singer in those years and Uncle Jim could really sing. He could sing, tell jokes, and keep a whole room entertained for an entire evening. In the daytime, he was a sportswriter for the International News

Service (INS). Aunt Taddy knew more about sports than anyone including Uncle Jim. They had no children but they both had a huge influence on my brother and sisters and I give them a lot of the credit for helping to form my character. They took us to bars, sporting events, and taught us poker—all wonderful character building activities. These types of relatives are absolutely crucial to any child's development. Besides treating us like their own children, without the financial burden of course, they were able to give us experiences that my parents couldn't afford. Aunt Taddy would ransom her life to get us the best seats at a football game or to make sure we ate in a "real" restaurant. One day, she came home with tickets to the Army-Navy game. She worked at the famous Bellevue-Stratford Hotel. Somehow, she managed to get four tickets. In those days, tickets to the Army-Navy game in Philadelphia were the toughest tickets in town to get your hands on. But we got to the game, thanks to Aunt Taddy. My younger brother Franny, Uncle Jim, Aunt Taddy, and myself sat in these beautiful seats in the old Memorial Stadium in South Philadelphia. Shortly after the game began my brother blabbed out loud, "Couldn't you have gotten us better seats, I can't see anything!" I cringed a bit. Across the aisle, I noticed then President Eisenhower sitting with his total entourage. I pointed to Eisenhower and then said to Franny, "I think you better shut up, there's the President of the United States, I think these ARE the good seats!" Even though I was embarrassed, Taddy didn't care. She got us to the biggest event of the year. She loved making us happy. After the game she took us "out to eat" which was like having a winning lottery ticket today. At that age, "going out to eat" was an event you were sure might only happen once in a lifetime. We went to a place called Cinella's, which to Franny and myself, looked like the Taj Mahal. The place had real tablecloths and their menus were larger than each of us. The waiter came over to our table and asked if we wanted an appetizer. I didn't know what an appetizer was but Franny, who ironically became a successful restaurateur, asked the waiter, "Do you have fruit cocktail?" The waiter replied, "Yes, we do." Franny followed with, "Is it fresh?" Franny unconsciously sounded like he was putting the waiter on the spot. I sensed the waiter thinking, "The nerve of this little 9-year-old questioning our food quality." Indignantly, the waiter responded, "We only serve the freshest fruit." Franny then followed with, "We only eat 'Delmonte' and my brother and me usually fight for the cherry." The waiter breathed a sigh of relief. I guess he realized Franny was a food critic from the newspaper! He came back to our table and made sure we each were served a cherry.

Good memories are like good smells, they never leave you. How did six of us fit in this tiny, two-bedroom house? Four kids packed into a 9 x 9 bedroom, yet no one complained. My parents, the eccentric aunts, the colorful uncles, all made for the happy beginning of my dash. If you are going to have a successful dash, you need to get out of the blocks with a great start like the one I had. Inside our tiny two bedroom house, we were poor but we were wealthy. There was a gold mine of love always available to us. Our parents were strict but always gentle. Outside the house, I had lots of freedom. At the risk of sounding like an old timer, it was a simpler time. We walked everywhere. We explored different neighborhoods throughout the city. No one owned cars so the major means of transportation was an eight-cent trolley ride, which amount I rarely had in my pocket. On Sundays, all the kids on my block would walk to Mass at Our Mother of Sorrows, which was a bit of a distance. After Mass, all of us piled in a trolley car for a ride home. A gang of kids would jump on the car and then leave me as the last to get on, with the only dime. I'd give the dime to the operator saying I was paying for everyone. It was my first foray into negotiating a deal, which would later come back to help me when I was sitting across from NFL agents.

᪥

I'd like to tell you that my younger years were full of athletic success and that I set lots of records. But I can only say that I was an all-star in the intense city games of stickball, half-ball, and box ball. I can tell you I led the league in fun. I enjoyed every moment of my youth. In actuality, my brother Franny was the athlete in the family. Later on, he played for the University of Pennsylvania's 150-lb. team. Some colleges used to have a team for smaller guys and if you did well sometimes they would put you in the big, varsity game. In the 1950s, Penn had a great quarterback named Hench Murray. One day a reporter was doing a story and he stopped in our neighborhood. He asked me if I was the brother of Hench Murray. I said, "No, I am the brother of 'Bench' Murray." My brother got very angry with me when the paper actually printed that. Ironically, Hench got hurt that season and Franny got in the game against Army. He made five first downs in the game on fear alone, making it one of the biggest days in Murray family sports history.

≈

One of the few uniforms that I did get to wear was that of an altar boy. I was small and dressed in a big white cassock, I looked like I had escaped from the nursery. Though I was undersized, I had a big voice. One day, a nun called on me for my first public speaking engagement. This event foreshadowed my love for the microphone. There had been a missionary bishop released from a Communist prison in Romania. He came to speak at our Church, probably raising money to fight other Communists. It was the exact same day that Franklin Roosevelt died. I remember Sister singling me out to give the welcoming address. I bellowed as loud as I could, "On behalf of all of the children of Our Mother of Sorrows, I welcome you home!" I felt ten feet tall with a voice like Karl Malden. I knew right then and there that I would never have a problem with talking in front of an audience. And the nuns! They were so pleased that they had a budding Fulton Sheen in their midst!

Oh the nuns! I remember all of the nuns who taught me in each of my eight years in elementary school. I can still rattle off their names, which for a person my age is a great mental accomplishment. Nuns had a big influence on me. In fact, I'll go so far as to say that besides my family, they get top billing in my story. Obedience, self-control, and personal hygiene were the markers of success in my education. It wasn't that I was a great or a well-behaved student, it was that I'm Irish. I was very adept at not getting caught and even more important, I was very neat and clean. Not so with one of my best friends, Bobby Ellis. Bobby could find trouble in an empty house. Parent-teacher meetings hadn't been discovered in the 1940s. Parents sent you to school and trusted the nuns. End of discussion. The nuns were the first "DI's" (Drill Instructors) I encountered. They actually made the Marine Corps a walk in the park. If you were caught by the nuns doing something wrong, there were three fairly routine consequences, though each increased with intensity. For a minor infraction, you lost your recess time and sat in with your hands folded while all of your classmates made noise outside the window. For the

Bobby Ellis and me...my best friend from childhood

repeat offender the sentence was a whole after-school session, with lots of writing. I have to admit I spent too many afternoons with writer's cramp writing five hundred times, "I must not talk in class." Hey, that might be a way to shut me up today at many of my long winded speaking engagements. Show me to a blackboard with chalk and I'd probably shut up. However, the last most severe punishment of Catholic school was the dreaded, "Report to the convent on Saturday" directive. For those of us whom the nuns deemed incorrigible, the torture of last resort was cleaning the convent on your day off. My best friend Bobby

Ellis was one such dangerous criminal and imprisoned regularly on weekends. Bobby reported bright and early one cold Saturday in January. One of the sisters instructed Bobby to clean the basement of the convent. Bobby headed downstairs with a broom and dust pan. Soon he was transfixed by contents of this secret cave. Nuns were mysteries to us. We were convinced that they came from another world. Discovering later that they were ordinary humans was a great disappointment. Once out of sight from the nuns, Bobby took to exploring the deep cave that lay before him. One thing Bobby discovered was that due to the large number of nuns in residence, food was purchased in large,

1948 - My brother Franny's first communion picture. Every Catholic kid has one of these.

oversized cans. Bobby couldn't resist a prank if his life depended on it. What could be next for Bobby after the convent? The rack of the Inquisition? A public hanging? Bobby proceeded to peel all of the labels from all of the cans stored in the basement, throwing the entire culinary routine of the Immaculate Heart of Mary sisters into chaos for the next several weeks. From that point forward, Bobby's gift to the Sisters was fourteen straight nights of corned beef hash. "Surprise!" The good news is that Bobby and I have remained best friends to this day—his son, Robbie, is a wonderful sports talk radio host at Philadelphia's WIP and my Godson. I still laugh out loud when I think of Bobby as a kid.

❧

Sister St. Terese was my first grade teacher and my first crush. I wasn't sure if that was a sin so I kept the crush to myself. She was dark skinned and strikingly beautiful. At seven, she took my breath away. I would sit for hours just staring at her, wishing that we would live happily ever after. I'm sure every young boy has a similar episode at some time in their schooling, but only I fell hard for a nun in a black and white habit. Later in life, I met Sister St. Terese and guess what? She was still as beautiful as the day I first laid eyes on her. And she remained a nun. I remember one day sitting in class day dreaming, how did a dark-skinned woman make it to the convent? Being an Irish neighborhood, the standard was white skinned that burned when the temperature got above 40 degrees. A dark-skinned nun was an anomaly. After her death, I attended her funeral and met her nephew, who told me her life story. She had a twin sister and they were born in South America and then they were adopted and raised in the United States. It turned out that her twin sister drank and loved horses. This meant that I was probably in love with the sister. But the impact of Sister St. Terese on me was so strong that I stayed in touch with her until she died. Up until the end of her life, she visited with my family and played with my grandchildren. Sister St. Terese was simply a wonderful woman and, to this day, I still visit her gravesite. She demonstrates the good fortune that the nuns brought to us.

I feel bad that nuns get a bad rap today. I hear people talk about nuns as if they were alien creatures. In many circles that have been discredited, or worse, considered irrelevant and unnecessary. Certainly, in hindsight, they have been the butt of many jokes in adult Catholic circles. Religious life in general has been devalued, but the nuns who taught me were selfless people. These good women gave up their lives to educate urchin kids like me and I will always be grateful for their sacrifice. Anyone who lived through that time must admit that they were grossly underpaid for their contribution to our communities. Many nuns were the stereotypical stern taskmasters, but I can call up instantaneously in my mind thousands of fond memories of genuinely kind, sweet women. Like the time when Sister Mary Ursula taught grammar by putting on a play with all her students playing the parts of speech. I was dressed as the exclamation point! Surprise, surprise! The strict sisters got me ready for my later stint in the Marines. Instantaneous response to a command! That was the Marine way and the nuns prepared me well. Of course, it was during World War II, and Catholicism, like all religion, flourishes during wartime. In my memory, it was the best of times. If life was a "Monopoly" board, our street wouldn't have made the cheapest street on the board—we were five hundred miles away from "Park Place"—and nobody would ever put a hotel on our spot. Still, it was the singularly greatest place in the world to grow up.

ʄ+

One memory in particular speaks volumes about my sainted parents. It was Christmas, 1946. For months leading up to my favorite day of the year, I had stared into the window of Wolf's Cycle Shop. My greedy eyes coveted a shiny, black Schwinn beauty, complete with matching white saddle bags. Imagine my face pressed against the window each day. I was like Ralphie in the *Christmas Story*. If you know the movie, it's the scene where Ralphie is hoping for an air rifle. Like Ralphie's mother, my mother knew my Schwinn obsession. She set out to get the bike for me. She sacrificed everything she had to put a bike under the Christmas tree. Day by day for a year, she stashed pennies in a jar so that she could purchase a bike. Christmas morning arrived. Lionel trains, tinseled tree, excitement everywhere. We waited on the stairs with our eyes closed. It was as rich of a Christmas scene as there ever was. Slowly I stepped downstairs. There, in the living room stood a Schwinn bicycle. But not the one I had been eyeing in the window. I had coveted a Ferrari but Mom bought the Volkswagen. It was the difference between Rita Hayworth and Little Orphan Annie. There was nothing close to a resemblance of my desire. True, it was a Schwinn but not the black Schwinn with the saddle bags. The long look of disappointment that hung on my face couldn't fool a mother. I broke her heart. In her eyes, she failed. It was probably one of the toughest memories I carry. Since that moment, there hasn't been one day in my life that I haven't regretted that moment. My mother never said another word about the incident. I, though, realizing what I had done, continued to apologize almost daily to her until the day of her passing. She sacrificed, and sadly, it took a mistake of that proportion to teach me the most important lesson of all. Expectation versus reality. Her love for me was so strong that in that one instant, I understood the depth of love a parent feels for her children. She would have gladly cut off her left arm for me and I would have said, "I'm a righty." So go the lessons of childhood. Later, I would experience the same deep, emotional bond over and over again with my own children and through my experiences at the Ronald McDonald House. Parental love is the greatest gift we are given. A red Schwinn bike taught me that in a split second.

Subtract a few mistakes like that Christmas and my upbringing was a seamless garment. Every human emotion was present and accessible to me. We weren't perfect but we were rich beyond measure. Life was a sacrament! I don't mean that in a corny sense but I experienced something sacred. I mean that as honestly and sincerely as I can express. We were aware that good times and the bad times were shared together. Most importantly we understood that God gave us each other as gifts. We were a team and we could handle anything that life threw at us, but more importantly we lived in a house where joy resided. Today as I travel around, I see many young parents. I often get the sense that parents are trying too hard to give their children everything that they wanted but maybe didn't get. Today, there's no debate on which Schwinn to buy. It's the norm that every kid deserves the best that money can buy. AND there's no need for pennies saved. Many of us can buy whatever we want when we want with money we don't have. I've often said that today, *we're overpaying our children but short changing them at the same time.* We're so busy that we think things we buy can substitute for moments well spent. My parents? My house? My youth? If it was the Monopoly game, I lived on Boardwalk!

CHAPTER 3

My Formation

*"You have to do your own growing
no matter how tall your grandfather was."*

-Abraham Lincoln

When I was in 7th Grade, our teacher Sister Patrice announced that we would be performing the Nativity as a Christmas pageant for our parents and the whole school. Like most of the other boys in the class, I fancied myself as Joseph, a tall and rugged carpenter. Unfortunately, Sister Patrice, as director, went for type casting. When the cast list was posted I was totally overlooked. This wasn't difficult since I was the shortest kid in the class. The role of Joseph went to a tall, Hollywood-handsome looking kid named Joseph, who by the way, wore the best bathrobe during the auditions. That was another early lesson for me. Clothes can make the man and your wardrobe closet can make a big difference in your career. After the sting of the initial hurt began to die down, I continued down the page. How about a shepherd? "Maybe I'm a shepherd." Nope! "Angel? Wise man? I could carry some frankincense and my nickname is Murr. Innkeeper?" No? The list of male characters grew shorter and shorter and still I hadn't made the cut. Finally! At the very bottom of the list, my name finally appeared. The Passover of all Passovers! The 3rd Innkeeper? What? Are you serious? Not Innkeeper one or two? No, Number three! The very last person cast! It was official. Sister Patrice had no eye for talent. The third innkeeper was all I was going to get and with a guaranteed sold out auditorium, I consoled myself that at least, I was still in the play.

The opening night of a one-performance run finally arrived. Mary and Joseph, weary after their donkey ride from Jerusalem, finally got to the Inn. Knock, knock, knock! "Can we have a room?" The first Innkeeper, on cue, angrily dismisses the couple with a, "There's no room at the Inn!" Mary and Joseph look a little further for a vacancy sign and Joseph knocked loudly on a second door. "There's no room here!" declared the second Innkeeper. Finally they arrived at Murray's Inn. Knock, knock! I opened the door and against everyone's expectations I said in a loud, clear, confident voice, "Sure, come on in, we've got plenty of room!" Sister Patrice turned fire-engine red. Veins popped from her temples! From offstage, she whispered an angry stage whisper to me through clenched teeth. "Are you crazy?" By then, I had the audience laughing and in a good mood. Everyone seemed relieved that Mary and Joseph would have lodging. I was feeling fairly good about my kind deed but Sister Patrice wouldn't stand for it. She said louder, almost in earshot of the front row, "No, the line is 'NO ROOM HERE!'" I shot back in as a defiant a voice as a 7th grader could muster, "I'm sorry, he's St. Joseph to me and I'm not turning him away!" It was my first and one of my only acts of civil disobedience and my very first job as a maitre'd. It foreshadowed my long career of trying to keep peace and build consensus in difficult circumstances. I wonder what a psychiatrist would say about this event. There's some developmental theme here if I look hard enough. Maybe I developed an overactive sense to please. But, play or no play, I led with my heart. My stage career was nipped in the bud in that one instant. I'm fairly sure Sister Patrice never recovered either. I'm positive she gave up directing theater. In fact later, she had heart troubles

Opening day 1952 at Augustinian Academy.
Mom (Mary Kelly Murray), Dad (James Murray), Taddy and me.
Was I ever that skinny?

and I'm sure the doctors, nurses, and anyone present at the play traced some of her health problems back to me. However, the incident revealed that at an early age, I knew that I was different. I couldn't turn off what had been part of my upbringing. You never turned people away, especially when they're on defense. Mary and Joseph were in a tough spot, as many others are, and we encounter many of these folks every day of our lives. Mary was having a baby and I was confident we had at the very least, a nice efficiency. Little things like that continued to happen to me in my formative years. Events seemed to manufacture themselves and present opportunities to me, where my gifts became apparent, at least to myself. I was a happy-go-lucky kid with the gift of gab. I relished in making others feel welcomed and wanted. At that time in my life, sometime during my 8th grade year, I met a priest, Father Lunney. He had come to speak at our school and for some reason his words seemed to be aimed straight at me. He was an Augustinian priest and he told us the story of Saint Augustine. You may or may not know the story of Saint Augustine. The short version is this. He lived a wild, licentious life, much to the chagrin of his mother, Saint Monica. His life was one of the all-time, feel good movies with the "bad boy makes good" theme. After years of unrestrained immorality and lots of prayers by his poor mother, Augustine converted to Catholicism. The rest, as they say, is history. He became a bishop, and then one of the premier thinkers of the Catholic Church and the Western World. Depending on what side of the religious fence you stand, St. Augustine could be considered a saint or an idiot. What Father Lunney emphasized, and what I tuned into as an impressionable teenager, was Augustine's restless searching. There was another side to my outgoing Irishness, and it was something akin to Augustine's searching. Incongruous with my outgoing easiness, I possessed a deep desire to probe the deep mysteries of life. Soon after meeting Father Lunney, I became interested in pursuing a priestly vocation, and after 8th grade I enrolled in a high school seminary in Staten Island, New York. Naively or stupidly, I would bypass Augustine's licentious phase, skip the fun and go right for the conversion. It was the 1950s and believe it or not, there was no shortage of other teenage boys con-

1953 - Augustinian Academy, Staten Island, NY with Father William Lunney

templating the same idea. I realize that this seems odd to people today, but I arrived to a packed seminary. Imagine a large building filled to the brim with adolescents wanting to imitate a 4th Century saint. Yes indeed, times have changed!

ès

Ultimately, the seminary idea didn't bear priestly fruit from my tree. I was kicked out! Believe it or not, this was a very sad chapter in my life. I could devote a whole book just to my Catholicism, but I'll give the abridged version so that you understand why I believe so strongly that everything in life is connected. As it says in Ecclesiastes, there is a time to every purpose under heaven. I was 16 years old and I was facing a big, life-changing decision. Should I or should I not become a priest? You may think that 16 years of age was very young for a kid to make that kind of momentous choice. But as I said, I was a serious kid, looking for serious answers. In 1952, I arrived in Staten Island, New York, where I would attend the Augustinian high school seminary. It wasn't really a seminary but basically a very strict, religious high school. Students were to discern whether or not they believed they were called to the priesthood. The downside of the place was that as a teenager, I found myself in living quarters with little to no recreation. There weren't too many outlets for pent-up teen angst. One day, a few of us decided that it would be fun to sneak out and see a movie. A group of us made escape plans and, lo and behold, we were caught. Afterwards, the rector concocted the worst punishment possible for anyone living away from home. His decision was that we were not allowed to go home for Thanksgiving. I've never been tortured by water boarding but I'm sure it is more pleasant than being left in a seminary away from home during a major holiday. I was stuck! Even worse? At the time, Perry Como's hit, "There's No Place Like Home For The Holidays," was a huge hit and it played every five minutes of our waking hours. Three classmates and myself decided that lockdown in Shawshank prison wasn't an option. Slattery, Walsh, Dunn, and Murray, the Four Irish Tenors of Staten Island, decided that we would challenge the gods one more time, sneak out and go to Manhattan for a big night on the town. There was a Christmas show in Radio City Music Hall that would provide us some much needed relief from solitary confinement. The plan began when we threw our winter coats out of a window. The escape included attending evening prayer, and after prayer when the lights were out, we'd jump from a window, claim our coats, and catch the Staten Island Ferry to our Manhattan paradise. The moment of truth arrived. We stood by the window and each of us had a "come to me Jesus, help me resist temptation" moment. We changed our minds and decided to skip the idea and go to bed. Upon awakening the following morning, we found ourselves in bigger trouble than if we had actually carried out the plot. The authorities, in particular the Rector, found the coats below the window and assumed we had indeed left the premises for an evening of debauchery. From that moment on, we experienced a frightening interrogation from the rector Father Barney Hubbard. It matched the "Manchurian Candidate" in intensity and fear. Each of us was called individually. They isolated us individually in what was an imitation Communist Chinese prison cell. It was clear Father Hubbard hadn't read up on, nor did he care about the concept of due process. As 11th graders in 1952, we weren't eligible for a trial by our peers. With a simple pointed index finger, we were shown the door. Kicked out! No money, no ride, no tearful good byes. It was a simple, "Get out!" Just like that! Standing outside shivering in the cold, we mulled over our next move. Dunn suggested we go to his house in Brooklyn. So we did. Upon arrival, his mother and grandmother let us know that we were not welcome to hide out in Brooklyn. All the time, I was wondering, *How am I going to tell my parents I was kicked out of the seminary?* We left Brooklyn and then we traveled all the way to Eddie Walsh's house in the Bronx.

Do we look like desperadoes who should be kept out of a seminary?
FRONT ROW, left to right: Gene Taylor, Jimmy Murray, ???, Eddie Walsh
BEHIND MY HEAD: Paul Dunn; With hands on Eddie Walsh's shoulders: Bill Klisham
(My apologies to old chums whose names escape me...it's been a few years lads!)

"Why were you kicked out?" asked Eddie's mother.

"We didn't do a thing, honest!"

"Sure! Sure you didn't do a thing now did you?" asked Mrs. Walsh in her brogue. "I don't believe a word of your nonsense."

Even worse, Mrs. Walsh wasn't interested in quickly adopting me, either. Now, unsupported in the Bronx, the decision to tell my parents was closing in on me. I had to call my father. "Dad, I was kicked out of school," I mumbled sheepishly.

"Nice Christmas present," he responded in a barely audible tone.

He didn't raise his voice but those simple three words cut right to my core. I felt awful. I had let him down for the first time in my life. We never talked about it again. I returned home and picked up my junior year at West Catholic High School for Boys, in West Philadelphia. So, if I didn't get kicked out of the seminary unjustly, the rest of my life would have turned out completely differently. Who knows, "Charlie, Charlie, I could have been a contender, could have been Pope, instead I got a one way ticket back to Palookaville!" But that one moment, the finger pointing exit from Staten Island changed everything. I returned to Philadelphia and the rest of my life continued in a new, unplanned direction. Looking back on that time, I've often wondered what might have happened if I followed through and became a priest. I still think I had the gifts that make a good priest. In hindsight, I actually don't think my young age at the time had anything to do with discernment. I was, then, and still am, trying to figure out what I want to be when I grow up.

I finished high school in a routinely uneventful way. Any teenager will tell you, transferring into a school in the middle of the year is not easy. Coming home and trying to fit at the halfway point of my junior year was difficult. Friendships and patterns in the school were well established. But still, I managed to reconnect with some of my old pals. One buddy, John Martino drove a spanking new convertible. That was special. It is every boy's dream to cruise through your town's streets in a convertible. I was lucky enough to have that fantasy indulged. John and a few of us would cruise the streets of West Philadelphia looking for the girls we would marry. Shortly after I returned home, I met my first high school sweetheart, Maureen Haskell. We referred to Maureen as Reenie. We dated for two years which included my first years of college. Reenie was one of the nicest people I had ever known. Certainly if a crazy turn of events didn't happen, who knows, we might have been married. However, I still had the priesthood in the back of my mind and this presented a quandary. Should I go back to the seminary or marry Reenie? Fortunately, Reenie helped make the decision for me. A friend of mine from the seminary, Paul Dunn, was getting married and I was in the wedding party. The wedding took place in Floral Park, New York. Paul had asked me to be an usher, along with another fellow seminarian, Dan Seminitis (who we called "Disease" for short). Both Paul and his finance were in a Romeo and Juliet type situation. Their families were against the marriage because of their young ages. The wedding went off without a hitch but at the event I had a fall off your horse moment. I was struck by a lightening bolt in the person of Nancy Fuller. Nancy was in the wedding party as well. We hit it off immediately. Quickly our romance swelled into a tsunami of love. After the wedding, I felt awful. My love for Reenie was true and, I thought as a person of high moral character, I had to come clean and tell her the truth about Nancy. When I mustered up the courage to break the news to Reenie, I couldn't get out a word before she confessed, "I'm in love with Jim Reuling." Jim Reuling was my best friend. How did that happen? I was crushed! The girl I loved was going to marry my best friend? How could she go behind my back when I was going behind hers? Double standards can sure hurt. But I took the news rather well. If I couldn't marry Reenie, I was happy that she would be marrying my best friend. To add insult to injury, my relationship with Nancy went nowhere. It was a short lived crush. Nancy wasn't as interested as I thought. A few years later, Villanova's basketball team received a bid from the NIT (this was when the NIT was a big deal). I was the sports editor for the school paper, so I was able to go to New York for a few days. For old times sake, I decided to look up Nancy Fuller. I was able to locate her working at an ad agency and I decided to give her a call.

"Nance, Jimmy Murray!

"I just got married!" she exclaimed.

Silence on my end. Disappointment only needs a few seconds to be heard.

"It such a coincidence you called," she continued.

"My mother was just talking about you and she was saying that she hoped you might drop by in the future.," She said with great sincerity, "Maybe we should get together."

"How big is your husband?" I inquired.

"For my sister!" she insisted.

Later Nancy, her sister and I met for lunch. I forget the sister's name but it was a pleasant time but it was clear that her sister didn't have the same feelings for me that I thought Nancy once had. After lunch the sister departed, and Nancy and I walked down

Madison Ave. arm in arm, that is, platonic arm and arm. In a few moments at an intersection, a bus stopped. Nancy's father, a Ralph Kramden sort of fellow, was driving the bus. He opened the door and screamed, "Hey pal, she's a married woman!" Platonic or not, I had some explaining to do. Then he smiled knowing from the look on my face that he had me on the hook.

He laughingly said, "Don't forget to come see her mother! She's got a sister you know!"

I didn't have to nerve to tell him about the lunch. I struck out all around. Back at Villanova I got busy and forgot all about Nancy and her sister. And Reenie? She's still married to Jim. They remain my best friends. What's the point of all of this? Another one of those crazy moments that at the time seemed insignificant became a big turning point in my life. A few changes in the weather or calendar, I could have ended up with Reenie or Nancy or her sister and my life travels a completely different arc. There are no accidents!

                                          ରଞ

After high school, I attended Villanova University just outside of Philadelphia. Even though I had an opportunity to attend the University of Pennsylvania free of charge because of my Dad's employment there, I passed. You think it would be a no brainer decision for anyone to attend an Ivy League school tuition free? That would make sense. But not for me! Though the Augustinian order didn't want me in their seminary, I still chose them by attending their University. Even after I was booted from their seminary, I talked my mother into borrowing the annual $400 tuition fee. Why did I have this unexplainable attraction? Who knows? But I began the four years that would entirely transform my heart and my future.

No one has ever accused me of being a great student. I wasn't the worst, but God knows, I wasn't going to break into the top 50%. I managed to grind my way through the coursework. It was during my time at Villanova that I met the man who profoundly influenced my life. Arthur Leo Mahan came into my world while I was in my junior year. Next to my own father, Artie impacted my development more than anyone. I'll give a more detailed account of my mentor in the next chapter because "Artie," as he was called, deserves his own spotlight. Both Villanova and Artie teamed up to change me. Artie used to say to me, "A college education is what you have after you forget all of the facts." He was spot on right about that. Villanova and for the most part, Artie, formed a great part of me, and prepared me for my career and the rest of my life. He taught me that life, like the story of mine, is an audible. Whenever I seemed to be taking myself or life too seriously, Artie would counsel me by saying, "Life's an audible, Jimmy." Let me conclude this chapter by saying that I left college at 21 with a rock solid foundation built on blocks from my parents and Artie. Schooled in common sense and love, I was ready to make my mark in this world.

CHAPTER 4

First Chances

"Coincidence is God's way of remaining anonymous."

— ALBERT EINSTEIN

My real life or let's say, my professional life, got its jumpstart from hitchhiking. Today, hitchhiking is out of fashion. In my day, hitchhiking was everyman's Ph.D. As I mentioned before, I had a free ride to the University of Pennsylvania but no, I decided to pass up an exclusive Ivy League education, and decided to go to Villanova University instead. For the next four years I would hitchhike to suburban Villanova rather than attend the more convenient and exclusive Penn. My predisposition or mild obsession with the Order of St. Augustine caused much dismay in our household. Despite my father's disapproving head shaking, I went off to the Main Line to continue my infatuation with the Augustinian friars. I quickly found out that when I stuck out my thumb, people would stop their cars and let me climb in. Furthermore once in the car, if I was polite, they would take me anywhere that I needed to go. It happened every day. I'd stick my thumb out with a big happy smiling face and eventually, someone would pull over and say, "I don't usually pick people up but you looked like a nice, friendly kid." Of course, I was a nice kid, I understood the hitchhiker's guide to universal transportation: smile and show lots of teeth. A big smile relaxed people enough to convince them to stop. Mostly it was the men who would stop. Inevitably, they would want to share their life's found wisdom with a wide-eyed college freshman. The typical conversation on a ride to school started with, "Kid, let me tell you something, you don't understand that today…" And I'd jump in and finish with, "Yeah, it's the greatest time of my life!" One driver chuckled and asked, "How did you know I was going to say that?" Because I knew instinctively that it was the greatest time of my life. From day one of consciousness, I knew I had a great life. Family, friends, neighbors…I was blessed.

After graduating from college (which by the way, surprised the entire population of Philadelphia and the tri-state area), I quickly found out that no one seemed to care that my services were available in the marketplace. I learned like every other college graduate learns, the world wasn't waiting for me with open arms. And, like most young people, I had no idea what I wanted to be when I grew up. If I had to pick something, it was to be just like my mentor, Artie Mahan. To me, he had the best job of all, Athletic Director at a university. How could I do better than to emulate Artie? One day, I asked him, "Artie, how did you do it, how do you get into sports?" For being the best mentor of all time, he gave me a dumb answer.

"I don't know, you just go over and ask," he said.

Ask who? I didn't know who was going to be that first person but at least I had some direction. "Go over and ask." So here was my life plan. Get into sports and be like Artie. It wasn't Dale Carnegie textbook, but I did have vision if nothing else. That summer I spent a great deal at the track, playing the ponies. My parents would let me know their feelings with, "Way too much time at the track!" Horse racing has and always will be one of my addictions. Now that I was a college graduate, I was hitchhiking daily to Delaware Park in Wilmington, with my newly minted Bachelor's of Arts degree. One day I walked through our front door excited after hitting the Trifecta, and my father asked me, "So what are you going to do now, really?"

"I'm getting into baseball!" I announced with absolute certainty.

I said it with such confidence that I sounded as if I already had the job.

My father smiled and gave me a surprised grin. "Really, baseball?"

I had zero prospects but loads of confidence. I was going to succeed. I was sure of it because I had my plan. A really bad plan!

≈❦

The Philadelphia Phillies, my home town team, had a General Manager by the name of John Quinn. Quinn had been the General Manager of the old Milwaukee Braves before coming to Philadelphia and he was relatively new to the city. My thinking was this (follow this if you can). John Quinn was an Irish Catholic. I'm an Irish

Catholic. If I could get in front of John Quinn and tell him I'm Irish Catholic, I could have a job with the Phillies. Not exactly a Wharton School of Business strategy. But I believed. Now, not only was my idea faulty, my timing was atrocious. It was winter and it was the off-season. Quinn traveled back to his home in Milwaukee for the holidays. Christmas Day arrived and I had no job and no means of support, AND I had developed an even bigger appetite for horserac-ing! My second father, Artie Mahan, called me on the phone and said in his thick Bostonian accent, "There's a guy at the Phillies, a personnel guy by the name of Jaahn Aagh-den (John Ogden)...I spoke with him and he'll see you. He lives in Oxford, Pa."

Oxford was and still is a small rural area on the Pennsylvania/Mary-land border. It's about a 45-mile ride from Philadelphia, which was my starting point. As any hitchhiker knows, to travel that long a distance you need lots of luck. And Lady Luck has always smiled down on me regularly. I had barely stuck out my thumb and the first car that came down the road stopped. I joyously jumped in. The driver was a bible salesman. He wore a cowboy hat, boots, and one of those thin western ties. He was as "country" as Hank Williams. He didn't contain an ounce of Philly. I was sure he was a thousand miles from home in Arkansas. He immediately informed me that he sold bibles and that he had just sold $600 in bibles to an old Baptist woman. He was bursting with extreme feeling for God's hand in the sale. "I'm full of the Lord!" he exclaimed and asked me if I was full of the Lord. Of course, I was. I had a ride.

"One good deed deserves another, the hand of the Lord done took care of me, and I'm going to done take care of you, right to that front door in Oxford," he exclaimed with a twang. "Now what do you think of that?"

We spent a good hour trading bibles quotes. Normally, Catholics don't stand up well to Protestant scrutiny on biblical knowledge, but I had remembered enough from my Catholic school days to impress even a bible salesman. He took me to Oxford and dropped me off at a farmhouse smack in the middle of nowhere. There, in a driveway in front of this house, sat three new Ford Thunderbirds. In its heyday, the Thunderbird was the precursor of today's Mercedes. John Ogden had three! I knocked on the door and the tall, handsome Ogden answered. He was a dead ringer for John Wayne. He invited me in to the house which looked like a scene right out of a John Ford movie, down to his Maureen O'Hara wife cooking up some grub on the old wood stove. After some forced small talk, Ogden demonstrated immediately that he was a no-nonsense, get-to-the-point-immediately, kind of guy.

"What do you want to do?" he asked with authority.

"To get a job in baseball," I said.

"There's only sixteen worth having."

"What's that mean?" I asked.

"GM's, General Managers."

"I'll sweep the floor," I pledged.

"New York and Houston are starting up expansion clubs. That's where you want to get to."

With that comment, he picked up a scrapbook from a coffee table and begins, "I've had every job there is in baseball. Player, Hall of Famer in Triple A. Done all there is to do in baseball. So I'm telling you, aim big!"

I replied, "You've got three T-Birds parked out there. That looks awfully good to me. I want to get in front of John Quinn."

To my great surprise, he agreed and said, "I can and will do that for you."

The process had begun. My plan was put in motion. Maybe it wasn't such a bad plan after all. Mano a mano with John Quinn! I might still be able to use the Irish Catholic bit! Two weeks later on a cold January day, I received a letter in the mail from John Ogden. In the envelope was a letter to Ogden from a place called the "Florida Baseball Placement Bureau, Inc." The letter read, "Thank you, Mr. Ogden for these prospects." The letter gave an overview of a school in Florida. At the end, there was a P.S. "We have a business managers' course." Ogden had circled the last line in red pen, and noted in bold letters, "Start here! It's a baseball school run by friend of mine Lou Handley. IF you go down there, you'll at least get a job in Class D ball." That sounded to me like a promise.

Immediately after reading the letter, I picked up a phone and dialed long distance to Florida. A man by the name of Max Whitman answered the phone. Whitman seemed excited to talk to an actual live prospect from Philadelphia. Maybe I was the first. At least at that moment, it sure seemed like I was.

"I've never been to Florida," I told him.

"Don't worry. We'll hold a spot for you. Be here by Wednesday with $300 and you're in." He spoke as if he was trying to put me behind the wheel of a used Chevy.

Now, I had a big decision to make. First, I didn't have $300. I would have to ask Mary Kelly, my sainted but frugal mom by getting down on bended knee. Of course, it was always better to go to Mom than to Dad. I tried softening my mother by telling her that the Florida Baseball Placement Bureau was indeed, "a rare opportunity and I am extremely fortunate to be invited to such a prestigious baseball academy." And then I added the topper, "it won't be long before I am a baseball executive!" Though oozing skepticism, my mom agreed to talk with Bob Carlin, our local loan shark. Neighbors would call Bob Carlin in times of extreme financial duress. Like any great mom who loves her children, Mary Kelly borrowed the $600 for my tuition for my executive training. (She also borrowed a few extra because a mother also knows that I would need to eat once I got to Florida). For the short term, Mom covered the $32.09 per month loan payment until Major League Baseball recognized my genius.

ॐ

If I was going to have to use my thumb to get to Florida, there was no way that I was going to make it in time for the first day of the class. I departed on a Monday on a Greyhound bus, packed tight

with retirees and mostly older women, going south to avoid the
cold Philly winter. The old folks, packed like sardines, left only a
sliver of a seat on a wheel well for me to sit. Twenty-four hours sitting on a wheel well? Just an hour outside of Philly I had charmed
all of the old ladies on the bus to the point where they all wanted
to adopt this chirpy leprechaun. They argued with one another
about who would "scooch over to make room for Jimmy." The bus
ride made me fairly sure that if I couldn't make it in baseball, I
could always find a job as a cabana boy on the Florida beaches. The
next day, we arrived in Florida, and it was heaven! Getting off the
bus and taking in the warm Florida sun after leaving the cold
Northeast is exactly what heaven is. I stepped off the bus in Tampa
and found my way to the Florida Baseball Placement Bureau, Inc.
The sound of that name just seemed to resonate executive job. Was
I ever in for a shock? The school was an old, run down army barracks. I'm talking old, old army barracks. World War II? No. World
War I? No, try going back to the Spanish-American war. But, at
least there were palm trees!

The first person I met was Mitchell Mick. Mitchell was the General
Manager of the St. Petersburg Yankees but he moonlighted as an
instructor at the "Bureau". All of the employees of the Bureau
moonlighted. Mitchell's presence was a good sign that real baseball
people were employed at the school. There were five guys enrolled
in my class. The first kid I met was Teddy Sorliss. Teddy was from
New York and Teddy was a New Yorker's New Yorker. Tall, dark,
handsome, and brash, Teddy had tried for every job in major league

baseball. Teddy was only in Florida to pass the time until his ticket to the big-time got punched. There were two very quiet Canadian kids in the class and two local Florida kids. I suppose everyone had the same dream and each of us was anxious to make that first connection to the big leagues. For the most part, the classes were uneventful. I don't believe I learned much. I think the most important lesson I took away was how to fold my arms. All sports executives must perfect the art of folding arms. Folding arms while watching professional athletes practice or perform is a sure sign that you know something. Even today, I can stand somewhere with my arms folded and people still think I know something. Try it. Stand somewhere with your arms folded. You'll look like an expert and people will naturally gravitate to you and ask you questions. It has been the foundation of my career.

Quickly, Teddy Sorliss emerged as the person most likely to succeed in the baseball business. Teddy had all the mannerisms and moxie of a budding star. We would travel on our free days to all of the training camps of Florida spring training, trying to impress major league executives that we were ready, executive material. Several weeks into the training, Teddy got a call and a subsequent interview from the Louisville Colonels. At that news, my eyes began to widen. I started to think that maybe this Florida jaunt was going to work out after all. If Teddy could get a job and I know Teddy, then it was reasonable to assume, I'd probably get a job too. I went to the airport to see Teddy off to Kentucky. Though I probably wasn't going to see him again, I wanted him to keep the name Jimmy Murray in his memory bank. "Remember, Teddy, don't forget us no names down here when you get that big job!" Three days later, Teddy returned to the school with his head down. He slowly shuffled back into the barracks one evening.

"Teddy, what happened?" I asked in a tone both disappointed but supportive.

Teddy quietly explained, "Well I got there, I got the interview. It was the GM and he was an old Irish guy. He asked me what job I wanted. I told him I wanted the chair. 'The chair?' he asked. I said, "Yeah, I'm gonna be commissioner."

I told you, Teddy was full of confidence. And, Teddy had lots of nerve if he didn't have anything else. And, he believed every word he spoke. However, the GM thought Teddy needed some more seasoning and a good dose of humility. So, Teddy returned to us. I was thrilled to have Teddy back even though my short cut to executive privilege had been derailed momentarily.

Soon after Teddy's return, he was contacted by the Tampa Tarps, their local minor league team. The Tarps were owned by a Miami millionaire by the name of Bill McDonald. Their GM was a guy by the name of Joe Ryan, who happened to be a dead ringer for the actor Jim Backus. Lou Handley, the school director, told me to go over with Teddy and "maybe you can get an interview too!" Again, Lady Luck followed me religiously. I was able to score an interview with Joe Ryan. Ryan's interview consisted of putting a piece of paper in front of me. He handed me a pencil and then, instructed me to "put down all of your qualifications for the job on that paper." I quickly blurted out, "I've got all the qualifications but the job!" It was a classic chicken or egg problem. You couldn't get the qualifications without the experience and you couldn't get the experience without the qualifications. But thankfully, Ryan took a liking to me.

"Are you ever going to be in Miami?" he asked.

"Sure," I said, even though I had no plans to travel south to Miami, although I had always wanted to gamble at Hialeah Park.

"We might have something with our other team, the Miami Marlins, " he said.

My time at the FBPB, Inc. was coming to an end and I had nothing better to do than to travel to Miami for an interview. I had a friend from Philly, Larry Levitt, who owned a bar in Miami, so I knew I would have a place to stay for a few days. I figured that in a worst case scenario, I could extend my time in Florida for a few days, interview, and then hitchhike home, finally surrendering the baseball experiment. I was down to $8 in my pocket when I called my brother Franny, who was in the Navy and stationed in Pensacola. I talked my brother into meeting me and taking a few days respite with me in Miami Beach. By this time, even Teddy became pessimistic about his future in baseball and packed up and went home. As I walked into the school's office to say my goodbyes, Lou Handley told me, "Hey, Jim, I'd love to hire you here at the school."

"We're offering an umpire's course," he said. "You can work here in our offices and take the umpire's course."

Great! an umpire's course? A great reason to stay. However, the $8 screaming in my pocket sobered me. I had a tough decision. Should I give up and go home? Should I stay around for awhile and see what happens? Quickly, I decided to go home. Again, God was watching out for me and in this moment, unbeknownst to me, He was redirecting my baseball career.

⁊❧

Mitchell Mick said goodbye to me and threw me a curve, "By the way, there's a job opening in Leesburg. It's on the way home. Wouldn't hurt to stop and check it out. You want to talk to a guy by the name of Bill Hurlong, the owner."

Next, I was standing on the road, thumbing it back to Philadelphia via Leesburg, Florida. The first truck that approached me stopped. It was a huge orange tractor trailer carrying what else? Oranges to Ocala! The driver pulled over and screamed to me to climb up in the cab. Almost as soon as we introduced ourselves, I saw a sign for Leesburg and screamed, "That's my stop, I've got to get out!" He jammed on the brakes and I jumped from the truck. When I hit the ground and dusted myself off, I had landed right in front of Hurlong Dodge. I had a suitcase and I was feeling a bit sloppy for a first introduction. I noticed a Catholic Church about a block away. I went into the Church figuring I'd change into a fresh shirt and say a good luck Hail Mary. I'd stash my things in the back pew, then go back and meet Mr. Hurlong. I freshened up and went back and entered the Dodge dealership where I thought I found Mr. Hurlong.

"Mr. Hurlong, I'm Jim Murray and I understand you have an opening with your baseball team," I said as I extended my hand.

He responded, "No son, I don't. But my brother does."

"And where might your brother be?" I asked.

"Oh, he's about 5 miles down the road a piece. He's in the produce business and I'm in the car business."

I made my way back to the Church where I realized I had to sneak in and sneak out with my suitcase. However, there was a priest watering the flowers in front of the entrance to the Church. Being comfortable around priests, I gave him a big, "Hi, Father!" He looked at my college ring and asked, "What's the ring?"

"Villanova University."

He had recognized the name."What was your major?" he quizzed.

"English. But I'm trying to get a job in baseball."

"Why aren't you teaching?" he asked disapprovingly.

"Why aren't you a Jesuit?" I shot back.

He laughed. That line loosened him up enough to drive me five miles to the other Hurlong on the opposite side of town. After driving me to my destination, we shook hands and departed old friends. Within moments of entering Hurlong Produce Company, I had nailed the interview. Mr. Hurlong was either desperate or impressed. With the excitement of a new Dad, he offered me a job as the General Manager of the Leesburg Class D team. John Ogden's prophecy echoed, "If you go to the Florida Baseball Placement Bureau, you'll get a job in Class D." I was so excited I didn't even ask Mr. Hurlong what was the name of the team.

Finally I did. "What's the name of the team?"

"The Phillies," he said.

Wow, I was now the General Manager of the Leesburg Phillies Class D baseball team with a real baseball park. I told Mr. Hurlong that I accepted his offer and that I would return in one week to begin the job. I wanted to go home and share the good news with Mom and Dad. Certainly, I needed to relieve my mother's anxiety generated from the $32.09 monthly payment to Bob Carlin. Back on the road hitchhiking to Philly, I got the dream ride of all dream rides. The first car that stopped was going all the way to Philadelphia. The driver was a Van Johnson look-a-like. Van Johnson was a heartthrob movie actor in the 1940s. This guy told me he was just coming home from Cuba where he was a mercenary for Fidel Castro. It was my first meeting with a military gun for hire. And he fit the stereotype to a tee. He was driving back to Philly to visit his mother. So I guess he was a mercenary with a tender side. Not only did he provide me with free transportation but he paid for all the gas, tolls and my meals. And an added bonus, he liked to eat well. I imagined after a revolution in Cuba you can get hungry for some home cooking. I didn't ask but I'm sure there weren't too many steak dinners camping on the outskirts of Havana with Fidel. But, what great luck! I was a General Manager. I was eating steak dinners and getting a ride to my front door. How long would this run of good fortune last? Turned out to be not very long.

I arrived home from Florida and immediately after kissing my mother, she informed me there was a special delivery letter waiting for me. The letter was from Joe Ryan of the Miami Marlins. It read: "Dear Jim, we've decided to hire you for the San Juan Marlins."

The Miami team was re-locating to Puerto Rico so back in Philly I went from no job to two jobs. To complicate my decision, the San Juan team would be playing Triple-A ball, which was a big step better than Class D. I had never been on a plane, and though geography wasn't my strong suit, I somehow remembered that to get to San Juan, you had to fly over water. It was an opportunity that would jump start my career but I had to turn down Mr. Ryan.

"I've got a job with the Leesburg Phillies," I said sheepishly to Ryan. I still had my sense of loyalty and I felt I had to keep my word to Mr. Hurlong.

"Are you kidding?" Ryan screamed. "You've got a chance to be in Triple-A? Call Leesburg and tell them that you've been offered a job in Triple-A."

"I can't do that," I said.

"Of course you can. He'll know the difference between D and A!"

I called Mr. Hurlong in Leesburg.

"Mr. Hurlong," I began, "I've been offered a job with the San Juan Marlins."

Suddenly, he sounded very excited for me.

"That's great! Triple-A! That's fantastic," sounding like he was jumping through the phone.

"But," I interrupted, "I've already committed to you."

He countered with, "Look Jimmy, I've got this sportscaster in town here who really wants the job badly, and to be entirely honest, you'd be doing me a huge favor if you'd back out and go to San Juan."

Really? Problem solved! My integrity intact! The planets aligned perfectly. I would just have to get over my fear of flying and get this baseball career moving. Not so fast. The next day Joe Ryan called again.

"We've got a team in Virginia," he began. "Marshall Fox runs the team. He had some heart problems in the last few days. We want you to go there and help out. You're going be the ticket manager. Be there tomorrow."

So that means no plane ride over the ocean? I was thrilled.

Marshall Fox proved to be one of the truly great teachers who ever mentored me. He was a character extraordinaire. Marshall got me ready for so many things in life and he set the table for me professionally. "Foxy"—as he was affectionately known—could sell anything, including second base with someone standing on it.

During my first conversation on the phone with him he barked, "You gotta car? You need a car and we need you right away!"

I had no car and no time to make other arrangements. Fortunately, my Uncle Bob lent me his 1954 Ford with bad tires. This made driving more dangerous than the plane trip to San Juan. Little did I know that this slight change in plans would radically alter the course of my life.

$$\approx$$

Several weeks passed and it was clear that I had arrived in a strange country. Not a state but a country. Unlike the one in which I grew up. Virginia was the "South." I had scant knowledge of its history or customs. On top of that, I had little to no experience with racial issues. Suddenly I found myself deep in the heart of Dixie. I was a Philly kid, naïve or stupid or a little of both. I assumed the whole world was one, big friendly place. The very first person I encountered during our first game was an African-American fan from Washington, DC. He was visiting and as I stood at a fence watching the game, he confronted me about the visible lack of integration on the field.

"Hey, notice that everyone on the field is white? Ain't there no black players in Virginia?" he asked.

I was taken back, momentarily caught off guard. He was right. I didn't have a response. It wasn't something I had thought about but suddenly here it was, plain as the nose on my face. I was forced to confront my own ignorance of one of the major social issues of my time. Quickly, I became aware that we did have a substantial black fan base paying to come watch our team but there were no familiar players for whom they could cheer. Immediately after this incident, I committed to righting the situation as best I could as a lowly ticket manager. First, I tried hiring the local minority residents to work in stadium jobs. Soon, I found myself bringing all of my energy to forging racial progress in Virginia. Though it was just a tiny effort, it had an immediate effect. One elderly gentleman, who I hired to handle the press gate, stopped me one day and warned me, "Mr. Murray, it took us 100 years to walk and talk slow. Don't you go thinking you can rush things. I suggest you get familiar first with the landscape and just take your time." This was my baptism into the segregated world. But a silver lining? I saw a glimpse into how sport could be used to address social issues and possibly create positive change. Even though I was mjust a ticket manager, Marshall taught me that the "only good ballpark is a full ballpark." I called this the "Marshall Law." And, that meant black, white, brown, and anyone else who could cough up a couple of bucks for admission. It was marketing boot camp under Marshall, and to his credit, he applauded any efforts I was taking to make the franchise more equitable in terms of race.

I was doing a good job in Portsmouth when Joe Ryan called me again. "I need you to go to Charleston, West Virginia and help out with a Marlins game."

The Marlins, who were now relocating to Charleston, were playing the Jersey City Giants in an exhibition game and Ryan wanted me to handle all the stadium and ticket logistics. I flew to Charleston and began a new crash marketing plan. First, I rented a room in a boarding house. Then, I began papering the town with flyers, as well as taking out ads in every town paper that existed. I rented the ballpark, hired staff, and handled all of the game pre-sales. For several weeks I was busier than one-armed paper hanger but increasingly, I was proving my worth to the organization. Ryan and owner Bill McDonald finally showed up, and they couldn't help but be impressed by my progress and youthful leadership. Fortunately, they were not aware that I was keeping several thousand dollars of ticket sales in a shoe box under my bed at the boarding house. Had they known, I'm sure my stock would have quickly nosedived. I had never met Bill McDonald. He was a dapper older fellow who made a ton of money in the trailer business, and he loved to dabble in sports. On his second day in town, he came walking into the stadium with pro golfer Sam Snead and a gorgeous blonde on his arm, one of the most beautiful that I had ever seen.

I introduced myself in a big, friendly way, "Hi, Mr. McDonald, Jim Murray…Hi, Mrs. McDonald, Mr. Snead!"

"This is my niece from Montana," he said quickly correcting me.

Sam Snead looked at me and burst out laughing.

"You'll learn, kid," he smiled as he walked away. I would. I would encounter that very same scene many times in my future. Wealthy owners and their hobbies, disguised as their niece from Butte or Poughkeepsie. Even though I came up short with my owner's greeting, he was sufficiently impressed that I would keep my spot in his organization.

The Vietnam War was in its early stages and while I was happily climbing the ladder in my chosen profession, I felt a pang of patriotism. So in the spur of the moment, I decided to join the Marine Reserves. I had been heavily influenced by a local priest and family friend who was a famous Marine chaplain and war hero during World War II. Father Francis "Foxhole" Kelly was a frequent guest in our house and I had grown up listening to his tales of Marine Corps life and his wartime achievements. Father Kelly was a decorated veteran and a role model for hundreds of kids in my neighborhood. He had the double whammy of admiration for being both a priest and a military hero. Father Kelly impressed me so much that I decided to join the Marines, hoping I could walk in his shoes.

∾❤

Again it was one of my ill-advised game plans. How do I join the Reserves, while keeping my hand in baseball. And, if called, serve. I visited a local recruiter and he asked me if I was sure I wanted to be a Marine.

"You have a college degree and a job. Why would you join the Marines?" he asked with a quizzical look.

I said emphatically, "I want to do my patriotic duty."

"You're going to hate us," he said with a grin.

Mr. McDonald gave me leave from the organization in order to attend boot camp at Parris Island, South Carolina. I was officially in the Marine Corps and immediately, because I had been to college, they gave me more responsibility. Though basic training was ex-

tremely difficult, I had a secret advantage. I was taught by nuns.
No Marine Corps drill instructor (DI) could compete with the nuns
who taught me in my grade school. I had a leg up on all the other
enlistees. Since Catholic school taught me IRTAC (Instantaneous
Response to a Command), the Marines simply echoed what was for
me second nature. I adjusted quickly and well. Everyone seemed
to like me but my DI. For some reason he couldn't figure out why
I would join as a reservist or "non-regular Marine." In hindsight, I
guess I didn't look the part. I'm sure he looked at me and thought,
"This guy is happy and obedient and does everything he's told. He
must be a spy!" One day he called me into his office and questioned
my motives for enlisting. We had a conversation which proved that
my presence indeed frightened him. Even now, I don't know why
he wanted to get rid of me, but for some reason he went to great
lengths to have me transferred someplace far away from his command. As I entered, I snapped to attention.

"Sir, Private Murray reporting, Sir!"

"Don't call me Sir!" he snipped. "You have a job in baseball don't you?"

"Yes, Sir!"

"Don't call me Sir!" he snarled.

He then offered me a job if I would go away. "Norfolk Naval Base
Security, easy job. How about it?" he asked.

"No, Sir!'

"Don't call me Sir! How about Honolulu? You ship over and I guarantee, you're on base with the easiest job you can have in the

Marines." He sensed he had me where he wanted me.

"Sounds good, but no, Sir!"

"Don't call me Sir. Okay, the best duty of all in Marine Corps, embassy duty. Any capital in the world. Paris? You wear civilian clothes. Marine Corps pays for everything. The sweetest duty in all of the free world. Sign here for embassy school."

He really, really didn't like me and wanted me out of his sight forever.

"No, sir!"

Frustrated beyond his comprehension, he screamed, "What is it with you? I want you out of here and I'm willing to give you anything. What's the matter with you?" His veins were popping from his head and he was reaching for the nitroglycerine pills to stem a bubbling coronary.

I added insult to injury. "If you made me a commandant, gave me a riding stick, gave me that great hat with the scrambled eggs, I'm not shipping out."

I was very comfortable with the situation I had developed and I didn't want to venture too far from baseball. I had no plan to give up my unique situation. This final rejection broke the camel's back.

Next, he proceeded to spew f-bombs up and down his office for what seemed to be an eternity but was in truth, a good five minutes. He just didn't like reservists. He released years of pent-up rage on me. He considered me a wimp. I was killing two birds with one stone. Serve my country and keeping my hand in baseball. To his way of thinking, this was a half-ass effort. The Marines required full, 100% dedication. For the next several weeks he rode me hard. He continually tried to get rid of me like the DI in *Full Metal Jacket* did to Vincent D'Onofrio. But, I outlasted his assaults and graduated. It was one of the greatest days in my life. I survived Parris Island, became an officer, and today, I still get chills listening to the Marine Corps hymn. Despite my instructor's efforts, I went on to serve a six-year stint as a reservist, with thirty active days per year. Admittedly, it wasn't a brilliant or heroic military career but I served. I always counted my experience as a Marine the most influential in my life. Even though, like my DI, people might argue a part-time Marine is not a real Marine, I performed well at Camp Lejune. Today, I'm proud of my Marine service. And, throughout my adult life, I have continually lent a hand to any Marine cause. I am one of the few, the proud, the Marines! However, by the time I finished with my training, the Charleston team was sold again. This time, the new owners were in Atlanta, Georgia. Miami, San Juan, Charleston, and then Atlanta. I was back in baseball! Yet I would only be passing time until my life would take another 180-degree turn.

Until his death in 2010, Arthur Mahan (Villanova '36), former Vice President of Athletics was a father figure and friend to his protégé, James Murray (Villanova '60).

CHAPTER 5

Some Crazy Detours

"When the whole world is crazy, it doesn't pay to be sane."

— TERRY GOODKIND

After a quick visit home to see my family, I was back on the road and on my way to Atlanta. Now I was the newly christened "Ticket Manager" for the Atlanta Crackers. I wasn't sure if the team's name "Crackers," was intentionally racial hat-tipping but Atlanta was deeper south than Virginia. I knew by this time, race was fast becoming a recurring theme in my young career. I decided to travel to Atlanta via Norfolk, Virginia. I didn't have a rhyme or reason. I just wanted to see some sights along the way. Weeks before my departure, I had read an article on Bill Veeck, the legendary baseball promoter and owner of the Cleveland Indians. He owned a house on the Maryland Eastern Shore and, due to some health problems, he was confined to his estate. I admired Veeck greatly as a sports innovator and I decided to write him a letter. My thinking was, one outgoing legend mentoring an incoming one. I wrote:

> *"Dear Mr. Veeck,*
>
> *I am a novice in Minor League baseball and you have always been one of my role models. You're a huge success, a marine, and a baseball legend! I'm a Marine and a green young baseball guy. I'm not a success, yet. I'd love the opportunity to meet with you and I'll be passing by your home on my way to Atlanta. Maybe I can get some career advice.*
>
> > *Sincerely,*
> > *Jimmy Murray."*

He wrote back to me immediately:

> *"Sure kid, drop by on your way to Atlanta."*

Veeck lived on an enormous piece of real estate called, "Tranquility." You can always be sure that if someone has a name attached to their house that they have made it financially. I arrived at Tranquility where Mr. Veeck greeted me. He smoked a big fat cigar and he gruffly invited me into his home saying, "Come on in, kid." I was thinking this was going to be a two-minute polite brush off, a kind of "Yeah kid, good luck kid, see you later kid," meeting. I thought that after a few moments of empty chatter, I'd be on my way. But, no! He brought me into his living room and offered me a drink. I don't drink but I was tempted if it would keep me there longer. Here I was with one of the biggest names in baseball and we were suddenly talking like we had been pals for years. It was my first experience in breaking through a myth. I realized in a few short moments, he was just a regular guy, who no doubt was smart and talented, but still the beneficiary of lots of good fortune. Veeck had a wooden leg. He lost his leg in the Marine Corps while fighting in World War II and now limped on his prosthesis. He had carved an ashtray in the artificial limb and during the entire time we spoke, he flicked his cigar into his fake leg. I couldn't take my eyes off of the cigar. I'm sure he enjoyed the effect this had on me. Interestingly, he was a different man than I imagined him to be. And here was the second lesson that I learned from my visit. Veeck had been married and was divorced. He was immensely successful by anyone's measure, rich and extremely comfortable. But sadly, he was all alone. There was a slight melancholy emanating from him. I sensed I was alleviating some of it with my visit. I exceeded my expected visit by several hours. We talked and argued and surprisingly we became as close as you could to a friendship in a first meeting. Here was the man who put a team together in Cleveland which won the 1948 World Series against the Boston Braves, and they regularly challenged the goliath New York Yankees in the American League. He owned the team that had some of the biggest players of his day, Bob Feller, Bob Lemon, and Early Wynn. And here was the kid from Brooklyn Street, sitting across from him in his living room. In a quiet moment, he confided in me that at the end of his long string of successes, he had no one to share them with. It was strange yet moving to have him reveal something so personal. Bill Veeck was as successful in baseball as one could be, yet he lived in splendid isolation. My little side trip had a reason. Again, God was trying to teach me something. Success in baseball was all that I desired. But, Veeck had some parting wisdom for me which would stay with me always. Before I left, he said two interesting things. One was, "Kid, Baseball is too much of a sport to be a business and too much of a business to be a sport." I had to munch on that for a while but it would come back to me many times in my future professional dealings in sports. The second and the more important thing was this, "And remember kid, success all alone with no one to share with, is no success."

Bill Veeck

⁂

What a side trip! Fortunately, I heard later that Veeck married a second time. I was disappointed and surprised I didn't get an invitation, proving that I was delusional. Why would he invite me to his second wedding after one visit? His wife's name was Mary Frances, and she was the public relations person for the Ice Capades. He was divorced and Catholic, which according to the Church meant that you could not remarry. Because of this, Veeck bribed a bishop to push the marriage through. I was happy to hear he found someone he loved and that there was a bishop who allowed the marriage. He and his new wife ended up having two children, so I imagine that Tranquility then became less tranquil in a good way. He had success and someone with whom to share it. A happy ending! Later in my career, I would contact him for some help with Ronald McDonald Charities in Chicago but imagine, my crazy impulse of a detour turned into a fantastic rich memory. And that's a third thing I took from my Veeck visit. Always trust your impulses. At least, this impulse allowed me the great fortune to pick the brain of one of the greatest showmen ever in baseball or in the entire entertainment world for that matter. And craft one of my best memories in sports.

I left Veeck and Maryland then headed south to start my new job in Atlanta which would become my Ph.D. dissertation in integrating a baseball team. Compared to Atlanta, Virginia was progressive. There were no black players and unlike Virginia, there were not even black fans. The Crackers were a St. Louis Cardinals minor team and I was again reunited with Joe Ryan. My charge with the Crackers was the same as it was at my former stops, fill the ballpark with paying customers. In my first week, I met Dr. Martin Luther

King Jr. Dr. King was a larger than life figure and he was in the throws of moving the country forward on the civil rights front. He shook my hand and looked at me straight in the eye and asked me directly if and when I (we) had a plan to integrate the Crackers. I explained to Dr. King that I was only the ticket manager. I wasn't trying to excuse the segregation but I wanted to let him know I wasn't the kingpin making decisions on the issue. However, I assured him that I would do my best to move things forward. He seemed genuinely grateful and thanked me for my attention to the matter. Little did I know the events that would unfold later. I shook hands with one of the most important men in American history. I went straight to Joe Ryan and told him, "That's Martin Luther King asking for more black players. Don't you think it would be a good idea to cooperate?" Joe agreed and so did a few other Cracker staffers. We

Dr. Martin Luther King, Jr.
He asked me the direct question "Do you (the organization)
plan to integrate the Atlanta Crackers, and if so, when?"

began to progress. It was 1963 and the young Cardinal farm players included Tim McCarver, Ray Sadecki, Nelson Briles, and Phil Gagliano. Timmy was the star and the MVP and within a year, this core group went to St. Louis and made it to the World Series, where they played the great Mickey Mantle-Roger Maris Yankees. But, the Crackers of 1963? Wow, that was some minor league lineup!

❧

Atlanta was and still is one of my favorite cities. It housed a great number of big corporations so I was able to ride a big promotions learning curve. No one had really thought about or reached out to the corporate fan. Joe Ryan though, had vision. With his advice, I started courting fans using the now ubiquitous "businessman special." We were one of the first organizations to tap that market. At the same time, I worked to keep my promise to Dr. King. I made a sincere effort to reach out to Atlanta's minority community. I worked with schools and churches to increase our African-American ticket sales and within a few months there was a marked improvement in minority attendance. Our scouts gave special attention to the lack of black ballplayers and started bringing in more black ballplayers, one being the famous Curt Flood. Flood would one day change professional sports by singularly ushering in the era of "free agency." I was working round the clock but I loved every minute of my time in Atlanta. Since we were transient baseball folk, most of the team's employees lived on the 16th floor of the Peachtree Hotel. Could a bachelor land in a better place than the Peachtree? I didn't sleep much and I had fun. Lots and lots of fun!

❧

Another reason Atlanta remains one of my favorite places is that it's the place where I met my wife. I'll never forget the day, March 25, 1964. I was driving past the local Ponce de Leon Park when I spotted this vivacious blonde pushing a little girl on a swing. I stopped the car, got out and introduced myself. I had no idea that she was a single girl, and I had no idea her father was the controller of the Crackers. I only knew she stopped me in my tracks. At the end of my first encounter, I bypassed all small talk and boldly announced, "I'm gonna marry you!" Dianne Gustafson had married Dennis Arlin Gustafson, had a baby and then divorced. She grew up in Coral Gables, Florida but she had recently come to work with the Crackers. How was it that our paths hadn't crossed? I was always a "wheel" (leg) man and Dianne had the best wheels I had ever seen! I had hair at the time. Alright, let me brag. I was cute and I appeared confident. Still, it took me five years to close the deal with Dianne but eventually we married and raised five children. I'll rave on more about Dianne and my family later.

The most interesting moments usually happened to me outside of baseball. This was certainly the case when I met Stefan Popescu. It was in one of our local hangouts, the Ship Ahoy Restaurant, where I met the owner, Stefan Popescu. Stefan, a debonair Eastern European immigrant, had come to the United States to escape communist Romania. I ate at his restaurant regularly since I couldn't cook and I liked everything on his menu. I should mention that I like everything on every menu. Stefan and I hit it off immediately. I was fascinated that Stefan spoke 12 languages while I was still trying to master one. Stefan had been a professor in his home country and I had a fascination for Eastern Europe. I peppered him with a thousand questions about Communism and the Iron Curtain. Even my future father-in-law loved Stefan. My father-in-law, a stereotypical accountant, also loved Stefan's Romanian stories. Stefan, a gifted orator, had led VIP tours around post-World War Europe and could speak on any subject concerning the contentious history of Eastern Europe. One night after hours, Stefan and I sat at the bar and he quietly described the time he spent in a Nazi concentration camp. Of course, I had no idea that Stefan was imprisoned in Buchenwald. He didn't offer too many details but from his outgoing, restaurant owner's personality, I would have never guessed he had that background. In a few short months, Stefan and I had become best pals and he encouraged me daily to get into the restaurant business. "Jimmy, you have own place, do very well." He had no knowledge of baseball and he would curiously ask me in his heavy accent, "How in America do you get job in game?" Stefan's advice to me was to diversify my talents and learn his business, "since Jimmy, you never know what things can happen." I wasn't making a ton of money with the Crackers, so I took up Stefan's offer and began moonlighting at his restaurant. One day Stefan said, "Jimmy, I buy 'nother restaurant, you friendly guy, you make people laugh, you be greeter at door." Stefan bought a restaurant called the "Red Barn Inn," and I became its maitre'd. Fortunately, this turned into one of my all-time smart decisions. I had begun dining with Dianne's father regularly, sweetening him up for eventually asking for his daughter's hand. But weeks later, the Crackers were sold again and which meant of course, I was out of a job. Here I go again. If Stefan doesn't survive

Buchenwald, he doesn't move to the U.S. of A. I don't work at the Red Barn. One incident changes the whole course of history. There are no accidents! Luckily, Stefan was there to pick me up. "Jimmy, you move in with me and my family." Stefan had a beautiful, Swedish wife and a young son. "You be fine," he promised. "You will learn business and work with Stefan." Don't you just love people with accents who talk about themselves in the third person? I replied, "Jimmy Murray work for Stefan. Stefan good friend to Jimmy Murray." Stefan, an old school European businessman, insisted on perfection. I guess he saw something in me though he'd have to have Superman's vision to see the perfection. How he'd sized me up, he never said, and I'll never know. I smiled and laughed a lot so I guess they were skills he valued. "Jimmy," he told me, "food, drink, and SERVICE!...food and drink they get at Woolworth's, at Stefan's you get European old world SERVICE!" Suddenly, I was too busy at Stefan's "Red Barn Inn," to miss the Crackers. Stefan catered to an upscale clientele and he insisted I buy and wear a crisp tuxedo each night. He recruited the four best black waiters in the city, which I learned was an important accessory for Atlanta's high priced diners. The downside of the Crackers sale was that my future father-in-law moved back to Florida and I lost my access to Dianne. The "Red Barn" was doing very well and I was quickly swallowed up in the restaurant business. My baseball dreams were going up in clouds of nightly cigarette smoke.

It was Christmas and no matter where I've ever traveled, I always needed to return home for the holidays. I arrived back home in

*Stefan Popescu who taught me the restaurant business at the Red Barn Inn in Atlanta
(Stefan spoke 12 languages, I spoke Philly); Me and Marshall Fox,
my first boss in baseball (Tidewater Tides - A Baseball)*

Philly two days before Christmas. Coming back home made me feel a bit sorry for myself. Returning home, I found my brother doing very well athletically and academically at Penn and my younger sister had just gotten engaged to be married. Staring into a mirror, and this has only happened a few times in my life, I began to engage in self-pity. My short-lived baseball career was in the tank, and though I had a job of sorts at Stefan, it wasn't the great sporting future I had plotted out for myself. I had no money to speak of, no car, (I had to return my Uncle's), and no girl. Everyone at home seemed to be moving on with their lives and I seemed to be stuck on first base. I had always told myself that self-pity was the single greatest waste of human emotion, but at this point I was drowning in it. But, in a split second, I pulled myself out if. I decided to go back to Atlanta and take my chances. "You like the town. Something good will happen to you. You just need faith!"

≈❈

January 2, 1965, I was back on the road with my thumb out and with a measly fifteen dollars in my pocket. The first woman who stopped and picked me up only took me a few miles and immediately brightened my spirits when she said, "If I wasn't married, I'd drive you to Atlanta myself." She was a bubbly woman and she had a few kids in the back seat. She assured me that the world was full of good people just dying to take me to Atlanta. It was a good omen. Immediately, I was optimistic and for the first time in awhile, upbeat. Sometimes all it takes is one friendly face or encouraging word to get you back on your horse. I was back on the road hitchhiking showing my gleaming teeth. Next, three New York cops stopped. They were passing through on the way to a racetrack. In a very serious manner they told me they could arrest me and take me in for hitchhiking. These guys were the quintessential New Yorkers, right out of the old 1950's drama, *Naked City*. They did an excellent acting job scaring me to death. My frightened face made them laugh hysterically. They backed off the joke and insisted that I accept their invitation to the track. By now I only had thirteen dollars in my pocket. As a horse player I briefly thought that I might double my money but then my prudent side quickly voted against it. My miles with these New Yorkers were memorable. They dropped me at the Pennsylvania-Maryland border. They departed with some advice for the rest of my journey, "You'd better wise up kid and lose that naïve little boy routine." In Maryland, I was standing on the road outside a diner when a man drove up to me and yelled, "Jump in." Later I found out this particular man was an important Maryland State Senator.

I told him my story and my Atlanta destination and he said, " Flat out, son, I'm damn envious of you, with youth and freedom to just go back down to Atlanta, do whatever the hell you please." I reassured him my life wasn't as glamorous as he imagined.

"I'm just going down to see if I can get something going," I said.

"You mean you're just going to Atlanta to see if you can get another job in baseball?" he asked.

"Yes, sir."

He said, "Kid, never forget what it's like to be young and free!"

I told him not to waste words on me and I gave him my normal hitchhiking retort. "I'm a kid who knows I'm in my prime." He laughed and as an added bonus to the ride, he invited me to stay at his house for the night. His wife made a delicious meal for me, and they sent me off the next morning with a great breakfast. Further south, where Routes 95 and 85 intersect, I was walking along the roadside with my suitcase, trying to decide which road to take. Dusk was approaching and I was getting a bit nervous that I might have to bunk down on the side of the road. A state trooper drove by me and thought I was lost. He stopped and asked, "Where are you going?"

"Atlanta."

He cautioned me that nightfall was upon me and warned me that if I was planning on camping nearby that I would be breaking the law. He offered to drive me down the road. We passed motel after motel with no vacancy signs. Finally, he dropped me off in front of one old place that looked a bit like the Bates Motel. He stopped the car and said, "Old Tex here, he'll take care of you." I exited the car, thanked him and then walked into the motel office. Sure enough, there was this southern gentleman with cowboy booted feet up on the counter, and his name was Tex. It was Virginia but it sure felt like Mayberry.

"Hey, my brother," he said with a drawl. "How can I help you?"

"Are you really my brother?" I asked. "I need a room."

"We got a room. Just one left before the no vacancy gets turned on…sleeps 16, almost a suite and it's only $20."

"I only got $10," I said. "I'm on my way to Atlanta and if you don't take it, I'd say you ain't my brother."

He took a long breath, exhaled some cigarette smoke, and said, "It's the last room. Take it and give me $4, cause a man's gotta eat, too."

Before turning in for the night, I took a stroll around the parking lot looking for any Georgia plates I could find. There were 4 cars with Georgia tags, a good sign. I asked Tex to wake me up early the next morning so I could try mooching a ride to Atlanta from some of his guests. The old hotel in rural Virginia seemed like the Taj Mahal and I slept like a baby. It was going to be a snap to get to Atlanta. When the morning arrived, I was 0 for 4. All of the Georgians were going north. I did however manage to land a ride to Duke University from a professor. He was a doctor of chemistry. Needless to say, we didn't have much in common. He didn't seem at all anxious to pass the drive with conversation. And I didn't have any questions about chemistry. If I told him I flunked biology three times, he might have kicked me out of the car. It was an annoyingly quiet ride. But I quickly rebounded in Durham, North Carolina. A slick Las Vegas card dealer picked me up and offered to take me to South Carolina. One thing is sure. Two gamblers instantly hit it off when talking about their addictions. We became fast friends. I shared my game plan of seeking fortune in Atlanta and he immediately became excited, almost like we were partners in a heist. By the end of the ride, he was considering coming with me. Then his sobering reality appeared. He was married and his wife had just recently giving birth to their first child. I guess he was in denial. In moments, we went from partners to the friendship that wasn't meant to be. We departed, promising like young people do to meet again someday. We never did.

I needed one more break to finish the last leg of my journey. My final drive to Atlanta was with two salesmen. When they found out my story and that I was flat broke, they treated me to a dinner larger than the Last Supper. I arrived in Atlanta in a sleepy haze from overeating. They woke me in front of the Red Barn at 8 p.m. I thanked them and promised that when I made it big, I'd repay them for the dinner. I walked into the Red Barn with just a few coins jingling in my pocket and no place to work or live. Stefan had no time to greet me. He was dealing with his own restaurant emergency. A 90-proof regular customer by name of Kelly had just driven his car in the swimming pool outside the restaurant. A staggering Kelly recognized me and slurred, "Murr, can you drive me home? I lost my car." Stefan, wanted Kelly off the premises immediately so he gave me the keys to his car and instructed me to get back to work.

"Get that drunk out of here!" Stefan barked.

In the first five minutes back in Atlanta I was hired back at my old job and Kelly handed me fifty bucks when I took him home. In a one snap of the fingers, I was back in the saddle.

I was working for Stefan full-time, having a ball with my new extended family which Stefan had created. The Red Barn was full of colorful Damon Runyon types and no one was more colorful than a regular by the name of Jim McDonald (note that the name McDonald and McDonald's in general, play an important theme in my life). One of the waiters tipped me off that "You gotta know this guy McDonald…you and him would be some pair." McDonald was a rich businessman, to say the least. Originally from Minnesota, he was a decorated veteran of World War II. He was the most remarkable storyteller I had ever heard, and up until that time, I was the most remarkable storyteller I had ever heard. Obviously, McDonald made a quick and big impression on me. On the flip side, he was an absolutely mean, nasty drunk. The first night back working for Stefan as the maitre'd, McDonald was sitting with two young, gorgeous women. I kept them happy and their glasses full with my calling card Irish charm. At closing time, he called me over then spoke to me like my commanding officer.

"Kid, I heard about you. Take a seat, have a drink with us!"

"I don't drink," I said.

"What do you mean you don't drink?"

"Exactly what I said, I don't drink?"

"Then what do you like?" he asked continuing the interrogation.

"Gambling and women," I quipped.

"We got women here, so let's play cards," he declared.

We began a card game and it was apparent that McDonald was easy pickings. Mac was the pre-cursor to my future boss with the Philadelphia Eagles, Leonard Tose. Leonard also happened to be a bad drinker and an even worse card player than McDonald. Quickly I snagged ten hands from McDonald and with each hand, he insisted with increased verve that we bet more. While playing, he downed an entire bottle of ouzo. I quietly tipped my hat to the Greek distillers for enabling such a large pile of money to accumulate in front of me. As the clock approached 5 a.m. and with the restaurant long closed, I finally announced, "I quit!"

An angry McDonald yelled and woke the sleeping Stefan with, "You can't quit! Double or nothing!"

It was double on the next hand. Again I won. A yawning Stefan rubbing his eyes, insisted that we leave and that I drive home McDonald and his two chippies. McDonald owned my favorite car, a Lincoln Convertible, otherwise known as a "Jewish Jeep." I drove McDonald and the women to Mac's house. We were now two couples. My pockets were full of cash and I was driving with two beautiful women. What was not to love about Atlanta? All in all the evening went very well. Being the only sober person in the car, I still managed to laugh loud and hearty at every bad drunken joke. Our luck ran out when we reached McDonald's house. The two lovers got into a vicious fight. The women cleared out of the Lincoln. Then, his girlfriend leaned over to my window and emphatically told me, complete with expletives, to go tuck McDonald into bed. She spewed a few other things as well, of which I wasn't physically capable or willing to do. I did manage to get Mac upstairs in his house before he passed out. I had a new friend and a potential employer. For the next several weeks, McDonald took me under his wing and adopted me as his protégé. He liked that I was a Marine and I liked the idea of cultivating a friendship with a highly successful, wealthy, decorated entrepreneur. After all, I knew I couldn't stay at Stefan's for the rest of my life and who knew if I would get another opportunity in baseball?

McDonald was a salesman's salesman, and though a brutal drunk, he was one of the smartest, most well-read people I had ever met. He wasn't always the most original thinker and often, he would, after a few minutes, become me. In other words, what ever idea I had, quickly became his, just seconds after leaving my mouth. The truth didn't necessarily set Jim McDonald free. What exact enterprise brought Mac so much wealth?

"I research big perfume companies, the ones that are monopolies and then, I act as their agent in the franchising world," was how he originally explained to me what he did. McDonald could convince anyone in 30 seconds that, "I can sell you anything!" And he could! And he wanted me to do the same.

"You're a natural," he promised me. "You're a born salesman." I believed him immediately.

One day he asked me, "What do you know about bass fishing?"

"I know there are fish, and I know that there are bass and I know that some fish are bass," I said. It was one of those syllogisms I remembered from logic class.

"Well, Jimmy, it's very big in the south (fishing and bass fishing in particular) and you are in the south," he began. "There's a couple I know that makes a living selling a rubber worm, 'Big Joe,' that bass fishing people down here just go crazy for. They got a place down in Lithia Springs (GA) and we're going to sell the hell out of 'Big Joe.'"

McDonald sent me down to this old sleepy Georgia town that was straight out a Tennessee Williams play. Slow, hot, humid with train tracks coming in and going out. I was waiting for Marlon Brando to shout, "Blanche, get the hell out of Lithia Springs." There were only four buildings in the town and the manufacturers of "Big Joe" owned one of them. The genius marketer Jim McDonald took out an ad in the New York Times that said, "Like Fishing? See Jimmy Murray!"

After signing a distribution deal with Big Joe's Mom and Pop, McDonald made side deals with every Japanese manufacturer of fishing lures and tackle. Then he created what was to be the first portable tackle display in the south. A fisherman could walk into a 7-11 convenience store or a gas station, and for $5 buy a "Big Joe" worm with, hooks, anchors, and flies. One-stop fisherman shopping. McDonald was way ahead of the marketing curve. Although he did make one major miscalculation. He entrusted me to sell and assemble these displays, all over the state of Georgia. I may or may not have mentioned this, but I'm not mechanical. Not even a little bit. I have difficulty with an electric can opener. Putting up a fishing tackle display for me was like building the pyramids…by myself. But, with practice, I soon developed the dexterity of an Incan stonemason. The New York Times ad and several others in major papers paid immediate dividends. Franchisees began to appear from everywhere and quickly the "Big Joe" display infiltrated the marketplace. McDonald called me on the phone one morning and I happily waited for enthusiastic congratulatory message and maybe even a bonus.

"I'm gonna give you some instructions," he barked. "When someone calls, you tell him you only have two openings for appointments. Don't appear anxious. Say, you got one tomorrow and one on Thursday, are you in or out?"

It wasn't what one would call positive reinforcement. McDonald's first major sales lesson was not location, location, location but perception, perception, perception! Limit the supply and make it appear like you can't possibly meet demand. You lure the customer in just like a large mouth bass. I descended on Augusta and placed our initial ad in their local paper. "Big Joe" franchises were next going for a $15-20,000 buy-in fee. I rented a hotel room, built the display in my room and then waited for appointments to arrive. Then I would close the sale. I began to see the scale of this operation and how my commissions could soar exponentially. My adrenaline pumped with the thought of actually depositing money in the bank. Images of Howard Hughes danced in my head. When finally I got my first call, I completely forgot McDonald's rule.

"Sure come right over," I blurted out. The potential buyer came to my motel room, saw the displays, and then immediately said, "Let's go to a bar and talk this over." Going to a bar with a customer was a definite no-no in the McDonald training manual. Despite my mistake, the guy turned out to be one of the funniest people I ever met. My first sales meeting turned into one of the most memorable nights of my life. I laughed loud and long and then we brokered a "Big Joe" franchising deal in an after-hours club over the South Carolina border. In a short time I was proving to Mac and to myself that I could sell. Mac busily worked in Atlanta lining up leads for me throughout the country. After Augusta he sent me to Norfolk, Virginia. I continued nailing good lead after good lead but for some reason the money wasn't quite trickling down to me. I was in hotels checking out perspective franchisees' financial statements with $3 in my pocket. McDonald Enterprises was establishing "Big Joe" all over the eastern seaboard and throughout the South, but Jim Murray was still eating tuna out of the can. In Norfolk, a very serious entrepreneur and fisherman came to my hotel room. After looking at my wares he said, "Mr. Murray, you do realize that you are in the Chesapeake Region and the Chesapeake is saltwater and all you're selling is for freshwater." I had no idea there was a difference. I told you I flunked biology three times. Maybe I wasn't cut out for this business after all. I called Mac in Georgia. I said that the only reason I can sell "Big Joe" displays is because I have no faith that anyone will catch a fish. I was sure of one thing, if they didn't catch a fish, they could recoup their investment with a yard sale selling off lots of tackle. After a few months I realized that though people loved fishing and fishing tackle, I didn't. My lack of ability to distinguish fresh from saltwater was God's subtle way of telling me to choose another profession. Though I was not cut out to sell fishing tackle, I learned a ton from McDonald. He had one of the great gimmicks of all time. With every franchise application went a cashier's check to a bank in Lithia Springs. In less than a year, we took "Big Joe" to every store front and convenience store from North Carolina to Georgia. The little old couple who first invented "Big Joe" grazed the cover of "Field and Stream" magazine and "Big Joe" production went from a basement to a six block factory and warehouse. Mac was a booster rocket entrepreneur with vision, nerve, and Jimmy Murray.

Jim McDonald's empire was not limited to perfume, fishing and the south. He owned businesses throughout the country and one in particular, was not doing well. He owned a bar in Malibu, California. The bar was bleeding cash because everyone knows you can't be an absentee owner in the bar business. Mac understood that my sales days were numbered and suggested one day that I go to Malibu and, "straighten out my joint." Mac gave me a firm pep talk about how I was one of the few people he could trust in a cash business. He promised that if I could right the ship, I'd never have any worries. I still hadn't seen much money from my "Big Joe" sales. But, I always wanted to visit California and here was as good an opportunity as any. So off I went to Malibu, to keep McDonald's bar "The Raft" afloat.

I lived 20 years of my life in one year in Malibu. I had never been west of the Mississippi and immediately I fell in love with sunny Southern California. Particularly, I enjoyed being around the creative people who migrated to L.A. to seek fame and fortune in the movie business. Everyone who came into "The Raft" drove a Porsche, had an unsold screenplay, and never paid their bar bill. Even still, there was a certain lack of hypocrisy among the patrons, though the Hollywood rule of thumb is to act like you are more successful than you actually are. My California education began on my first day on the job. A kid walked into the bar. He was stereotypically blonde, blue eyed, and he wore a powder blue bathing suit.

"What do you do?" I asked.

"I surf," he answered.

"All day?"

"Yeah," he said, "all day, everyday."

"How do you do that?" I asked, though I couldn't even carry a surfboard.

He explained, "I have a wake up call. I sleep in my car. Someone from the Beverly Hills Hotel calls me at first light on the public phone in the parking lot near the beach across from Trankas Restaurant. I wake up and surf. That's how I do it."

There were scores of people with no visible means of support who suddenly appeared in a Marlboro cigarette commercial. The life was free and unpredictable. I particularly enjoyed kibitzing with writers and actors who were waiting to be discovered, because in a way, I was waiting to be discovered. I held court every afternoon and at the risk of sounding brash, I could make the customers laugh. My easy going nature seemed to make them forget that they weren't making it in Hollywood. Most of the customers thought I owned the place, which for all intent and purposes, I did, though it was more based on the Soviet model. It was the first bar cooperative in history and I had the role of Lenin (not John, Vladimir). In retrospect, I got to know some of the most interesting characters in my life and who knows? Maybe I should have tried my hand at acting because I dazzled a host of big Hollywood types. Actually, I gave the place a Philly atmosphere. I tried to create a neighborhood feel, like where I came from, and everyone tuned into that energy. Before 24/7 cable news, most people came to bars to get their information. In Hollywood, everyone wanted to know about the latest scandals brewing. As a kid, I went to local taprooms with my father and uncles. There I learned to play liar's poker, tell a joke, and just enjoy the company of others. Bars were happy, sad, celebratory, and somber depending on the occasion and the patrons. Growing up, bars were the gathering place and the pulse of my neighborhood. My success at resurrecting "The Raft" for Jim McDonald hinged on this exact approach to business. Or as Stefan preached to me at the Red Barn, "Don't rush them, let them stay."

As a people person, I was aces. As a business manager, I was the joker. The bar was a rocky ship, surviving day to day on nothing but good cheer. In the days before computers and credit cards, you could manipulate the financial system to buy time until profits started turning. I remember one of the tellers at our bank, the Bank of America. Delia was a soft-spoken bespectacled girl who, if cast, would star as the spinster librarian. She had the exact look of a trustworthy, model bank employee. Anyone who met her would immediately trust her with the keys to the vault. In order to make up a cash drawer for the weekends, I would write a bad check on Friday afternoon for $2,500 and return the deposit on Sunday night in the night drop box to cover the check. Finally, Delia caught on to my method but she liked the attention I showered on her, so she turned her eyes away. She continued to enjoy this excursion to the dark side because of my regular flirtations. "What if we get caught?" she asked nervously one day.

I laughingly assured her, "Malibu jail has only one cell and we'll finally be together. And, the judge is Catholic and drinks every night in my bar so I think we're safe." Even after she discovered my method, she continued to let me pull the same jig, week after week.

I was starting to turn the bar around. My employees became my great friends. John O'Connor was a funny Bostonian bartender, who had the identical accent as my mentor, Artie Mahan. Another Philly guy name Jack Baandes helped reinforce the Philly feel I had developed. The big stars of the day, Lee Marvin, Robert Mitchum, Dodgers pitcher Sandy Koufax, were regulars. Even actor Ronald

Reagan stopped in for a drink on the way back to his ranch. I loved the action! "The Raft" was unique in that you could come in, in a tuxedo or a bikini, and just relax. Peter Lawford, fresh off of the original "Ocean's Eleven" and of Rat Pack fame, used to sit in an alcove that we called the "Kennedy Table." Once he invited me to his house for a game of naked "Password." I hadn't quite developed the confidence to strip down in front of strangers and play the home version of the famous game show. Blake Edwards, Neville Brand, Carl Reiner. I could name drop forever. All of these big stars were part of Mac's circle and now I was vicariously living the surrealistic star life.

◈

My favorite star from this entire experience was Lee Marvin. Marvin built a reputation in his films as a no-nonsense tough guy. He was often cast as the street smart, tough cop or just as often he was cast as the evil bad guy. I learned Marvin didn't play anyone other than himself in all of his movies. He was the kind of actor who could get away with just showing up. Like myself, Marvin did a stint with the Marines and his unpretentiousness made him a real deepwater guy. He was dating a girl or a "thrush" (a singer) as he called her. They eventually married. He was starring in a movie at this time and he had to travel back east on a publicity tour for the film. While back east, he visited his hometown and ran into his high school sweetheart. This woman proved to be tougher than Marvin. They began having a bi-coastal relationship but unbeknownst to her, he was married. Somehow, a reporter got wind of the affair and disclosed it publicly. Remember, this was pre-tabloid days and instantaneous gossip had not yet been developed into a full blown industry. Newspapers employed reporters to comb the city for any dirt on the stars. After the reporter divulged this story, the entire town knew of the affair. One night after he'd had too many drinks, I drove Marvin home. He insisted that we go to Mac's house and so we did. There waiting for him was Mrs. Marvin. Sure enough, a war broke out between them. And here was little Jimmy Murray caught in the crossfire. Apparently, Marvin had also fathered a child outside of his marriage with the girlfriend. It turned into one of the first mega-palimony suits in Hollywood and one of the biggest soap operas Hollywood had ever seen. Regardless of his personal foibles, Marvin remained one of my all-time favorites.

Lee Marvin
One of my favorite pals from "The Raft"

The biggest life changing experience I had in Malibu involved the return of Jim McDonald to California. Mac arrived back at "The Raft" one day with "Crazy Peggy." This was the same girl I met back in Atlanta the night he crashed his car into Stefan's pool. Mac and Peggy finally had decided to tie the knot. Marvin was to be in the wedding party. Mac was a name dropper and loved the fact that he could brag that Lee Marvin was standing in as his best man. Better yet, Marvin invited the entire cast of the *Dirty Dozen* to a party for Mac. It was a night to remember though not as exciting for me as what was to follow. After the party where we met such notables as Charles Bronson and Telly Savalas, Crazy Peggy proposed I meet her girlfriend. Mac insisted I meet her. For some reason, Mac thought we'd make a pretty pair.

Film Director, Blake Edwards

Neville Brand
*Hollywood actor and
highly decorated soldier
in WWII*

Carl Reiner

Charles Bronson

British actor Peter Lawford (one of "The Rat Pack")

The Dodgers' Sandy Koufax —one of the greatest pitchers of all time I may have also served him a pitcher or two!

Telly Savalas When this guy orders, you "make it snappy!"

Robert Mitchum - a familiar face at "The Raft"

Some of the old "Gang" from "The Raft"

"I got you a date and she's gorgeous, come over to Peggy's house later on," Mac barked. It was the same tone he used to inspire me to sell "Big Joe" displays.

Being an obliging employee, I obeyed. When I arrived, my blind date, Jeanie, was a dead ringer for my favorite actress, Doris Day. Blonde, blue eyed, she was the kind of girl you wanted to take home to mother. The four of us traveled from club to club. At one stop we were serenaded by Jim Nabors, who was famous for his role as Gomer Pyle, USMC. Nabors was a great singer as well as a comic actor and he sang opera at our table. After years of watching him on television, I had imagined he was like the lovable hillbilly Gomer Pyle. He wasn't. He was a very personable guy with one great singing voice.

Jim Nabors (seen here playing Gomer Pyle, USMC, being called to task by his forever-exasperated gunnery Sergeant Carter, played by Frank Sutton)

Jim had an amazing voice and, one evening, sang opera at our table

After hours we stopped at a place called Zucky's Deli where by then everyone had "ice cube poisoning" (drunkeness) but me. Remember? I never drink. Jeanie and Peggy began to argue over something nonsensical because drunks argue nonsensically. My experience with Peggy was that she woke up each morning arguing. Peggy wanted to take a one-minute argument and make it twelve rounds. But I stepped in to defend my date saying, "Jeanie, you don't have to take this from her." Jeanie and I stood up and then left. Suddenly we were standing outside where Jeanie was amazed that little, chubby Jimmy could perform such a brave, chivalrous act.

"You mind if I smoke," she asked. I didn't smoke either and I didn't mind if she lit up. As she did, I smelled a scent that until that moment, I had never smelled before. She asked me if I had ever smoked "weed." I said I couldn't smoke something I couldn't spell. She then asked me if I knew the effect that marijuana creates. I replied that as far as I knew the long term effects of marijuana caused the body to be locked up for a long period of time. Either the drug or my joke caused her to laugh for the next twenty minutes. What I know now about the drug, it was the marijuana that caused the laughter. Then, Jeanie confessed to me that she had kids at home who were being watched by a nanny.

In her Doris Day voice she asked, "Jimmy, be a sweetie and drive me home." She was too drunk and high to drive, even in the days when everyone drove drunk. She gave me the keys to her Porsche, which somehow was magically parked at Zucky's. At this point, I was in way over my head, a mere rookie with a seasoned veteran. I drive a bad stick shift. Like, my first time. But, there I was, driving up the Pacific Coast Highway in a car that was worth more than the entire net worth of my family. Eventually, I had control of the car and I whipped it into the driveway of a palatial Malibu beachfront house, safely getting my date home. The pool alone was bigger than the street where I grew up. She said, "I really like you and I want you to stay with me. Don't go back to Mac, I'll take care of you." An offer I couldn't refuse from Doris Day's stand in? Apparently, she had some huge bucks. It was tempting! The thought flashed in my head. Husband? There had to be a husband, because she mentioned she had kids. What if he sees me in front of his house with his wife?

"What about your husband?" I quickly asked as my eyes scoured the premises. And those kids that you talked about?

She pulls me closer, giggling like a drunk Doris whispering to Cary Grant. "I'll let you in on a little secret. I'm divorced."

The truth was that her husband and she were going through a divorce, which of course meant that technically, I was out with a married woman. I was committing a litany of sins according to my religion, and in particular that 9th commandment, "Thou shalt not covet thy neighbor's wife." I might have gotten off on a technicality because I couldn't afford to have these people as neighbors so how could I be expected to keep this woman in the manner she was accustomed. To make matters worse, I found out later that the husband was "connected" in a matter of speaking, as in a Tony Soprano sort of connected. My first date in Malibu and I would have been content looking for a Mass schedule and a church. But no, I was dating the wife of a made mobster. If Mary Murray had witnessed this scene, it would have been sudden death for me, and not the playoff kind. As it turned out, the sober Jeanie turned out to be a lovely girl and we actually dated for several months after this unpredictable first night. The good news was that no one threatened to break my legs for the next several months. Also, Jeanie expanded my vocabulary with new words like "joint" and "good shit." To this day I'm still a huge Doris Day fan. And, I still carry the knowledge that on that first crucial romantic overture of my career, I was just an awkward rookie!

Right after Jeanie and I parted ways, I came back home for a visit. Dianne from Atlanta was still on my mind. I had tried several times from Malibu to pop up on her radar screen. I sent her 13 roses, not 12, with a card that said, "You're the extra rose!" Not bad, huh? I'm still proud of that line. Surely, I was in love and clearly she wasn't buying the Jimmy Murray corn. Returning back to Philly, I saw my friends and family members moving on, getting engaged and married. I had dated a local girl off and on for years by the name of Judy Jones. Judy was a cute, very sweet nurse I had met in college at Villanova. In my loneliness, I began to contemplate that maybe Judy Jones was the one for me. Suddenly, I had this crazy notion that I would propose to Judy because after all, we had dated off and on at some point in time. Follow this logic if you can. I came home from California, so why wouldn't she want to marry me? Can you see why people have called me the "cockeyed optimist?" Letter writing was never my forté but nonetheless I sat down and wrote Judy an epistle that would have made St. Paul jealous. I suggested that she listen to a song that I had christened "our song." I hinted that maybe it was time I settled down and that I was going to get serious about my future. After confessing my love and proposing marriage, I suddenly got cold feet, then folded up the letter and put in my pocket. A few days later, I went to New York City to see the 1964 World's Fair. Bell System had a pavilion at the Fair where you could call anywhere in the world for free but only for three minutes. I chose to call Judy. I held a new fangled, high tech phone which meant it had buttons instead of the old rotary dial. I pushed the buttons and I was magically connected to Judy's house and immediately she picked up.

"What's all that noise in the background, your engagement party?" I asked being cute.

"How did you know?" she asked, popping my balloon.

"I hope he's a doctor," I said covering my embarrassment.

"He is!"

"Well, good luck!" I said hanging up the phone with one hand and reaching in my pocket for the letter with the other. I didn't even use the entire three minutes. Immediately, I tore up the letter and remained crushed, for about five minutes. Then, I walked over to Shea Stadium with my two friends and enjoyed a terrific Phillies-Mets game where outfielder Johnny Callison hit a walk-off homer. I always felt that Callison was able to hit that home run because I took all the negative karma from that day. I delivered good vibrations to Callison. Years later I met Johnny and told him the story of Judy Jones and he thanked Judy through me. "I hope Judy and the doctor are happy," he said. They were, and I went on searching for the woman of my dreams. I knew it was Dianne but she wasn't yet convinced I was anything other than a recurring bad dream.

෨෫

Two weeks later I was back in Malibu with young Martin Sheen. Sheen was a "Raft regular," and a real down-to-earth guy. He gave me glimpses into what it was like to be a struggling actor. The Hollywood scene was a tough one to break into and it was taking its toll on Sheen. Both of us were Catholics and we attended Mass at the same Church. We really hit it off. I haven't seen him in years but whenever I do, it seems like success never went to his head.

Martin Sheen—one of my "Raft" regulars who attended Sunday mass with me at Our Lady of Malibu Catholic Church

Genuine as they come, he was a memorable friend. And every night and every patron in Malibu was memorable. Sundays were the best! For some reason, Sunday afternoons were like the Academy Awards show. People would come into the bar dressed "to the nines." So I integrated high fashion into a regular event. Each Sunday we would present a best dressed Academy Award. I succeeded in converting Mac's dive bar, which had treaded water, into an intimate neighborhood experience. The place was jammed all the time and eventually money started to flow in like a Vegas casino. Mac couldn't have been happier.

One day, actor Peter Lawford said to me, "Jimmy, you know what's missing here? There's no place to dance."

We had an outside storage area which was just a place where junk had accumulated. One evening I pointed to the storage room and announced to the entire bar, "Let's make a dance room!"

Mac wasn't going to give me money to expand because he had just started to turn a profit after five miserable years. Comedian Morey Amsterdam, who starred as Buddy in the old Dick Van Dyke Show, had a brother who owned a bar in Santa Monica. Morey's brother was selling his place and giving away some old supplies. I solicited the regulars to help me build a dance room. Many of our customers were artists, so we got together and began to build a dance hall. We cleaned out the storage room, put a few old tables from Amsterdam's place, and painted the place with a spectrum of wild colors. It was pre-psychedelic. We just might have paved the way for San Francisco's Haight-Asbury district. In a few days, we dedicated the new dance room as "The Zoo." I decided that we needed an opening night, like a

Hollywood premiere. I was bursting with excitement but as always God has a sense of humor. I hired a great band and the place was sold out with wall-to-wall people. The band was rocking and the joint was jumping. We had created the perfect nightspot. That was until seven cops appeared. About a mile down the road there was another club called Tranka's which was also on the beach. Our music broadcasted to the beach, ricocheted off the canyon rocks, then traveled up the beach, and cancelled out the music being played at Tranka's. Without any sound engineering experience, I had created the world's largest natural stereo. But in all of the opening excitement, I forgot to get zoning approval for a dance and music establishment. The cops joked with me, "Murr, they're complaining up in San Francisco." Phones at the Malibu station were ringing off the hook and my one night as Don Kirschner, rock promoter, ended with a sniffle. I killed the live

*"The Zoo." Peter Lawford suggested it and with help from some celebrities I created the place for dancing .
I opened the joint and then tried to save it after neighbors in far-off canyons
complained about the loud music!*

The Raft

music and escaped the nightclub experiment without a fine.

❧

I worked at "The Raft" night and day, around the clock, and I never took a night off. I rented a one-room efficiency apartment nearby but I rarely stopped long enough to sleep there. One night, I set the alarm but left the apartment before it went off. When it finally kicked in, it blared for five days before I eventually returned home. It was one of the few times where the Malibu residents wished I was really dead. A few evenings later they almost had their wish. At the end of the night shift, the waitresses had a bad habit of putting the trash cans in the big walk-in fireplace that occupied a wall in the bar. After everyone went home, I fell asleep on the office couch. In the night, I was awoken by a burning smell. The cigarette butts in a trash can had ignited a fire that spread through the entire bar.

Luckily, one of the first things I did when I took over managing the bar was to update our business insurance, including making sure we had the most critical feature, business interruption coverage. I got out the building alive but the fire was so intense that it melted our American Express Card machine, which was solid metal. The bigger loss, of course, was the loss of my artistic creation, "The Zoo." The insurance money equaled the debt on the whole place. I'm sure that if the same fire occurred today, investigators would surely have dogs sniffing the joint for arson. Mac eventually rebuilt the place but the fire signaled to me that it was time for me to go home, like Philadelphia home. I had come to Malibu, saved the joint for Mac, but for several months prior to the fire, my second father Art Mahan was calling me back to Philadelphia for a job in sports. He exerted pressure on me to come back to Villanova. Later on I would periodically return to visit "The Raft" but my days as the manager were over. It was one of the great experiences of my life and, painful for me to leave. It was time to get serious again about my chosen career. What I loved most about Malibu was that the culture lacked hypocrisy. People lived so differently than in my home town but they reveled in each other's individuality. When I returned home to Philly, I felt as if I was traveling back to a foreign country. It was a long while before California's laid back counter-culture became normalized throughout the country but I was grateful that I had several years of an insider's view of Hollywood. And, I had lots of memorable tabloid star gazing that today still lives in my memory. As for Mac, he gave me lots of useful learning experiences from the "Red Barn" to selling "Big Joe" to running "The Raft." Later he suffered a stroke and sadly ended up being cared for by his driver and a private nurse. I do have a confession to make. After I heard of his passing, I secretly hoped there were some profits still left in his will. For a brief moment I thought I might cash in for all of the fishing displays I sold. Nor did any of the profits that I turned in from Malibu come back to me. I only hoped that people who took care of him at the end of his life got a piece of the action. I'd like to think that I did my job of increasing this millionaire's net worth. I helped to create a "1-percenter." I returned to Philly as a "99-percenter." It wasn't long before I would be working for another colorful rich guy—Leonard Tose. I never forgot Mac. He was a true Hollywood original.

With my mentor, former employer and friend, Jim McDonald a former USAF bomber who flew over Berlin in daylight raids. Jim was a successful businessman who gave me my entrée to Malibu, CA where I managed his restaurant "The Raft."

CHAPTER 6

Settling Back Home

"Man never legislates, but destinies and accidents,
happening in all sorts of ways,
legislate in all sorts of ways."

— PLATO

I came back to Philadelphia but I took the long road, by way of Florida. Two great things happened at this time that would dramatically alter the course of my life. Art Mahan, the Athletic Director at Villanova University, offered me the job as Sports Information Director and Dianne finally reacted to my romantic overtures. I made a secret stop in Florida and I did what no good Catholic boy ever did. I married a divorced non-Catholic at a Justice of the Peace. I was so in love and after some charming sweet talk, Dianne said yes to marriage. I was ecstatic. I didn't even think about what my very strict, dogmatic parents would say when they found out. It was common practice in my family tradition to look for a nice local girl, preferably someone of the same ethnic and religious background, date for awhile, get engaged. And then with large fanfare, top it off with a large church wedding. Again, my life is an audible and in this moment I called a big one. I threw caution to the wind. What happened when I got home? We bought a house, eventually had the big Church wedding, and naturally my parents fell in love with Dianne (which no one can help when they meet her). And on top of marrying Dianne, I received a bonus immediately. I started working at Villanova. In short, it didn't just work out, it worked out great! I settled into a job I loved, working for Artie Mahan. He was the man I admired second in all the world, after my Dad. Oh, did I mention I was Irish? So of course, kids started coming faster than a hurricane. I was happy. How couldn't I be? A great wife, great kids, great job with my favorite mentor. Could life get any better?

Quickly, cut to an inconsequential event on May 1, 1969. Unbeknownst to me, this day would forever alter my universe. Leonard Hyman Tose, the son of a large wealthy trucking executive, purchased the Philadelphia Eagles football team from then owner Jerry Wolman for the paltry sum of $16 million. After winning their only NFL Championship in 1960, the Eagles became the perennial NFL doormat for the next decade. Though in 1969, the $16 million price tag seemed like Mr. Tose got taken. Actually, it turned into a bargain for it was the eve of the coming NFL explosion. From that point forward, football stepped in front of baseball as the national sport. Tose's first hire, in his newly acquired organization, was Pete Retzlaff. Retzlaff had a Hall of Fame career with the Eagles as a great tight end and receiver. After Pete retired from football, he became the Sports Director for local television station, WCAU. Pete was a mild mannered guy from South Dakota, who by sports fate, came to play for the Eagles. He stayed in Philadelphia where he became a household name. I knew Pete from Channel 10 since I dealt with him in my role as the Sports Information Director at Villanova. The sports community in Philadelphia is small and tight knit. Pete was well respected, and Leonard Tose as the new owner needed to prove to critical Philly fans that he knew what he was doing. He trusted his new image to Pete.

Arthur Leo Mahan

≈§

One morning, Art Mahan walked into my office and said in his thick Bostonian accent, "Hey, Jimmy, why don't you go down to the Eagles and check out one of those jobs? I hear they're hiring." What? Why would I go down there for a job? I had a great job at Villanova and Dianne and I were having kids every five minutes. I was the happiest guy in the world. Go down to the Eagles and check out one of those jobs? Even though the Augustinian priests who ran the University took the vow of poverty, I was living it. But I didn't care! I worked for the guy I loved, at the school I loved. But Artie insisted, "Jimmy, go down there and see what they've got to offer." Artie knew school politics inside out and at this particular time there was great political turmoil on the campus. In his wisdom, Artie sensed that the Villanova ground was shaky. Instinctively, Artie knew that his own job was in jeopardy. That meant that my job was in jeopardy as well. Artie was father to 11 children and he demanded that I acted unsentimentally. "You watch out for what is best for your family's future!" he shouted. If he was nothing else, Artie was a straight, no nonsense guy. His kind of directness never flies well in an autocratic institution like a Catholic university. At first, I resented Artie's suggestion. Seek refuge in self-protection? That wasn't the Artie way. "But, Artie," I protested, " I'm working for my best friend and mentor, come on, I don't want another job." Thankfully, Artie doggedly persisted and fortunately I eventually heard his message. Thank God I listened, because several months later, Artie was indeed fired as the Athletic Director. It was a sad day in a lot of lives. Even today, when I think about it, I get a lump in my throat. It seems that organizations always get these types of decisions wrong. Top-down thinking seems to always say, "Let's get the old guy out of here...he's seen better days." In my life, I've never witnessed a bigger mistake by an organization than the day that Villanova let Artie go.

I contacted the Eagles' office just as Artie commanded. They called me in to interview for the very coveted job of Assistant Publicity

Director. Unlucky for me, it was for the big NFL team in the city of Philadelphia. There weren't too many sports jobs to begin with and they were few openings. If you were lucky enough to get in with one of the three city teams, you would never be dumb enough to leave. ୬୫

I had my initial interview with Pete Retzlaff. It was cordial but I can't say that my heart was in it. I only interviewed to please Artie. I came back to my office at Villanova and Artie asked, "How did you do?" Artie knew me well. He could see me hem and haw and shuffle my feet. Artie's voice boomed as he pressed, "You didn't do your best job, now did you Jim?" Not satisfied that I did, Artie insisted that I go back and interview again. "You didn't do your best! You've got to call him and go back for another interview."

"But I don't want to leave here," I protested.

"I don't want you to leave either, but you've got no future here. You're going to go back and get that job and you're going to do better this time!" Artie spoke like a parent and I listened like a son.

୬୫

Pete Retzlaff was a bit stiff. He came from a German background, and no one would have ever nicknamed him, "Mister Yucks." I was embarrassed that I had to call him back but I never disobeyed a command from Artie.

"Pete," I said with a quivering voice, "this is Jimmy, I've got to come back."

"What? You were just here!"

"Yeah, I know, but I've got to do my Gene Kelly impersonation. I've got to dance on your desk and do a better job," I pleaded. "Please, can I get another shot?"

The next day, embarrassingly I went back to Pete's office. This time I was as bubbly as Mickey Rooney dancing with Judy Garland. For some reason, Pete said, "You're right, you didn't do your best job. And, I want you to work for the Eagles." I was in.

☙

At Villanova, as the Sports Information Director, I was fighting for publicity with the local media each and every day. On a good day, I would get the school mentioned on the bottom line of a church newsletter. When suddenly I became the Eagles guy, I moved from the back page to the front page. SID's in colleges, in terms of coverage for your school, spent the bulk of their days, pitching for just a crumb of publicity. I was batting 0 for 10, each and every day. At Villanova, I lived as the ultimate cellar dweller. I merely serviced the Villanova account like Willy Loman with bad leads. It was as if I were selling insurance to my brother's brother-in-law's neighbor. Moving to the Eagles was like moving to Exxon—immediate public relations on steroids!

The first day on the job defined my entire career. It firmly established a humility from that day forward that has never left me. The Eagles' offices were located in the same building that was home to the *Philadelphia Bulletin* newspaper. *The Bulletin* was the late great evening Philadelphia paper that went the way of the Edsel. They sat directly across from 30th Street Station in downtown

*Jimmy Murray with Eagles' Vice President
and General Manager (1969-1972) Pete Retzlaff*

Philadelphia. I showed up excited, and dressed like a Main Line cover boy. I wore a blue blazer and corduroy pants, the official outfit of the conservative Villanova University and Republicans everywhere. Immediately, I was escorted to a small cubicle that was my new office. The pencils could barely fit. I got my big promotion to the NFL, and then I got an office that was the size of the coat closet at my old job. Jimmy Gallagher, the Publicity Director, was my new boss. Jimmy had been with the Eagles since the beginning of time and was a *mensch* of a guy. The only thing that was bigger than the size of Jimmy's heart was the size of the ulcer in his stomach. He

Jimmy Murray, Jimmy Gallagher (my first boss at The Philadelphia Eagles) and my brother, Franny "Bench" Murray

drank antacids by the gallon. Jimmy had held every job in the organization and knew more about the Eagles than anyone before or since. One day Jimmy said, "Here's what it's like at the top, now go in your CUBICLE and familiarize yourself with the files." It was a George Constanza moment, right out of the sitcom "Seinfeld." I sat awkwardly in the cubicle for eight hours looking over files and trying to appear busy and important as George did when he worked for Mr. Kruger. In the bottom drawer of my desk sat a huge pile of folders that turned out to be the files of everyone who applied for the Assistant Publicity Director's job. I counted the files. 142 people applied for my job. Suddenly, I was curious. Why did I get the job? Who did I beat out? As I looked through the résumés, I decided to invent my own ratings system. I needed to see where I stood. For some reason, I fit in with Pete Retzlaff. He liked me from his days at Channel 10, maybe it was my Irish charm. Objectively, after looking over the files, I didn't even deserve to get a cup of coffee from the organization. Using my own estimations, I came in 88th for the job. I beat out guys who looked like Adonis and even those smart looking other guys in tweed jackets smoking pipes and talking like a Ph.D. There were a few serious journalists that I hurdled over. And when I was a Sports Information Director, I did a rather poor job playing serious journalist. But, it was luck at first sight. Behind these files in the bottom drawer were Jerry Wolman's personal files. Jerry Wolman, the previous owner somehow left some things behind. I glanced through his letters in the file and I soon came to know that Jerry was a terrific guy. And, he was, up to his recent passing. That stack of letters in the file drawer testified to Jerry's character and popularity. Jerry and I become great friends, and up until his death we called each other regularly. He remains one of the great people that I've met in sport. Jerry wrote his memoir, *The World's Richest Man*...it is a wonderful read that I highly recommend.

"Dear Mr. Wolman...congratulations on being named 'Man of the Year'...Dear Mr. Wolman...thank you so much for your generosity...Dear Mr. Wolman...B'nai Brith would like to honor you with its annual..." etc. etc.

Jerry had built a large, successful construction business after coming from very humble beginnings in upstate Pennsylvania. His story is the quintessential "rags to riches" tale. When he was young and dating his future wife, Wolman had a fight with his future father-in-law. His wife and he decided to leave their small town for greener pastures. Like most newlyweds, they wanted less family interference. At the time, his wife asked him where they were planning to go as they ran away from home. Jerry said that they would go to the same place as the first hitchhiker they spotted and picked up. Where ever the hitchhiker was headed, that's where they would end up. Then they picked up a college kid who was going to Washington DC. So Jerry and his wife settled in the nation's capitol. Jerry started his business, set out to make his fortune, and indeed, he made his fortune. He went on to purchase the Eagles for $5.2 million. As I said earlier, Jerry sold the team to Leonard Tose for the bargain price of $16,155,000. It was more money than anyone had paid for a professional sports franchise up to that time. Compare that to today's billion-dollar Eagles price tag. A trivial amount today but at the time it was big news in Philadelphia.

❧

Jimmy Gallagher saw me reading Jerry's history and joked fortuitously, "Murr, don't get a big head working for the Eagles because the former owner ended up in the bottom drawer of the Assistant Publicity Director's desk." I repeated that line to Jerry years later and we both laughed loud and long about it. Jimmy's words turned out to be more prophetic than I could have ever imagined. I speak more about this later on.

❧

I quickly became acclimated to my new circumstances as an employee of Leonard Hyman Tose. There could easily be an entire book

Leonard Hyman Tose
A proud Notre Dame grad and very colorful
owner of The Philadelphia Eagles

dedicated just to Leonard and there may well be some day. Leonard Tose was as book worthy a fellow who has ever walked the earth. He was one of the great characters of all time and certainly the most colorful man that I've ever met. And, I'll add, one of the great friends in my life. Len was a Jewish kid from Norristown, a working class town outside of Philadelphia. Norristown sits on the Schuylkill River, just a few miles west of Philadelphia. The Schuylkill (pronounced "skookul") is the main body of water that cuts through Philadelphia and no one ever spells the name correctly twice in their life. You have to live in Philadelphia for at least twenty years before you can pronounce it. There is the famous Schuylkill Expressway that runs from Philadelphia to the western suburbs. It's not an expressway at all for the residents of Philly. It's a four-lane parking facility and if you need to be late for an occasion or need an excuse to miss an event, just say you were trapped on the Schuylkill and people instantly understand and forgive you.

Len's father founded the successful Tose Trucking Company. Len's father became very, very, very, wealthy. Leonard was an out-of-control teen, who liked cigarettes, drinking, and women. He didn't care much about what the order they came in. His father had a priest friend and the elder Tose asked the priest for advice. How many times did a Jewish man ask a priest for advice? Well, this time it benefited the Catholic university and the Jewish scholar! It just goes to demonstrate the extreme personality of Leonard Tose. His father needed to rein in Leonard from the wild side. The priest recommended that Leonard be sent to the University of Notre Dame. A conservative Catholic always thought that the discipline and tradition of Notre Dame was a sure fire way to improve character. The elderly Jewish father apparently agreed. Mr. Tose sent Leonard packing for South Bend, Indiana. The priest was right. It turned out to be the perfect fit. Leonard loved football and quickly fell in love with Notre Dame. After college, Leonard came back to Norristown to work in the family business, but he continued to be a lifelong "Golden Domer." After he secured his fortune, Leonard served on the Notre Dame's Board of Trustees. He played a huge part in putting Notre Dame back on the road to prominence as a national football power. Not bad for an out-of-control Jewish kid, whose kosher father sent him to a Catholic school for some discipline.

Leonard developed a close relationship with the legendary Irish coach Frank Leahy. Allow me to digress for a moment about Frank Leahy. Normally, I'm not a star struck guy. Throughout my life I've had the good fortune to meet all types of people, celebrities and non-celebrities. But, I stood in wide-eyed awe the day I met Coach Leahy. Soon after I got the job with the Eagles, I was invited to help with a charity benefit back at my alma mater, Villanova. I went to Leonard right away and asked him if he could possibly help out with the affair. He volunteered to invite Frank Leahy as a keynote speaker for the evening. Leahy was up in years at this time and he could barely walk without the aid of a walker. He was weak to the point he had to be carried into the room. I anticipated that he would have a difficult time addressing such a large audience. Coach Leahy took the microphone and then delivered one of the most memorable talks I have ever heard. He was a cross between Burt Lancaster in *Elmer Gantry* and the legendary Bishop Fulton Shee-han. In fact, no clergy person in my experience ever delivered such a powerful sermon. He mesmerized everyone down to the last bus-boy. Leahy hit it out of the park. He received a five-minute standing ovation. After his talk, I ran up to his seat and asked for an auto-graph. I stuttered like a bubbly teenager but he was kind and gra-cious. He posed for a picture with my young son, Jimmy, and me. I carried that picture in my wallet for a long, long time. Sadly, one day a few years later, I was a victim of a pickpocket. I lost that pic-ture in the process. I'm still angry about it. I only pray that the pickpocket was a Notre Dame fan and could appreciate the spoils of his theft. The night with Leahy is one more example of a great life experience I chalked up as a gift from Leonard. There would be countless more while being under his employ. Working for Leonard Tose became and remained for years to come, a thrill.

≈✤

As I mentioned, Pete Retzlaff was Leonard's first hire after he purchased the team. Leonard understood that Philly fans were and always remained vocally critical of sports management. Any sports person worth his salt understands the depth of passion that Philadelphians have for their teams. And, any owner understands the scrutiny that awaits his or her every move. Leonard wanted to put the city at ease immediately and let them know he was a competent owner. Pete was a fan favorite so Leonard felt that Pete's hire would get him off on the right foot with Eagles fans. Pete, as the new General Manager, inherited a disaster. His first words to me after putting me on the payroll were, "Jimmy, just make sure we fill up the seats." My minor league experience with all my exposure to crazy promoters, left me poised for the challenge. You might remember this, you might not. Before the NFL exploded into the mega-billion dollar business it is today, selling professional football required work and creativity. This was especially true for my very first task.

"Jimmy, we want to sell out the pre-season games," Pete said.

The four exhibition games were not obligatory for season ticket holders as they are today. I like to put it in Catholic terms: they were not holy days of obligation. I stood on Franklin Field in 1969 with our very first game against the Washington Redskins. Franklin Field, on the campus of the University of Pennsylvania, was the home of the University of Penn "Quakers" on Saturdays but on Sundays it was home to the Philadelphia Eagles. Soon after I began with the team, we moved to Veterans Stadium but Franklin Field still remains one of my favorite football venues of all time. It is a stunning, classic football stadium and like they say, "they don't build them like that anymore." This particular game with the Redskins was an afternoon game in August. The temperature was in the high 90s with a dose of close Philadelphia humidity thrown in for good measure. I lost five pounds just waiting for a hot dog. The University of Pennsylvania had recently installed AstroTurf, one of the first stadiums to experiment with artificial surfaces. AstroTurf was the granddaddy of all of those to follow. AstroTurf was legendary for holding heat. The temperature on the turf hovered somewhere in the neighborhood of 140 degrees. A skeletal group of Redskins quarterbacks and receivers took the field for the pre-game warm-up. We should have called it the pre-game stroke. They were soaking wet with perspiration snapping their chinstraps. I stood in the back of their end zone taking in the scene just pondering my amazing luck. Despite the heat, I was giddy with the thought of working for the Eagles. For a brief moment, I felt extra full of myself. The stadium filled up nicely for the first game. Same as today, exhibition games are where marquee players take three snaps then hit the showers so the 97 rookies trying to make the squad can break each other's necks impressing coaches. I, too, had to impress my new bosses. So, I had papered the house, so to speak. Anyone who could walk, talk, or drive a Tose truck got into the stadium for free. Luckily, the new management wasn't counting dollars, just fan interest. As I stood bathing in my momentary glory, I heard an aggressive voice from a few feet behind me.

"Hey, what are you going to do about this?"

At first, it sounded like some cranky guy complaining to someone else so I didn't turn around.

"Hey, I'm talking to you! What the hell are YOU going to do about this?" The second comment seemed directed right towards me and it was much louder and harder to ignore.

I still pretended that I didn't hear.

"Hey, you simple son of a bitch, I'm talking to you! I want to know what the hell are you doing about this field? It's a 150 goddamn degrees!"

Finally, I turned around and within six inches of my face stood the legend himself. The great Vince Lombardi! With the sun blinding me, it was like an apparition of Mary. It was like a holy card of a beautiful figure appearing from heaven that only the three children at Fatima could see. Although, I'm sure Lombardi was a much angrier apparition. This Mary would appear to me wearing a brimmed hat. He was hot, bothered and frothing at the mouth. Like any good coach, his angry concern was for the health of his players. Honestly, with the house filling up, the heat on the field wasn't exactly my immediate concern. He then stood glaring at me for several long minutes, his nostrils flaring, looking like a bull running in Spain. I flinched.

I said, "You're God and I'm only an altar boy. What the hell are you going to do about it?"

Lombardi paused a few seconds and then burst out laughing. That was my first "real" moment in the NFL. I defused the greatest, most intimidating, and in that moment, the angriest football coach of all time. In just minutes, I experienced his larger than life presence. Reacting to his demands, I ran around like a crazed chicken for the next

*Franklin Field on the University of Pennsylvania campus where the Eagles played
home games. Vince Lombardi with the Redskins after he left the Packers.
On one of the hottest days imaginable, he was testy but you can't
argue with the greatest NFL coach of all-time, so I took care of him!*

hour making sure that ice, water, and operational fans were delivered
to the sidelines and that towels were placed at every player's fingertips. The game went on in front of 65,000 fans, with only about $500
collected at the gate. Today, I would be fired for a similarly over-
booked flop. But everyone was happy! And me? I breathed a deep sigh
of relief knowing that the Tose train was pulling out of the station.

෫෫

Several weeks later I went to New York for an NFL press event. It
took place in the swanky Waldorf Astoria where reporters could
fraternize with players and coaches before the opening of the season. Coaches stood in different parts of the large ballroom taking
questions from the press about who were that year's best teams and

their season forecasts. You could tell the big shots of the NFL from the little guys by the migratory patterns of the reporters. A throng of a hundred or so writers flocked around Lombardi. I took a spot in the back of the crowd and listened to him talk about the Redskins and his quarterback, Sonny Jurgenson. But, Lombardi was more than a football coach. He could cover any topic within or out of football. This was at the height of the Vietnam War and he enjoyed waxing political and philosophical about America's battle against the Red Menace. It didn't matter what topic, Lombardi commanded attention. I stood and watched a man who was at the top of his powers and the journalists couldn't write his quotes fast enough. What a thrill it was to be in the middle of the action, pinching myself for the luck of being part of this great scene. Several weeks later, in the blink of an eye, Lombardi was diagnosed with cancer and he died within the year. The lesson of "one moment you're here and the next moment you're gone" wasn't wasted on me. At that particular moment at the Waldorf, Lombardi seemed to have it all. This man, who epitomized the game itself, was only moments away from his last quarter. I have always been grateful for the opportunity to meet and witness Lombardi's greatness. And when I say greatness, there's not an ounce of exaggeration here. Yet, the whole experience fed my deep Irish side. I couldn't help but feel the strange twists that the life seems to weave. We Irish can feel the melancholy in these moments. This man, Lombardi, stood like a Greek God one day but soon faced the inevitable fragility of life.

The challenges in Philadelphia were huge. The Eagles weren't any good. No, change that. They were abysmal. Or as the typical Philly fan might whine, "They stunk!" I was not only an employee but also a lifelong, suffering fan. We hadn't been good for a long, long time, like since Eisenhower was president. Philly fans historically get a bad rap, but they had been patient throughout the 1960s. However, when Leonard took over, they were full-blown, mature cynics. Unlike Pavlov's dogs, they had been conditioned to have zero expectations and had completely stopped salivating![1] The team was oftentimes referred to as the "Bungles," and we were the perennial town joke. I possessed no illusions that I would suddenly change the course of this downward spiral. After all, I was the lowly Assistant Publicity guy. Despite my pauper status, I was thrilled to go to work every day for an NFL franchise. I did have a burden of carrying one secret around with me. I was a press guy but I couldn't type. Throughout my life I have been mechanically challenged. I was the sports information director responsible for getting words out to the public with no means to complete the task. My whole life is incongruous. What was so different from any other job I ever held? I worked in baseball and didn't play baseball. I managed a bar and didn't drink. I sold "Big Joe" lures and didn't fish. Once at the NCAA Final Four in Houston in 1971, I accidentally got on the radio and did an entire radio broadcast on the fly with no prior experience. So, add radio announcer who never announced to my list of accomplishments that grew out of no skills. Actually the NCAA story is a funny one. Villanova had made it to the Final Four and naturally being a die hard 'Nova fan, I decided to take the ride to Houston, without a ticket for the game. I had complete faith in my natural gift of blarney and as I've said, I have faith in God. Despite no ticket, I was able to finagle my way into the Astrodome. While I stood at courtside, one of the local Philadelphia announcers covering the game recognized me and called me over to the announcer's table. It was during a commercial and he asked if I wanted to go on air and say "hi" to all of the fans back in Philly. He introduced me and quickly we became engaged in a conversation about the game. We never took a breath from that moment on. I sat there with a headset on for the entire game, offering my two-bit analysis. It was a "Forrest Gump" moment. I've had a ton.

One day, Pete Retzlaff called me into his office. "We're opening Veterans Stadium and you've got one job, make sure that we're not embarrassed." Veterans Stadium was the new jewel of Philadelphia. This was years before it fell into disrepair and became a civic embarrassment. Many of the major cities were building similar all-purpose stadiums for their football and baseball teams. Pittsburgh had Three Rivers Stadium and Cincinnati had Riverfront. All of the stadiums were cookie cutter designed and eventually were knocked down and replaced by the new ultra-modern facilities we have today. Teams now charge a year's salary for a ticket and no one flinches. Gee, where's the challenge to today's ticket managers? Veterans Stadium became a huge liability to Philadelphia in the last part of the millennium and was eventually demolished in 2003. But in 1971, my job was to fill it to the brim for the opener. This meant even more pressure than my first experience at Franklin Field. We were coming off the previous 2-12 season and again, the annual Eagles forecast appeared bleak. Everyone predicted that once again, we would sleep in the basement. The exhibition opener was against the Buffalo Bills, who happened to be the only team in the league worse than us. They were 1-13 the previous year but with the number one pick in the college draft, they selected their new franchise player, O.J. Simpson. Still, even with a heralded rookie like O.J., finding 65,000 people in August to watch two doormats play exhibition football was an uphill struggle.

Immediately, I conjured up images of old Bill Veeck's tactics and all of the crazy promotion people who tutored me over the years in minor league baseball. I needed to sell out the entire stadium and from the tone of Pete's voice, my life and job depended on it. And unlike my first days at Franklin Field, Pete wanted to see paying fans. Who would pay for the new stadium? Certainly not the freebies from my "paper the stadium" tactics. Sometimes, when my back is to the wall and I lay in bed tossing and turning over my inevitable demise, I come up with some clever ideas. Fortunately in this particular stressful moment, my creative gene indeed materialized. I came to my own rescue. A lighting bolt hit me. Marlboro cigarettes! Cigarettes? What kind of lightning bolt is "cigarettes"? Cigarettes would sell all of the tickets. Until the late 1960s, cigarette companies advertised everywhere. You couldn't turn on a television or radio or pick up a magazine without seeing a cigarette commercial. Everyone smoked. The most recognizable ad in the country was the "Marlboro Man." In every magazine, the "Marlboro Man" sat on his horse looking out over some canyon in the old west, the picture of ruggedness. What made a tough American male? A Marlboro cigarette dangling from your mouth cinched it. Tough guys and Marlboros went hand in hand, like mustard and hot dogs. However, big news suddenly hit the stands. The Surgeon General of the United States released a report and a subsequent health warning about the hazards of smoking. Next, the Federal government stepped in and stopped cigarettes from being peddled on television ads. If I was judged by today's morality, the entire health profession would want my hide for my ticket idea based on cigarette smoking. Fortunately, in 1971 I didn't have to worry about any fall out. Today, I'd be tarred and feathered!

෨෪

My first move was to engage a young artist by the name of Dick Perez to help me visualize my ideas. Dick grew up in Puerto Rico and loved baseball. I met him during my minor league days and eventually helped him land a job with the Philadelphia Phillies. As a friend, Dick is a number one draft pick. As an artist, he is a Hall of Famer. He is a quiet, no-nonsense guy but he has one of the most creative minds of anyone I had ever met. Later in his career, Dick would become the official artist for the Baseball Hall of Fame in Cooperstown. But in 1971, he played a key role in my career path. I was always an idea guy. I loved and still love to manufacture a million-dollar concept. Sadly, I never seemed to possess the skills to execute my genius. Dick Perez knew how to execute and God sent him to me at precisely the right moment. My plan was to get Marlboro (Phillip Morris Co.) to buy out Veterans Stadium for the opener. I came up with the phrase, "Eagles Country, Marlboro Country." I heard the theme from the film, *The Magnificent Seven*

Dick Perez and Jimmy Murray

play in my head and it was the perfect music for the campaign. Today, I wouldn't get past the security guard at Phillip Morris with such an elementary idea. Keep in mind, this was before the advent of mega-sports marketing. There were no computers, no Power-Point presentations, no fancy graphics. I had an idea and I had an extremely talented artist who listened to me. Added to this vision, I included Pete Retzlaff, who was rugged enough to be the real Marlboro Man. Pete would be sitting on a horse dressed as a cowboy. I got Eddie Mahan, Artie's son and Eagles' team photographer, to take some pictures of Pete dressed as the Marlboro Man. Pete wouldn't sit on a horse, so we improvised with Pete, standing with a saddle over his shoulder. We stuck a visible pack of Marlboros jutting from his shirt pocket. I had special lighters made with the Eagles emblem on one side and the Marlboro logo on the other. Dick and Eddie came up with a great poster of the new Veterans' Stadium with our Marlboro Country motif. Then, we made this amazing pitch presentation with music and a photo montage of Marlboro and the City of Brotherly Love. It was spectacular. We were way ahead of our time and the presentation, even by today's standards, at the risk of bragging, it was as impressive as anything you would see in the digital age. Dick built an oversized box of Marlboro cigarettes. Each point of our presentation was highlighted on a cigarette sticking from the box. If it was a term paper, I'd have made the Dean's list. There was just one small detail that I overlooked. I didn't have any way to get my masterpiece in front of the Marlboro executives. Who was I going to present this too?

The Leo Burnett agency in New York represented Marlboro and it was crucial that I obtained an appointment. Pete Rozelle, the commissioner in waiting, was still a young junior NFL executive. Pete was single and ran around New York with his good friend Jack Landry. Jack was the head account executive for Marlboro at Burnett. I had met Pete a few times but we were far from close friends but, he was my only chance to gain access to Marlboro. I called Pete and asked him if he could get me in front of Jack and his staff. Pete obliged and then he called me back to tell me that he secured a face to face meeting for me. Up until the last meeting, Dick and I worked furiously on the final touches of the presentation. Just like two colleges kids, we pulled an all-night cram session. We had Pete Retzlaff and another radio personality, Dick Clayton, do some great voiceover work and at 4 A.M., deliriously finished the whole thing. Dick Perez and I took a deep breath, rehearsed the presentation one time and agreed we could knock the socks off of any audience. Early next morning a group of us boarded the train from Philly to New York. I looked ridiculous carrying an oversized Marlboro box and Pete just shook his head. For the entire ride to New York, Pete skeptically asked, "Do you really think they'll buy this?"

We walked into the conference room and met five guys who today, can be seen on any episode of "Mad Men." Landry liked athletes so he invited Pete to sit next to him. Trying to appear calm, I arranged the audio and slide show. Next, I distributed bound books of the Eagles portraits with the Marlboro brand displayed prominently throughout. Leo Carlin, our ticket manager was seated at one end of the table. Leo, another one of the great people I've been privileged to meet in sport, was busy saying a silent rosary for me. It was abundantly clear to everyone present that I had climbed out on a far limb. It was a total all-in Vegas bet. At the other end of the table sat this expressionless character, who looked as if he jumped out of a Charles Dickens novel. In fact he was a dead ringer for the ghost of Christmas past. He was Burnett's assassin. One thing that I learned that day was that every big decision meeting with an organization comes equipped with an assassin. The assassin is clearly there to shout a loud "No!" to any proposal. This guy was ready to send me off the prison for wasting their time with a stupid idea. In hindsight, I should have been intimidated but I wasn't. For some reason, I always loved this type of excitement, even though I had no idea just how unsure Pete Retzlaff was feeling about my presentation. Later Pete confessed, he was unsure of me altogether.

Fortunately for me it was a case of, what you don't know can't hurt you. I turned the lights down and the presentation went off flawlessly, even better than we had anticipated. The crescendo of the Philadelphia Orchestra's Beethoven music built to a fever pitch with the last frame displaying a cigarette that said, "65,000 seats in Eagles Country for $500,000!" Voiceovers, bells, and whistles! Even these bored Madison Ave. executives, who had seen it all, sat breathless. Even the assassin stood up and applauded. He then said, "Who the hell came up with this idea? It's magnificent!" Trying to contain my excitement, I humbly nodded, giving credit to my team of Dick and Eddie. I said to myself what I always say to myself when I feel I've been successful. "Game, Set, Match!" Clearly, we nailed the winning point. They even asked if I could leave the cigarette box behind as a souvenir for their office. The meeting ended on an incredible high note with my boss Pete, beaming. Who would imagine that this no-name Assistant Publicity Director just barreled over the Burnett advertising establishment? Afterwards, we went to a restaurant down the street called Rose's, which was next door to the famous Toots Shors'. Pete ordered drinks and raised his glass to me saying, "Jimmy, I was so proud of you and what you did, I'm going to make you Assistant General Manager." Wow! I sat speechless, which by the way, is an occurrence as rare as Haley's Comet. I hadn't been speechless since birth. It was the best high I ever had. But like all drugs, the highs don't last. Even though the Marlboro and Burnett folks loved the idea and were ready to sign the check to buy out the Vet, lawyers got involved. Someone either on our side or their side asked a question that flashed a red light. The question was whether or not the Eagles wanted to promote a product that was known to cause cancer. I never was privy to all of the details but the whole idea quickly got derailed. My great idea was dead and, I would have to quickly come up with another flash of brilliance to sell out the Vet. Later, Jack Landry and the Burnett agency subconsciously lifted my exact campaign idea. Soon after, Marlboro began buying up sporting events all over the country. Sports marketing, as we know it today, was born. I'm not egotistical enough to take the credit for inventing the marriage between sports and advertisers, but soon after this event, Marlboro and auto racing forged a relationship that was christened the "Marlboro Cup." Suddenly other companies were buying naming rights to horse races. Please Anheuser-Busch, don't thank me. But, I'd like to think that I was one of the early guests at this game. After I struck out at Marlboro, my creative genius would have to wait for another opportu-

Jimmy Murray and Leonard Tose (Veterans Stadium)

nity. Yet as the saying goes, sometimes when a door shuts, a window opens.

₰

There was a happy ending to the story. I became Pete's new Assistant GM with a nice, tidy raise. What great timing! Since Dianne and I were having kids at a rate that seemed monthly, an increase in pay was a Godsend.

₰

The first game with O.J. was a huge sell out. The public address announcer echoed that there were 70,000 in attendance but the ticket manager knew that we only got money from 20,000. It's safe enough to admit today that I resorted back to my papering tricks. Little leaguers, cub scouts, cloistered nuns, Hindu high priests. It didn't matter, if you had a pulse and could stand without assistance, we let you in! O.J., the Heisman Trophy winner was carrying the future of Buffalo on his shoulders. Despite that fact that the Bills and the Eagles had a combined three wins from the previous season, the name O.J. Simpson generated excitement. It's hard for people to remember that O.J. was once known for his ability to run a football and O.J. could do that as well as anyone I ever witnessed. I still can't get over how his life turned out. Only Shakespeare could have written that ending. The National Anthem played and I winked above and I whispered a small "Thank you, God!" Pete and Leonard were happy and that's all I cared about. The next day, the newspapers were abuzz with the fact that Eagles managed their first sell out in their history. Even Mayor Frank Rizzo came to the game. Rizzo, a former cop and resident South Philly tough guy, commented that "the police were caught off guard because normally no one watches the Eagles." With a new stadium and an unexpected turnout for the game, the police called in a ton of reinforcements then invented new traffic patterns in and around South Philadelphia. It was a watershed moment for the Eagles. After the game I walked on cloud nine. I was the Assistant GM and my future looked rosy!

CHAPTER 7

The School of the NFL

"We are not always what we seem,
and hardly ever what we dream."

— PETER BEAGLE

I started to penetrate the inside of the Philadelphia Eagles' business organization soon after my success at cramming Veterans Stadium for several meaningless pre-season games. The first moment I realized I was suddenly taking part in bigger decisions was the firing of our coach Jerry Williams. Jerry had come to the Eagles from the Canadian Football League, where he had won the Gray Cup. The Gray Cup is Canada's equivalent to a Super Bowl. Though, in reality, comparing Canadian football to the American counterpart is like comparing an asteroid to Earth. It was the first time I participated in the firing of a coach and to be truthful, it is an awful task. Firing someone gives you an empty feeling. And the feeling stays awhile and there's no antacid or pill that relieves it. It's one of those things in life you wish didn't happen. When you tell someone that they've lost their job, the whole time you examine yourself as well, and you understand perfectly your own inadequacies. Williams was a very nice guy and the reasons for a team's poor performance normally go well beyond the coach. As is always the case in business, someone has to take the blame for poor performance. Most of the time, justice doesn't prevail. In the end, Leonard thought Jerry Williams had to go. Fans have to perceive that the owner has a clue even when he doesn't. I felt very bad saying goodbye to Jerry. He had relocated his family to Philadelphia and no sooner had they settled down, we fired him. Such is the life of a professional sports coach. As they say, it comes with the territory.

As Assistant General Manager, I traveled with the Eagles posse, the insiders, the dealmakers, the movers, the shakers. The first indication that I had arrived in the big time took place at an NFL owners meeting in New York. Pete Rozelle, who was the commissioner at the time, called a meeting to discuss some of the league's marketing issues. I'll talk about Pete Rozelle momentarily because to this day, I'm still one of his biggest fans. Ironically, Pete was not the first pick of the owners. His past résumé included working for a public relations firm in San Francisco. When the owners were searching for a commissioner, they originally wanted a lawyer, as that's the common pedigree of business leaders. The commissioner's main job was and is to negotiate deals, whether with unions, networks, or advertisers. Logic demands a lawyer as the rational choice for the job. However, Rozelle was a very smart guy

Pete Rozelle

who never went to law school. I know lawyers might have a hard time conceding that there are smart guys in the room other than lawyers, but Pete convinced a cadre of owners that he was the man for the job. One of his first official moves was to relocate the NFL offices from Philadelphia to New York—410 Park Avenue, to be exact—high rent district. Why? Rozelle's thinking was simple. He wanted the league offices to be within walking distance of Madison Avenue, which of course, was the home of all advertising agencies. Rozelle, an incredible visionary, foresaw the coming mushroom cloud that would be the marriage of football and television. The league needed a drop-in relationship with the product pushers. For some reason, Pete liked me right away. Mainly, I think he realized I was able to translate Leonard Tose for him. Len, as an owner, was a rebel without a cause and often, one without a clue. Len, more than anyone I've ever seen, could consistently throw a monkey wrench into the smoothest-sailing meeting. At the league meetings, the owners usually sat at school desks, lined up in rows, very much like a group of rich prep schoolboys. Len never liked meetings and he sure as heck didn't like school or desks. He proved this early in his stunted academic career as a boy growing up in Norristown. On one trip to a New York meeting, Leonard sent me on an errand. He instructed me to go out of the hotel and find a furniture store.

"Get me one of those La-Z-Boy recliners," he snapped. "And make sure it's green!" he added.

He demanded absolute comfort during the meetings. Thus, my regular duty for the next several years was to attend to Leonard's coziness. No matter where a meeting would take place, from New York to Los Angeles to Miami Beach, Len would expect a comfortable chair in which to recline while he participated in important league business. The legendary Cleveland owner Art Modell, who later was hung in effigy for moving the Browns to Baltimore, would sit in the chair before Leonard arrived. Modell, despite what Clevelanders remember about him, was a very funny guy. I'll go as far as saying he was one of the nicest guys I ever met in sports. Art radiated warmth and charm that made you feel that you were important to him. I always felt he was forever misjudged because of his actions in Cleveland. The truth of the move to Baltimore was rooted in the fact that Modell was losing his shirt in Cleveland. As a businessman, he had no choice but to take a better deal in Baltimore. The sports business model changed rapidly and Art reacted to changes in the new realities of the business. Okay Cleveland fans, you can hate me for saying this, and I know that this might hurt book sales in Ohio, but Art Modell was a genuinely great person. His generosity was legendary to a fault and anyone who knew him well can substantiate my testimony on his behalf. He was a compassionate and caring friend. I was extremely saddened to hear the news of his passing. I have one vivid memory of Art. Whenever he would enter a meeting and spot Leonard's chair, he would tease me with, "Murr, can I sit in THE chair before the boss gets here?" Art made me laugh and I count him as a great mentor. He continued to help me after I got my big break becoming the General Manager.

ஐௐ

Len was chronically late for meetings, no matter who was on the guest list. Presidents or Popes, Len kept people waiting. However, when he finally arrived, it was in style. His hair perfectly coiffed and he dressed to the nines. One memorable time, Len got so bored with some mundane piece of business at an owners' meeting that he left the meeting. Len walked outside on Park Avenue, took a stroll and landed in a Mercedes dealership. In just a few minutes, he bought a huge, blue Mercedes. Can you imagine that? Leonard, at this time, had sufficient funds to satisfy any impulse that grew from his boredom. After the meeting, he made me drive the new Mercedes and him back to Philadelphia. I didn't feel comfortable driving my own car, which was usually a jalopy. Driving a spanking new Mercedes, which was worth more than the collective worth of the Murray family tree, was a nail biter. The next day Len decided that he needed a full-time driver for his new purchase. I'm sure it came from driving home from New York with me. Naturally when Len had a sudden flight of fancy, he looked to me to execute it. This particular impulse of Leonard's almost cost me my job. There was a young kid in Philadelphia who was the recipient of an award called the "Hero Scholarship Fund." The fund was set up for children of fallen police officers, those who died in the line of duty. One morning Leonard read an article in the *Philadelphia Inquirer* about some of the scholarship recipients. Always generous, and always wanting to help the community Leonard said, "Get me one of those kids from that police scholarship thing to drive me around." I made a few calls and I found a nice South Philly kid named Jimmy. I forget his last name but Jimmy was a cross between Rocky Balboa and Michael Corleone. Leonard, who was bad with names, took to calling him "Jimmy Front Seat," because Len sat in the back while Jimmy was the driver. Soon after Jimmy's hiring, we were scheduled for a meeting in Philadelphia City Hall with then Councilman George Schwartz. If you know your Philadelphia history, this was the same George Schwartz of "Abscam" fame. (Schwartz and several others were pinched by the FBI for bribery and sent to prison.) On this day, a classic Nor'easter storm blew through Philadelphia. The rain measured inches per second. Jimmy Front Seat was having a difficult time negotiating his new position as a young, no-experience limo driver. The storm brought high winds, driving rain, and a foggy windshield making Jimmy's job more difficult. As usual, Len was in the back seat dressed in a thousand dollar custom suit with hair gel still drying. I figured I would crack a window slightly to get some air circulating in the car, and possibly improve Jimmy's visibility. Unknowingly, I hit the button which operated the convertible roof. The roof opened widely letting buckets of water pour into the car. The water soaked Leonard's expensive suit and stiff hair making him look like he had been sprayed by a bottle of seltzer. He then proceeded to break his own record for F-bombs in a single sentence. The previous record was set on the plane ride from San Francisco. Such was life with Leonard.

᯽

I was awed by the NFL executive scene. I'm not embarrassed to say this but I loved rubbing elbows with the bigwigs of pro football. Leonard lobbied for me to be the team's representative for NFL Films and NFL Properties committees. Film and licensing were fast becoming the cornerstones of the league's image-building machinery and Leonard wanted the Philadelphia Eagles to have a prominent position at the decision making table. "This is where it's all going, Jimmy. Make sure we're leading the troops," he instructed me. Like a sponge, I soaked in everything I could about the business of pro football. Being in close proximity to Pete Rozelle was like being a graduate student in an MBA class. He was the consummate deal maker. And, he single-handedly created the vision for the league's future and successfully steered the NFL to that future. Two decisions by Rozelle demonstrated how far ahead he sat on the sports marketing learning curve. First, Pete struck a deal with Ed Sabol to form the infant NFL Films. This seminal move proved to be the smartest marketing tool in sports history.

Let me stray off the subject of my career for a few pages so I may tell you about Ed Sabol and his son Steve. These two brilliant guys changed the way America watched football. Both father and son became my dear friends and greatly influenced my life. Ed, who was recently inducted into the Hall of Fame in Canton, is one of the great Philly stories. Ed fell in love with film accidentally. He began filming his son Steve's football games locally at the Haverford School in suburban Philadelphia as a small hobby. Don't forget, this is the days when film cameras where rare and not every single moment of life was captured with someone's cell phone. Ed described himself as seller of *schmatza*, disparaging his years as a raincoat salesman before discovering his film talent. That made Ed a salesman first, but in the early days, Ed had a camera and Ed had a son. He became obsessed with cameras and experimenting with interesting techniques to document Steve's games. Steve would go on to play football for Colorado State and Ed followed Steve west and continued filming. Believe it or not, the simple act of a father shooting his son's games became the seed for NFL Films. Ed quickly built his small hobby into an empire. Ed and Len were buddies, and soon Len asked Ed to film some of our games. With Ed's talent and imagination and Beethoven's music, he could make a 0-14 team look like a Super Bowl champion. I'm positive that Ed hooked Leonard as an early advocate by filming our only two good plays of the season, and then by looping them over and over in slow motion from eight different angles, he made us look like a first place team. Ed and NFL Films turned football from sport to ballet. Coupled with the masterful voice of Philadelphia newsman John Facenda speaking underneath the footage, the result was hypnotic. Facenda was a local newscaster and he possessed one of, if not the most memorable voices in television history. There has never been anyone since who has come close to capturing the magic of his voice. If God could pick a voice to speak to us, he would use John's. Together, Sabol and Facenda soon captured the nation's attention with their skilled highlight reels. The rest, as they say, is history.

The first hire by NFL Films was a man by the name of John Hentz.

John Hentz, NFL Films Director

John Hentz was a local Philly kid who attended North Catholic High School. John answered an ad in the paper for a typist job. According to John, typing was the only class in high school he passed. John became one of my closest and dearest friends. In short, John went from office typist to running NFL Films. The Sabols founded and owned the company but John became the brains behind their expansion. John and I were racetrack buddies. He would pick me up after an Eagles practice in his pink Cadillac and we'd spend the rest of the day at the track. John was Philly through and through, and horseracing was in his genes. His grandmother was a bookie and as a child he flushed betting slips down the toilet when cops closed in on her operation. John was brilliant but humble. Once, some executives from CBS Sports were visiting Philadelphia. I took them to NFL Films and introduced them to John. In just moments, John Hentz, the typist was tutoring the network experts on how to visually cover an NFL game. He was a curmudgeon who thought everyone was phony, except of course, John Facenda. But, he was very generous with his talents and always was willing to share what he learned with others.

We became brothers over the years and we spent entirely too much time at the track. One time John headed out west for a project and called me from Malibu. I instructed him to find his way to "The Raft" and introduce himself to Jim McDonald. They talked about me over several drinks and had lots of laughs at my expense. When John got back from Malibu he took ill. He had never been ill a day in his life but he was diagnosed with a disease called Guillain-Barré Syndrome. He suffered greatly and when he died, Steve Sabol and I gave his eulogy. I cried hard that day and I still tear up at the mention of John's name. He had one daughter, Tracy, and I gave her away at her wedding. After John died, Ed Sabol said, "I guess that's the end of NFL Films." It shows how crazy the world can be sometimes. Everyone has a destiny. There is an old saint, St. Irenaeus, who once said, "The glory of God is a man fully alive." That was John Hentz. He found his passion and never stopped working at what he loved until he could no longer physically perform.

❧

As I mentioned, Ed Sabol and Leonard were close friends. They used to travel by train to South Bend to see Notre Dame football games. Ed was fast becoming a vital cog in the NFL machine but ironically, he never had a contract with the league. Rozelle formed a committee to give Ed a contract and Leonard assigned me as the Eagles representative. Initially, most of the owners didn't get the importance of NFL Films to their bottom line. The committee had to lobby the owners to give Ed a contract. I was assigned to St. Louis Cardinals owner Bill Bidwell. Bidwell did not have a reputation as a big tipper so I had to convince him that Ed and NFL Films were indispensable to the future of the league. One time, while in St. Louis, I asked Bidwell which was the best hotel in the city. He said, "There isn't any," and then he moved his team to Arizona. Eventually, the Sabols got their contract and I can say I was there to see the seed grow into an entire forest.

ès

Years later, I was driving to Chicago for a Ronald McDonald House event and I got word that Ed Sabol was going to be inducted into the Hall of Fame. I asked my driver, Dianne, to stop in Canton. I had to be there. Steve Sabol had been recently diagnosed with brain cancer and he was to be the presenter. I had no tickets and no hotel, but in traditional Murray style, I was going to crash the event. The evening before the actual event, Dianne dropped me off and she went off to book us a hotel. There was a pre-induction event taking place at the Hall where each of the inductees was given their gold, Hall of Fame jacket. A huge crowd had assembled inside the Hall to witness the event. The entire Canton population seemed to turn out. The event had started. I walked in and all heads seemed to turn and ask, "Who's this little fat guy?" Immediately, I was face-guarded by a cadre of ushers asking, "Where are you going pal? Do you have a ticket?" Like John Wayne, I spoke with a tone of command with the authority of a four star general.

"I have to be in there right now," I said to an usher.

"Sir, do you have a ticket?" He asked.

"Who's in charge," I barked.

Two remarkable talents: Steve Sabol of NFL Films and Walter "Sweetness" Payton and Jimmy Murray

With that, a beautiful woman approached and I could tell by her walk she was in charge.

"Can I help you," she asked.

"I have to be in there. Ed Sabol is getting an award and I have to get in."

The woman not only took me into the banquet room, but she led me to a seat overlooking the entire event. Next, I heard a voice. "Murr, what are you doing here?" It was the voice of Ray Didinger, the Hall of Fame sportswriter. In a moment, I was sitting with Ray and his wife. I looked down across the room and I looked at the history of the NFL. It was a extraordinary moment. Steve Sabol, as ill as he was, introduced his father. Tears started flowing down my cheeks as I witnessed one of the proudest moments in my sports career. After the event, I ran into Roger Goodell, the NFL commissioner. I said to Roger, "I don't want to be presumptuous but next year it would be great to have father induct son, if he's still here." Steve made it one more year but the induction didn't happen. I saw Steve one last time before he died. It was a sacred moment and both of us knew it was the last time we would see each other. Nothing can be said in these moments. We just sat in prayerful silence. Everything is there just to feel. I had that moment with Steve and days later he passed. I hope I'm still here when Steve gets inducted into the Hall of Fame. The Sabols contribution to the NFL is one of the largest in league history. I have my own Hall of Fame—Steve and John were two of my first inductees.

Now I'll get back to my NFL narrative. Pete Rozelle's second brilliant idea was to take the NFL brand and team logos to the mass clothing market. The NFL discovered that they could put even more money into their coffers by selling merchandise as well as tickets. Television and product revenues ushered in a completely new era of professional sports. At one meeting, I watched Rozelle raise a concern about the manufacturing of clothing with the NFL symbol. He addressed the meeting saying, "I don't want our logo or team logos fading after the second washing. If we are going to sell NFL clothing to the public, it better be the best quality because we want our name associated with quality." Pete paid attention to detail like no other and that is why he ultimately was the right guy at the right time. Then, he hired Proctor and Gamble experts to design the official NFL line that would stand up to multiple washing in P&G's detergents. Smart? Why not corner the market from shelf through machine washings? From that point on, the NFL dominated the sports merchandise business and Rozelle's foresight changed the entire landscape of professional sports for all time. Through television and merchandising, Rozelle prepared a new generation to adopt football as the nation's game. It was only a matter of time before he achieved that goal.

Pete had a great attitude toward Leonard. Leonard early on, established himself as a somewhat difficult owner. No matter what the discussion, Leonard never presented himself as an easy going guy. Every time Leonard walked in a room, Pete would chuckle then ask me to act as a liaison between Leonard and himself. The big, oversized green chair symbolized life with Leonard. Sitting on his giant throne, he would loudly impose his will on his minions. Even the General Manager, Pete Retzlaff, had to admit that I was the most adept at handling Leonard's commands and volatile mood swings. Pete was low key and direct. His style was one hundred eighty degrees opposite on the emotional protractor. Even Pete would turn to me in difficult moments to appease Leonard.

In the first few years of Leonard's ownership, the Eagles continued to stumble and the fan chorus of "boo-birds" continually grew louder. We were stuck in a cycle of mediocrity because we were on the tail end of a period where all our high draft picks were dealt away in previous deals by the former management. In professional sports, when the fan base gets restless, owners usually go with their first instinct. They fire the General Manager. Random blame is the occupational hazard of any management position. One morning with no warning, Leonard walked in and fired Pete. There wasn't any concrete reason for letting Pete go other than the natives were restless. Leonard believed he had to demonstrate assertiveness as an owner. Pete played the public scapegoat. It was wrong place, wrong time, but it satisfied the public's thirst for blood. Pete had brought me into the organization so I became upset. I had deep loyalty to Pete. It was painful for me to witness the whole unfair process. Immediately after Pete's firing, Leonard split Pete's duties between a longtime Eagles executive, Herman Ball and myself. Herman had spent his entire career with the Eagles and was their veteran player personnel guy. Naturally Len entrusted him with player decisions, while giving everything else to me. It was funny at the time that I was taking the next step up football hierarchy since many people in the Philadelphia sport scene looked at me and then shook their heads. Suddenly, I was in the spotlight. It seemed as if the entire city was asking Leonard, "What are you thinking, hiring Jimmy Murray?" One sportswriter wrote, "Jim Murray is not a football guy." Certainly, I couldn't deny that accusation. I wasn't a football guy per se. I'm sure shaped like a football but my career didn't take the prescribed path of a so-called "football guy." I hadn't played the game. I hadn't coached in the game. I didn't have any inside contacts. You could say I sneaked in the back door. One day suddenly, I was a General Manager in the National Football League. I always ask the question, how do you define a football guy? To me, hiring a coach who coaches the players is what a football guy is supposed to do. I tried not to worry about the label or my lack of pedigree. According to my way of thinking, the General Manager's job was just like any other job. What amazing surprises were going to happen with the Eagles that I wasn't prepared for? All my years with Artie and my father prepared me for anything coming my way. I learned from the best. They taught me everything I needed to know. According to Artie, my job was to be problem solver in the organization. "Jimmy," he said, "you close the door, you deal one on one, and you always be one hundred percent truthful every moment and you'll always do fine." And guess what? Artie was always right! My dad? His mantra to me had always been that *"you look at people straight in the eye, tell the truth, and you never look down on anyone."* One of the reasons I had risen as far as I had was that I had cultivated a very direct relationship with Leonard. I followed my Dad and Artie's lessons to a "T." I tried never to be a "yes" man but neither did I ever offer an unsolicited opinion. If asked, I gave my honest viewpoint. Leonard liked this trait of mine. From my first days with the organization, I demonstrated openness and honesty. After Pete was fired, I expected Leonard to wait a few weeks, name a new GM, and then have Herman and me go back to our old jobs. Leonard arrived in the office one morning and announced a press conference. The media showed up and a host of microphones were quickly put in place. The press anxiously awaited a big announcement from Leonard. Moments before the press conference began, Leonard turned to me and whispered, "I'm going to name you the General Manager." What? I stood shocked, dumbfounded, but I didn't have the luxury to show my cards because reporters had filed in and were waiting.

In a low voice I replied to Leonard, "Don't you think you ought to tell the coach first?"

"No, I'm not," he said. "And," he added, " look surprised!"

Looking surprised was easy. Actually, I stood dazed like I had been tasered but I followed Leonard's lead. When Leonard asked that I step forward, I smiled big for the cameras. The folks watching the press conference at home, must have thought that Leonard had just hired "Gomer Pyle, USMC."

It was official. I was the new, conflicted General Manager. Here's Jimmy Murray: a dead ender from Brooklyn Street, a student manager, the erstwhile son of Art Mahan. I took some minor league baseball course, mixed it with some restaurant greetings, and shazam, now I was a "football guy." Point of fact, I became the youngest GM in the history of the NFL whose father didn't own a team. Even today, I still hold that distinction. Even in the excitement of the moment, I was sad for Pete. It was my first look, up close and personal, at the hard realities of the sports business. However Pete, a first-class individual, wanted me to have the job. In my first months on the job, he was extremely helpful to me. Pete taught me a one lesson…to take a punch in the gut, stand tall, walk away, and trust in your ability. He has remained a very close friend.

❧

One of the first orders of business was to hire a new coach. It was the first "big" decision in which I played a role. We hired Mike Mc-Cormack. Mike was a Hall of Fame player, who played and was mentored by the legendary Cleveland Browns coach Paul Brown. An NFL lifer, Mike always looked like he ate a bad tuna sandwich. Sadly, it didn't take too long to see that Mike wasn't going to turn the franchise around. Actually, I helped Mike find a house near where I lived and we would ride together to Veterans Stadium every day. We became very close friends which made it very difficult when, only a short season later, I had to break the news to him that we were letting him go. "Letting him go" is fancy speak for "you're fired." Mike, a Hall of Fame person as well as a player, took the bad news surprisingly well and like Pete, he never let business get in the way of our friendship. He understood, as rapidly as I had begun to understand, that the NFL can be fickle and cruel. When the owner takes the heat for the big numbers in the loss column, a change of blame takes place. Quickly, I discovered that I was in the big time because decisions had big consequences. I never took myself seriously as a football executive but I took the job seriously. Initially, I had failed to take into consideration how my actions affected so many lives from players to coaches and their families. Firing Mike McCormack was my baptism, so to speak, into a new phase of my life where I would face many tough, gut wrenching decisions.

After hiring me, Leonard gave one specific directive to me. "Win!" he said without a smile. Leonard's makeup was completely different from mine. He didn't waste much time blubbering in the human fallout of the decisions we made. That was my style. He was a businessman. He saw his role as providing top notch entertainment to a city starved for a winner. My Irish genes couldn't help but make me consider the dichotomy of professional sports. Yes, on one level, football on Sundays was entertainment. However in Philadelphia the Eagles and the fans are of one body. Philly fans live and die with their Eagles. Marriages can succeed or fail based on how the Eagles play on Sundays. It might sound like a cliché but the truth of the matter is, Eagles football is religion! Leonard understood that much like Caesar understood the Roman Empire. The only way to keep the people from rioting was to feed them the Detroit Lions and a winner.

During my first full season, I began to get a feel for the substance of the job. Immediately, on the sixth day of our summer camp, the new head coach Eddie Khayat and I had to post the first cut list. Unlike Leonard, I couldn't separate my emotions from the cold hearted reality of the football business. Here I was literally driving players home from camp just after we cut them. One day there was a big, strapping 300 lb. boy, sobbing in the front seat of my car. I shattered his world and destroyed his hopes. Or another day, it was a poor kid from the south who had all the intention of making it financially as a professional, so that he could ease the burden of poverty at home. These rides away from camp were long and deathly silent. I am a guy who normally has something to say at every moment yet I never found the right words that could put someone's psyche back together. But that was the crucial part of the job. I realized that a big part of my responsibility was to help young people sort out the reality of sport, moments after they were humiliated in a very public, embarrassing way. Again, my Dad and Artie prepared me for the human side of things. Unconsciously, Leonard began training me in the Eagles' business the only way he knew, delegation. He hated meetings and as I said previously, he had no attention span for committees. The NFL, like most corporate entities, is governed by committee. Suddenly, I was involved in every bit of football business because Leonard refused to participate. I took to this part of my job like a fish to water. I loved the marketing aspect of the league and where could I find a better tutor than Pete Rozelle? Pete had the unenviable task of building consensus among a large group of millionaires. The NFL ownership is a millionaires club. These are successful men who know what they want and how to get it. Each owner believes he is the king of his own domain. Pete Rozelle was not their first choice for commissioner. Just to prove to Pete that they were in charge, they elected him on the 34th ballot. From his first day on the job, he operated from a deficit. In terms of support, Pete had to swim upstream. Nevertheless, Pete possessed the unique ability to focus on the big picture. He didn't sport a large ego and I studied carefully how he controlled the big money decisions. He also knew how to massage the big egos and build consensus where there seemed to be none. His job was the ultimate problem-solving challenge. My job description, on a lesser scale, was the same. I like to think that Pete was learning on his job just as I was. We continuously improvised and I kept writing my term paper as I went along. After all, life is an audible.

≈

A General Manager's job, as I would come to know, is often a reflection of the owner. Take Jerry Jones of the Dallas Cowboys as an example. Jerry Jones played football in college and he views himself as a person with a keen football mind. His style from day one has been, "I own it, I run it." Throughout his ownership, he exercises full control over all franchise decisions from player personnel to cheerleader boots. If you work for Jerry, you had better know how to operate under that umbrella. Robert Isray of the Indianapolis Colts on the other hand is pure business. He hired Bill Polian as his GM, and Bill is a real football guy. Isray gave Polian full reign over football decisions and Polian never disappointed him. I'll use the Peyton Manning draft pick as evidence. When Polian made the decision to draft Manning with the first pick in the draft, there were legions of skeptics who raised their eyes thinking Polian had got it wrong. Look how right Bill Polian was about Manning. Throughout his tenure, all of his football decisions have been solid. Other owners don't care or refuse to get involved in the minutiae of a multifaceted organization. They build a systematic operation, whose one overriding goal is to build a successful franchise and increase the team's market value. Leonard was none of the above. Leonard did not fit into any category. That's what made him so interesting. You just never knew what would catch his fancy or get his attention. It was the rare occasion when you could get him deeply involved in anything. He had zero interest in the day-to-day operations of his team. He spent a large part of his time in a bar. He'd call from a bar to check in and whatever the decision awaiting him, he'd take a second, then reply, "You take care of it, that's what I'm paying you for." Quickly I recognized my role as the person in charge of utilizing other people's gifts. Throughout my career I had operated under one very simple principle: recognize everyone's contributions, appreciate them as people, and they will always be there for you in a pinch. Our organization was a team sport underneath a team sport. At Christmas, I had Dick Perez draw a picture on a Christmas card of everyone in the entire organization. As a manager, I was a total socialist. I valued everyone, and Leonard complained that "you're too much of a lovey-dovey." I'm not positive of Webster's definition of a lovey-dovey but it's a label I proudly wear. To his credit, Leonard let me be me. The strange thing was that in his own quiet way, Leonard wanted everyone to be happy, too.

One of the funniest GM stories I remember happened after my first few years on the job. In 1978, teams still had to schedule their own pre-season games. Big television contracts and league packages hadn't evolved into the mega-deals they are today. If a team did not have a guaranteed sell-out for a pre-season game, or in other words, couldn't guarantee the gate, the opponent team could turn you down and refuse to play the game. It was my responsibility to arrange the pre-season games then find a way to fill the stadium. This particular time, I had contacted the New York Jets and we agreed on a game at Veterans Stadium. For some reason, the Jets found a better deal than the one we were offering. Their executive at the time was Jim Kensel. Jim was a Philly guy and a friend of mine. He called me and told me that they were cancelling. Next Jim informed me that, though he was backing out, he heard that the New Orleans Saints needed a game and that they were planning on holding an exhibition game in Mexico. Mexico? Would I be interested? Sure. Mexico? I was desperate! When you were desperate in 1978, you considered Mexico. This doesn't sound strange today because the NFL regularly schedules games abroad cultivating an international audience. At this moment, we needed cash flow from the pre-season and traveling south of the border was better than not having a game at all. I called New Orleans. "We're in!" I promised. We'll come to Mexico. Then I flew to Mexico. I needed to check the Mexico City landscape. I worked out the deal with New Orleans. Leonard's first response was, "Mexico? Are you crazy?" No one in the organization from coaches to players specifically, was happy about going to Mexico for a football game. There was no precedent. Never had anyone in the organization traveled outside of the continental United States to play football. Besides, who in Mexico even knew what football was? Were Mexicans going to know or care about the Philadelphia Eagles? Despite everyone's pessimism, I told Leonard, "I promise there's going to be a huge crowd and we're going to get a big gate!" He shook his head and said, "We'd better have a phenomenal gate." Meanwhile, back in Mexico, President José López Portillo held the biggest press conference since the execution of Emperor Maximilian! It was the press conference of all press conferences. It rivaled what you would see before today's Super Bowl. Despite their lack of football knowledge, the Mexican people were thrilled to have an NFL game played in their capital city. However, there was one small detail we didn't consider. There was no venue to play the game. Mexico's national game is soccer so the country naturally is full of soccer stadiums. How were we going to create a football field with people who thought football meant soccer? A seemingly high level government official stepped forward to a microphone and promised that the game would be played in Aztec Stadium.

New Orleans sent their advance man and like me, he developed an ulcer dealing in Spanglish. I spoke loud and slow like the obnoxious gringo I was, but I kept smiling. I figured if I kept smiling no one would shoot a friendly, rotund GM. But still the process wore me down. Exhausted with my own creation, I did the sensible thing, I went back in Philadelphia. Next, I sent down a representative by the name of Jack Gross. Jack did some PR work for us and I instructed him to "go down to Mexico, see what's going on, and call me back with some good news." Two weeks before the game, the entire organization planned my execution. They had a rifle and a wall and lots of folks were happy to pull the trigger. Jack called me long distance and I sensed panic in his voice as he screamed, "Jimmy, we've got real issues here…you know, we're playing in a bull ring!" A bull ring? One bull would be better than our whole offensive line. Three days before the game, we transported enough equipment and personnel to invade the country. I should have declared a junta and installed myself as dictator.

No one arrived in Mexico in good spirits except me. No matter what ever happened I tried to keep a jovial outward appearance. But the walls were closing in on me. I did the second thing I always do in a crisis. I pray. Conveniently being in Mexico, I went to see Our Lady of Guadalupe. There was a shrine to her outside the city. I took a few young players with me under the guise they needed to have a cultural experience. If you ever get the opportunity to go to the shrine, be prepared. There are a thousand steps to the top where the statue resides. Of course, overweight but great me, struggled for each breath getting to the top. I watched an 80-year-old Mexican women sprint past me. It was that same woman that you've seen in hundreds of *National Geographic* magazines. Wrinkled and hunched over but could she ever fly up those steps. When I reached the top I prayed a "Hail Mary." I specifically asked the Blessed Mother, "If you like football, can you please give me a sign?" The day of the game finally arrived. I thought I had problems? Things were just warming up. I got to the stadium and then the real issues surfaced. First, the military and a hundred of their armored vehicles thundered into Aztec Stadium. The army arrived to transform a bull ring into a football field in four short hours. If you every watched the Woody Allen film, *Bananas*, then you can imagine the scene. The first person I met was a scary, stereotypical looking Latin American general with a moustache. This guy looked like every General that has ever appeared in a Hollywood movie featuring Mexicans. Each soldier had his gun strapped to him, and they seemed to have planned to do field maintenance while at the same time keeping national security. First, the soldiers had erected the goal posts. I said to the General, "We need nets for the ball or our kicker will kick into the stands." I was comforted when he assured me, "If they take de footbol we shoot them." I felt better. I left the stadium and then visited Leonard. Where do you find Leonard in Mexico? Where else? A bar! We were sitting in a rundown bar and the Saints brought in their cheerleaders which further added to the Fellini atmosphere. With all of the stadium issues, Leonard was as hot as a jalapeño pepper. He threatened me in a loud voice with, "Another one of your great ideas? I hope you prayed to your Blessed Mother for a miracle!" Little did he know that I already hedged my bets and, I had Mary on my team. I was confident. The game was televised back in Philly by a local television station and Leonard just kept repeating his warning, "I'd better not be embarrassed!" And he wasn't! It turned out that Mary liked football and she made sure the Mexicans turned out in full force. The game turned out to be a huge financial success and Leonard stood on the field and shook his head in amazement. Smiling, he said, "Either someone up there really likes you or you're just the luckiest son of a bitch on the planet." A little of both. During the game, I sat in a press box that looked like the prison box in *The Bridge On The River Kwai*. I reflected on one of life's valuable lessons. Never be afraid to take a shot even when you're swimming upstream. The whole experience of executing the entire Mexico excursion, along with some help from above, stays with me today. When I think about that experience, I still get goose bumps. Today, it's commonplace for a hundred thousand people to watch NFL games in Mexico or London, but the fact is, the Philadelphia Eagles were the first to do it.

There was another "first" that I was involved in that changed the face of sports in America. That was the birth of *Monday Night Football*. Leonard sent me to New York to represent him on another owners' committee. During one meeting, a simple pitch was made, that would change forever, the way America watched football. Way back when, before cable, there were only three major networks, ABC, NBC, and CBS. Each competed voraciously for their share of the television ratings. Huge television deals between sports and networks were non-existent. Salaries for players were miniscule compared to today. Players played for cigarette and beer money. In the 1960s and '70s, each network made a cursory effort at contracts for the broadcasting of our games. Football was simply a necessary item they had to appease viewers. Advertisers hadn't quite discovered or capitalized on the coveted 18-45 demographic. Once they discovered this Holy Grail, the NFL was primed to explode. As a member of the publicity committee, I attended a few lackluster network presentations for our business. Everyone was low-key and polite, and business was normally transacted with little fanfare. Our committee was the liaison with the networks and our task was to maintain the television status quo, which translated into a slate of a few weekly games. There were pockets of interests but there was nothing close to approaching today's national games of the week. One day when we were assembled in New York, I sat through two presentations by both NBC and CBS. During their presentations both networks stressed the relative unprofitability of broadcasting NFL football. Imagine that, football unprofitable? Each network gave doomsday predictions about the flat growth of football and it's limited future. A chorus of whines cried about the perils of non-existent television viewership.

I sensed they were low balling our committee. Understandably, they were trying to get the best deal for their networks. But then, a third presentation was introduced. ABC took their turn. Into the room walked three men: Roone Arledge, Howard Cosell, and Chet Forte. Cosell was immediately recognizable as a boxing commentator, made famous in the 1960s by Cassius Clay/Muhammad Ali. His signature punching vocal delivery was seared into everyone's brain. I had no prior knowledge of Arledge or Forte but they were about to become household names. I'll never forget their opening line to our group. "We ARE going to change the way Americans watch football!" I remember thinking to myself, "Wow, these guys are brash!" What? Change the way Americans watch football? Really? How? And besides according to NBC and CBS, no one was watching football.

"We're going to do something that has never been done before… we're going to broadcast a nationally televised game on Monday night," explained Arledge.

My first response was, "Are you crazy? Who would ever watch a football game on Monday night?" It's the first night of the work week. Everyone is unhappy about being back to work and everyone is in bed by 10 o'clock. Weekends are for fun. Weekdays are for work. Right? Wrong! Arledge proceeded to take control of the meeting. He became ABC's wonder boy by turning the Olympic Games into a major television event and making a huge profit for his bosses. Now, those same ABC bosses were turning him loose on football.

He then explained to us, "We're going to have two entirely separate crews working the games. One crew will focus entirely on the game action. The second crew will be entirely devoted to something we call, 'Instant Replay.' This, I guarantee will revolutionize the way football is viewed."

The three men were not just sure of themselves, they were annoyingly cocky and I have a short fuse when it comes to annoyingly cocky. But, they overwhelmed the committee with their style and self-confidence. Even I was forced to admit, these guys had their ducks in order. They bought the sizzle! No one was quite sure what to expect but it was clear to the committee that we had a unique opportunity with ABC. And then they executed exactly the vision they promised. Instant replay made football on television. They out "Steve Saboled," Steve Sabol. Suddenly, viewers could watch a game, leave the room for a beer, and never miss a moment of action. Watching the play over and over again was better than seeing the game live and in person. *Monday Night Football* became "Church" for a sports hungry nation! All of a sudden bars were full on the deadest night of the week. Beer companies found nirvana… drunks on Monday night. People were cancelling meetings to get home to tune in. In effect, ABC added a third day to the weekend. This was and still is the power of football. It has completely revolutionized a culture and our way of life. As general manager, I had a front seat on the space shuttle. I had been nursed on baseball, that conservative, staid institution. Baseball had dominated the country's attention since its founding. But, after Arledge, this other sport, football, was going to the moon. This sport, my second sport so to speak, from that day forward was going to be THE sport. Not only was ABC switching game days to Mondays, they changed the way we viewed sportscasters. No longer were the guys calling the game just broadcasters. Now, they were entertainers. Howard Cosell played straight man to a wise cracking good ole boy from Texas by the name of Don Meredith. Meredith, whom Cossell referred to as "Dandy Don," had been a successful quarterback for the Dallas Cowboys. He peppered the broadcast booth with a steady stream of funny inside stories from his playing days. For the first time in television history, fans got a taste of what it was like behind the scenes of a pro sports team. They started to hear who was smart, who was lazy, and what kind of beer they drank. It was sports gossip but gossip was entertaining. And gossip kept people tuned in which meant ratings. Cosell's role had forever been the in-your-face, ask any embarrassing question guy. A Cosell interview knew no boundaries. ABC shrewdly marketed him as the man America loved to hate but loved to watch. Viewers expressed dislike for Cosell but they never changed the channel. From the first broadcast, ABC struck gold and it paid them dividends for the next forty years. A few geniuses at ABC, with a bit of imagination, transformed NFL football from sport to entertainment. And personality—both on and off the field—became as important as athletic ability.

I remember one day I was sitting in a league meeting in the Arizona Biltmore. I loved that hotel because they had a fabulous buffet, one that I would gladly die for. On this day, the last two standing in the buffet line were John Madden and me. Madden was an ex-Eagle, who was drafted in early 1960s as an offensive lineman. His career as a player was uneventful but he went on to coach the Oakland Raiders and won a Super Bowl in 1977. Thankfully he wasn't the coach of the Raiders when they beat us in the 1980 Super Bowl. John and I both were Catholics and we attended Mass regularly. Whenever we played the Raiders, John and I would go to Church together. I guess some people might find this strange but it was an activity that bonded us deeply as friends. The great thing about

John Madden is that he is exactly the person he appears to be on television. He is funny, warm, and he has that ability to make you feel like you have been his friend forever. John became a household name, not so much from his coaching career, but from his time on *Monday Night Football*. Just as it did for so many, MNF made Madden a bona fide superstar! As we stood in the buffet line, John said to me, "Jimmy, I can't be-

John Madden
(CBS "eyemark" Logo is a Trademark of CBS Corporation)

lieve how much ABC is paying me to be myself." I couldn't believe it myself. Again, football evolved to be more than X's and O's. The viewers intimately knew the broadcasters. Madden appeared to be a special guy because he lacked any pretense at all. He was totally unaffected by his success. And, his success grew out of his genuineness, and television cameras don't lie. Madden did and still does provide a great lesson for anyone interested in success. John may not have been the smartest or richest guy at the time but the only role he played was himself. Truthful, natural behavior always sells. It has been my experience that the public has an insatiable appetite for sincere, real people. Who doesn't love the truth? I was fortunate to be around John Madden and he's always been a role model for me. I've tried to emulate his tremendous comfort with himself.

॰৺

If life is an audible as I claim it is, then I was really put to the test in 1979. I always prided myself with an ability to go with the flow. Since I was a child, I cultivated the skill of letting things roll off my back. However, during that year I was stymied by a tragic event. Blenda Gay was a late round draft pick of ours, a few years prior. He was one of those players who comes along once in a while who won't be denied a spot on the team. Blenda was not a natural talent but he made the team with his combination of guts and determination. I quickly became close with Blenda and we would have frequent talks about life in and outside of football. He was a extremely warm guy, who could easily open up in close, personal talks. I love these types of guys because they mimic part of my Irish nature. We were priests for one another. He would talk about his problems. Blenda struggled with depression and I'd talk about my obsession with Twinkies. But we formed a trusting bond. I was closer to Blenda than any player I had ever met. He had a tough upbringing as a kid, and I could hear in his voice how he carried around painful baggage. One day, Blenda and his wife had a bad argument. Later, after an argument, his wife stabbed him while he slept in their bed. The news the next morning stunned me and it rocked me and the organization to our core. We were heartsick. I took the news very badly. I felt like I had lost a close relative. The incident put into perspective for me exactly what my job as general manager was supposed to be. The players, coaches and all of the organization couldn't come to terms or make sense of the tragedy. One moment Blenda was part of us, and with a snap of the finger, he was gone. Our total collective being had narrowly focused on the outcome of an athletic contest. Blenda's death brought life's hard reality crashing down on us. In the final analysis, professional football is exactly like everything else. The cliché is true. *It's only a game.* And the game really doesn't matter after the whistle ends it. The only thing that does matter are the people and the relationships you form because of the game. I had lost a great, young friend in the prime of his life. Winning and losing football games would take a back seat for some time.

≈❄

I'll finish this chapter with a question that I have been asked hundreds of times in countless conversations. What exactly was my job as a General Manager? I answer by saying that I did a million things. Most can't be written in a job description. I can tell this. It was a totally possessive job. It consumed me. It took my entire attention every minute of every day. And the pressure? Constant. My family suffered greatly for my job. The rise to the top of an organization does not come without significant costs. Fortunately, my wife Dianne was and is the rock of our relationship. She kept things running smoothly on the home front while I moved up the sports ladder on the Philly sports scene. In my small world of football, I was given lots of power. There existed between the organization and fans a sacred trust. How the Eagles fared on Sundays affected thousands upon thousands of Philadelphians. Looking back at the experience I've asked myself, was I a capable NFL executive? I evaluate myself with a simple criterion. I graduated from the Art Mahan school of inclusion. I did my job to the best of my abilities. I made my share of mistakes. I'm sure I probably hurt some people. But always, I led with my heart. Hopefully, I never took anyone for granted. It was tough living under the microscope of 24/7 criticism by the fans and, especially the media. But even today, I wake up each morning and pinch myself because I had the dream job of a lifetime.

When you have a job you love, it seldom seems like real work...and, occasionally, I had time to relax with guys like Tom Brookshier and Jim Leaming, both local sportscasters.

CHAPTER 8

The McMiracle

"I am realistic – I expect miracles."

– DR. WAYNE DYER

In the middle of all the activity swirling around my responsibilities with the Eagles, the words of Dr. Audrey Evans, "Get us a house!" altered my life forever. These words unleashed an international movement. I walked out of the Spectrum in Philadelphia after my meeting with Dr. Evans and it felt as if she had handed me the Ten Commandments. I'll bet Moses didn't feel the weight I felt on my shoulders. Dr. Evans spoke in similar tones to the Almighty. She intimidated me with her weighty authority and unflappable conviction. The order had come down. It was a final examination time for me. I had danced and jigged my way around life and I always relied on my quick wit to disarm any problems that found me. Until this day. Finding a house for Dr. Evans? How would I do that? I reacted the way I always do when I have no direction. I prayed! The entire ride home, I prayed specifically asking, "God, don't let me disappoint Dr. Evans." She and a whole hospital of sick kids were depending on me for something. I can't say that anyone was counting on a house because we had just come up with the idea. Yet, it was clear that the patients of Dr. Evans were looking for miracles anywhere they might materialize. Now I had to provide my own miracle. I felt a self-imposed pressure to deliver. And privately, I was counting on the help of God.

I returned to my office knowing that I had this new responsibility. Locate a rather large house somewhere in Philadelphia. And then, of course once located, I needed to find the money to buy it. After my meeting with Dr. Evans, I came back to my office to find a note sitting on my desk. The message said for me to call a man by the name of Don Tuckerman. Don worked for a company, the Elkman Advertising Group. One of Don's accounts was the McDonald's Corporation. McDonald's and the Philadelphia Eagles had a great business relationship and this is where God chose to start working the miracle. I called Don and immediately without any premeditation, out of my mouth popped the words, "Don, what's your next promotion?"

"Murr, you're Irish. You know what's coming."

"What?" I asked.

"Shamrock Shakes, St. Patrick's Day," he said.

Green milk shakes? What a concept!

I said , "I need some help."

"What help?" he asked.

"Here's the deal, Don. If I get our quarterback Roman Gabriel (he was a big name in Philly at the time) to do a commercial for shamrock shakes could you give me a quarter from each shake?" I asked.

I then proceeded to tell Don about this house that we had to find for Children's Hospital.

"Any consideration that we could get from McDonald's would be a terrific boost," I added.

Don informed me that that type of donation decision would have to come from the local McDonald's operators because each store was individually owned. Don recommended that I talk to a man by the name of Ed Rensi. Ed was the regional manager for the company. Ed would later become the president of McDonald's. So let's review this one more time. We have an Irish guy, Murray, calling a Jewish guy, Tuckerman, who tells me to call an Italian guy, Rensi. You see how God was thinking? Let's make a salad. Within 48 hours I received a call from Ed Rensi.

"This house you want? If we give you all of the money, can we call it the Ronald McDonald House?" Rensi questioned.

I shot back, "If you give me all the money you can call it The Hamburgler Castle or Rensi's Hideaway!"

Today, if you walk into any Ronald McDonald House around the world (and there are 360+ houses, and counting, in 63 countries),

Local regional manager Ed Rensi was vital to our campaign to buy a house for Dr. Audrey Evans at CHOP; Ed later became the CEO of McDonalds and Ronald McDonald Houses are still being built around the world.

you'll see the hand of God in the whole idea. The symbol of Ronald McDonald's character has evolved into the universal welcoming sign for kids throughout the world. Kids are never afraid when they're greeted by Ronald's happy face. Even when they're sick, their hearts are calmed walking into a house where Ronald symbolically asks them to think happy thoughts. That's the magic the world has come to know.

But, let's get back to the story. The promotion turned out to be a huge success. We had the money we needed to buy the house. Next, we found a house that seemed to fit the bill. It was at 4032 Spruce Street in Philadelphia, right near the campus of the University of

Pennsylvania. "House" might have been too kind a word. The house, to put it mildly, was in disrepair. It was a vintage college student house, so use your imagination. Let's just say it made the Deltas' "Animal House" look like the Four Seasons Hotel. It was battered, beaten, and with a stiff wind, it might have fallen from three stories to a rancher. There were several students living in the house and when I first walked in, I whiffed enough marijuana smoke to get my first high. For a moment, I thought I was back in Malibu. Dr. Evans and I looked at each other and we tried to say something positive. She broke first. "Maybe we can find someone to rehab it!" Yeah, sure, and maybe Hercules is available! "Oh Jimmy," she said with her Welsh accent, "we can find a contractor or someone who can help us."

Sure enough within three weeks, she found the magic beanstalk. Dr. Evans had a patient by the name of Babe Canuso. Babe's father, John, had a large construction business in South Jersey. John was a Villanova guy and though we were roughly the same age, I didn't know him from my VU days and that surprised me, because I thought I knew everyone. We showed John the house and he stared at it as if he just witnessed a tornado hitting it. "What a mess?" he declared.

"John, do you think we could get this fixed up within three weeks?"

"What? You're out of your mind!" he barked.

I joked, "John, you're Italian! I never met an Italian who couldn't build a house in a day!"

John shot back, "Jim, you're Irish, you could probably move in here today!"

But I was convinced that if we could get this up as quickly as possible, I could get Ray Kroc, the McDonald's founder on board with this idea. I had met the McDonald's founder earlier and I was impressed by his simple no nonsense demeanor. I was sure he'd see the value of the company's involvement in such a worthwhile cause. I knew if I had a few moments with him in front of a new house, I could sell him the vision. Canuso agreed to do the repairs and the house was quickly becoming a reality. I understood very clearly from the beginning that building a house was just the start. The Eagles and their partner, McDonald's, were actually going into the hotel business together. There was going to be an ongoing need for funds and personnel to operate this new concept. It was crucial for the success in the future that we have the total support of the president of the corporation.

Next, John Canuso performed a miracle I'll never forget. Not only did John deliver the rehabilitation of the house on my ridiculous schedule, his work was stunningly beautiful. He didn't remodel a house, he built a castle. Within a month of our initial meeting, we were ready to have the grand opening. I don't think that kind of schedule could ever be duplicated again. I have a hard time getting a plumber to fix my leaky faucet so I can't imagine accomplishing today what we did back then. On the steps of the house on that day of the opening, we assembled the "Who's Who" of Philly sports. Former Eagle legend and CBS broadcasting great Tom Brookshier, Eagles' linebacker Bill Bergey, wide receiver Harold Carmichael, and legendary Mayor Rizzo were all on hand for the ribbon cutting ceremony. Rizzo, the former tough guy police commissioner, had only recently been elected mayor. He walked into the house and looked around and then exclaimed, "looks like it was done by a goomba!" He was right! The whole place was paneled in beautiful cherry wood. It was a stunning sight. I lined up all of the dignitaries assembled for a picture. Finally, I winked at God, saying to myself, "I think this is the genesis of something very big."

The Opening of the World's First Ronald McDonald House, October 15th, 1974 at 4032 Spruce Street, Philadelphia, PA

Ray Kroc the McDonalds founder (with walking stick) and Mayor Frank Rizzo being interviewed by Tom Brookshier.

Tom Brookshier interviews Jimmy Murray. Behind them stands #17 Harold Carmichael the great Eagles' receiver. Above them on the steps is the irrepressible Bill Bergey, one of the greatest linebackers in the history of the NFL...he holds a #7 shirt to present to Ray Kroc.

FRONT ROW: Dr. Audrey Evans & Richard Wood (Chairman of CHOP. COB of Wawa, Inc.), receiving $100,000 from The Eagles Fly For Leukemia, Leonard Tose, John Canuso, Roman Gabriel (Eagles quarterback)...the signature on the check is Leonard Tose's
SECOND ROW: Tom Brookshier; Ray Kroc (founder of McDonalds), Frank Rizzo (Mayor of Philadelphia) Bill Bergey, Harold Carmichael.

೫ఔ

The first house had opened and was in full operation. What a great feeling it was to go from a tiny seed of an idea to the full bloomed house. But God wasn't finished with me. Shortly after, I received a call from our next angel, Charlie Marino. Charlie was a successful Chicago attorney and his daughter was suffering from leukemia. Like so many parents, Charlie found himself sleeping every night on the floor next to his daughter in a hospital room. One morning, Charlie was having a conversation with their oncologist, Dr. Baum. Charlie asked the Doctor where parents might stay when they are not from Chicago but their children must stay in town to receive chemotherapy treatments. Baum responded by telling Charlie that he had heard of a place in Philadelphia called the Ronald McDonald House. He explained to Charlie that it was a new idea which gave families temporary housing and support during the cancer treatment process. Immediately, Charlie called me and then he flew into Philadelphia for a visit. We gave Charlie the full tour and it was quickly evident that this native of the windy city was a mover and a shaker. "Let's do this in Chicago!" he said almost before we took the first step into the house. Charlie reminded me that McDonald's headquarters were in Oak Brook right outside the city.

"Why don't we have a house like this in Chicago?" asked Charlie.

At this point, God was putting on a full-court press. This was to become a huge moment in the continued growth of an idea that just months before was a mere accident. Charlie understood and convinced me that a house near Oak Brook was an important chance to influence the entire McDonald's organization.

"This is a revolutionary concept and we've got to make them see it," Charlie exclaimed.

Immediately, my marketing brain thought of linking the idea of a Chicago house to my old acquaintance, Bill Veeck. Veeck, who owned the Chicago White Sox, was a master of marketing. I thought he was the natural partner for this new venture. Unfortunately, Veeck was occupied with some personal health issues. I called him and he jokingly responded to me, "Murray, you're a football guy now, you left baseball. Call the Bears!"

That's exactly what I did. I turned to George Halas and the Chicago Bears organization. I was hoping they would play the same role for the Chicago House as the Eagles did for the Philadelphia project. When I called the Bears front office directly, I was able to talk directly with Halas' son-in-law and the Bears' Vice President, Ed McCaskey. McCaskey, who liked me, loved the horses. Immediately I had an ally. The horse betting fraternity is a tight one so Ed and I kibitzed about the ponies for a few minutes. After he was comfortable, I gave him the pitch about the Chicago house. After giving him a quick overview, I asked, "Can the Bears partner with McDonald's on the Chicago house?" Right away, McCaskey agreed it was a great idea. He put their public relations man in charge. Bill McGrace a wonderful guy who held up the Bears' end of the deal. McGrace, was the former Minnesota Vikings PR guy. Also, he was an old friend of mine from my baseball days. Both of us came up through the minor league ranks and ironically, we both evolved into NFL guys. Bill was a nervous, one-after-another chain smoker but a smart, quick guy. I arranged a meeting with the upper echelon of McDonald's in a downtown hotel. I asked Bill to help me with the pitch.

"Murr, what do you want me to do? I don't know anything about cancer and houses!" he said lighting another cigarette.

I told Bill, "Just relax and just say yes to everything I say!"

Preparing for the meeting of the McDonald's Chicago operators, I reached out to our All-Pro linebacker Bill Bergey. My minor league marketing education taught me never to go into a meeting without something exciting to catch their eye. May I brag for just a second? I decided to have Bergey fly out to the meeting dressed in his full Eagles uniform. Just maybe that would catch someone's eye. I flew back and forth to Chicago one more time before our big meeting to finalize things with Bill McGrace. Bill had already gotten to work scouting locations for a house. He explained that there was one particular area in Chicago called Lincoln Park, which was the part of the city closest to the hospital. Bill said that this was the logical location for a house but at the same time, it was going to be a tough place to find a house that fitted the model which we had established in Philadelphia. Even though he presented a pessimistic outlook, he had already scouted a very promising house. But, there was one problem. It belonged to a local Catholic parish.

"It's the perfect location!" he exclaimed. "But there's a problem. The head guy is an old Irish priest who's not returning my calls. We just can't seem to get to Father Fahey on the phone."

St. Clement's Parish had an old convent for sure.

Bill assured me, "This is the place! Absolutely the best place for the house."

"Then let's go see Fahey," I said.

Bill protested, "Jimmy, I told you, I've tried calling him for weeks and he's impossible to talk with. Besides you're not from around here. You think you've got some kind of magic pull or something?"

"Yes, I do! Yes, I have magic pull."

Moments later, as I stood in front of St. Clement's, Father Fahey came riding down the street on an old bicycle. Fahey took a long look at me and saw a round Irishman. I was in my element. One-on-one, blarney style. Irish-on-Irish! Let's have a drink and get this done! I didn't drink but I could sit down and do the Irish familiarity thing with the best of them. I got off on a good foot with Father Fahey.

He walked me down the street and like a good real estate salesman he said to me, "I've got this house right here, 18 rooms, perfect for what you want and need and I'd love to offer it to you but we have one problem."

"Problem," I said, "I can fix any problem."

"There are three nuns living there and one, Sister Katherine, won't want to move," he said.

I asked Father Fahey if I might take a crack at softening Sister Katherine.

"Be my guest," he said, "and good luck to you boy."

Later, I came back to the convent with Charlie Marino and Dr.

Baum. The Italian lawyer, the Jewish doctor, and the Irish altar boy (there's that same theme again!). We knocked on the convent door. Sister Katherine, a small yet spunky elderly nun, answered the door. I had grown up with lots of Sister Katherines and it was clear that for many years this little woman had struck fear in the hearts of many. But these are the situations that I love. I was sure I could disarm her. I was still sure even after her initial greeting.

"You're thinking you're going to take our house? Because, you're not!" she barked.

I can't say it was my very best sales job but certainly it was one of them. After explaining in detail our plan to use the house, Sister began packing her bags. I'm not even sure if she found another place to live but within minutes, we had a deal to buy the house. From that day forward, the spry Sister Katherine would become an active booster for the Ronald McDonald House in Chicago and others elsewhere. We made a friend for life. After shaking on the deal, Charlie, Dr. Baum, Father Fahey and I were stood outside the convent in a celebratory mood. Everyone shook their heads in disbelief that Sister Katherine surrendered without a fight. It was easier than Reagan's 1985 Grenada invasion, and if you remember, that lasted about two minutes.

As we talked, Father Fahey said "Jimmy, you did such a good job here today, we should give you something…what do you want?"

In front of the convent stood an 8-foot, 1400-pound statue of the 14th century Saint Francis.

"I'll take St. Francis!" I joked.

Six months later, I was sitting at my desk in my office when my wife called and asked, "Do you know anything about a two-ton casket sitting in our driveway?"

So since 1974, a St. Francis statue that dwarfs Kareem Abdul-Jabbar, sits in my backyard. Today, I still pray to it daily. And the Chicago House? It grew and it grew rapidly. It became part of the corporate tour. It became a showpiece that was shown to anyone who visited the McDonald's headquarters. The house and the idea became reality in two cities and established the Ronald McDonald House as a cornerstone of the McDonald's organization and American culture.

Back home in Philadelphia, our original house on Spruce St. was quickly becoming antiquated. Dr. Evans, who once would have been happy with her "Island Rooms," now wanted "100 Rooms."

"Jimmy, we need to expand!" she said to me one day outside the house.

A few days later I was attending a funeral at the Oliver Bair Funeral Home nearby at 3925 Chestnut Street, just a few blocks from the house. I might have mentioned earlier that I've always been a big funeral guy. Some people have compared me to the character in the 1970's movie *Harold and Maude*. Like Ruth Gordon, who played Maude, I enjoy the ceremony of funerals. It's an important thing in life to be there for others in their grief. Again, this must be an Irish trait or maybe it just because I've met so many people. On this day, I walked into the funeral home and took an accidental turn into the wrong viewing room. The deceased woman I was supposed to see was a relative of a friend of mine. I didn't know her well and since she was embalmed and made up, I didn't recognize her. I stood over another woman and said a prayer for the wrong corpse! (I'm sure that my prayer wasn't wasted because I believe it helped her on her journey.) Next, I had a real "Seinfeld" moment before Seinfeld was in existence. In a true sitcom style, a small, very unassuming man shimmied up next to me. He whispered, "I noticed you were looking around earlier when you walked in...you wouldn't want to buy this place would you?" Not consciously but I was admiring the place before praying over the stranger. He was right. He sensed I was buying a house in my subconscious.

"Absolutely, I'll buy this place!" I screamed disturbing a whole room of mourners.

They seemed to all whisper in unison, "Who is this oblivious real estate salesman? And who invited him?"

On the spot, the owner of the funeral home and I shook hands on the deal. This little "Casper Milquetoast" turned out to be one of the Bair family members and he had the rights to negotiate. $200,000 bought the perfect site for the new Ronald McDonald House. And there was an added bonus! The house was a historic landmark. It was a mansion built by the owner of the *Philadelphia Public Ledger* newspaper way back in the 1890s. This guy was a titan of industry and he had money. Big, big money! How did I know? His children's faces were carved into the woodwork. I'm not sure if that's a sign of obscene wealth but I had never known anyone who had the money, or the idea, of carving family portraits in the woodwork! It was spectacular. Here in Philadelphia was a Newport, Rhode Island-style mansion—like the Vanderbilts'—and we were taking it over for Ronald. Guess who I called next?

"John Canuso, surprise, it's Jimmy Murray!"

Picking up his phone, John sounded a bit like a weary Leonard Tose.

"How much and when do we start?" Eventually we put $1,000,000 into this old funeral parlor and today it's still stands as the sacred shrine that we began in 1974.

ะ

From that day till today, the miracle continues and the good that has come from the first request, "We need a house!" has continued to grow exponentially. Audrey Evans came to Leonard Tose with a meager request for a few bucks for a few sterile hospital rooms. A bored Leonard turned to me to take it off of his desk. From Leonard's inability to pay attention for more than thirty seconds grew one of the great humanitarian efforts in modern history. The Ronald McDonald Houses have and continue to give families support in the gravest times in the life of a family, the diagnosis and treatment of a child with cancer. What a simple idea!

"Put families together with the same problem and they'll help one another."

Dr. Evans understood one of the most basic human needs. Give hope where there is no hope. Mother Teresa understood it. Gandhi understood it. Jesse Jackson understood it. Jackson, who's taken some political heat in his life, has always received my applause for the mantra he spouts, "Keep hope alive!" That's something we need to always remember.

ලෑ

It never ceases to amaze me but stories come in from all over the WORLD about the spread of the McMiracle. I was recently in the Philly house and saw across the room the shining face of the Madonna from Iran...the woman was so serene and stunningly beautiful that they would launch a thousand ships in her name... which, I'm sorry to say I forget, but her story put me on my knees.

She was from Iran and had lost her 1-year-old son (her only child) to cancer...she was in Philly at CHOP but her baby was called to the Lord, or Allah, and she was naturally bereft. What did she do? Of course, she mourned and dealt with the incomparable grief of losing a child. Then, seeing the squalor that parents in Iran suffered as they, like American parents, camped out while their children were being treated, she was inspired by the Ronald McDonald House. SHE RAISED $140,000 that has opened a facility in Iran which helps families and offers a sterile environment for bone marrow transplants. This blew my socks off and left me humbled...she is now witnessing children and their parents united under a comfortable roof dealing with one of life's greatest challenges...saving gravely ill children.

And, guess what else I learned, only recently? There are now (2019) 525,000 volunteers working with Ronald McDonald House Charities...almost 200,000 more than the population of Iceland! As the Brits say, "I was gobsmacked!" And I love being gobsmacked by such news.

CHAPTER 9

Two Giants in Eagles Costumes

There is nothing I would not do for
those who are really my friends.
I have no notion of loving people by halves,
it is not my nature.

– JANE AUSTEN

I must dedicate space to two great men that I was lucky enough to work for and with, Leonard Tose and Dick Vermeil. Working with Leonard and Dick was a marvelous learning experience and defined so much of my life. The life of an NFL executive or coach is all-consuming. There is room for little else in your life. In certain respects, Leonard, Dick, and myself were swallowed up in the business of the NFL. It's a double-edged sword but I wouldn't trade the experiences I had for anything.

№

The expansion of the NFL in my lifetime is one of the most remark-able marketing stories in the entire history of capitalism. The New York Giants vs. the Baltimore Colts overtime championship game in 1958 set the stage for an entire new era in American sports. The game was played in Yankee Stadium in New York with players who would later become household names. Pat Summerall, Frank Gif-ford, Alan Ameche, Gino Marchetti, and Johnny Unitas were just a few of the big players to play in the game that day. In all, seventeen players from the game would eventually be elected to the NFL Hall of Fame in Canton, Ohio. That is a remarkable statistic and one that

NFL Commissioner Bert Bell (1945-1959)

might never be dupli-cated. The game had the distinction of being the first sudden death over-time decision in history, with Baltimore edging New York 23-17. The commissioner of the league, Bert Bell, made up the overtime rule specifi-cally for this game. No one anticipated that this rule would set the stan-dard for how all future tie

games would be decided. Alan Ameche scored on a 1-yard run to win the game that is today is remembered by some as the "greatest game ever played." It would take an entire book to recount the events of that day and many things have been written about the game and its impact on football history. There are several brilliant summaries available, yet I suggest Mark Bowden's 2006 account of the game. I mention the game only because that day in 1958 signaled the first salvo fired by the NFL for control of the nation's sports attention. Several significant things happened as a result of this contest. 45 million people watched the game as it was covered by NBC. There weren't 45 million television sets in the entire country but people crammed into bars or watched it in storefront windows, where previously, the NFL had trouble selling out any live game. The game also featured two assistant coaches for the Giants, who both would grow into football legends. Vince Lombardi and Tom Landry were the offensive and defensive coordinators, respectively. One year after the game was played a Texas billionaire by the name of Lamar Hunt formed the upstart American Football League (AFL) to compete against the singular National Football League. This rivalry, which then quickly turned into a war for talent, extended into the late 1960s. Eventually both leagues would cooperate to form the Super Bowl Championship and later a subsequent league merger. The biggest winners of the day were the television networks. The massive interest in the game by the American public was not wasted on NBC or its advertisers. The game signaled to the networks that Sunday football could routinely capture large audiences, providing a regular money spigot for advertisers.

I saw the whole NFL evolution first hand from a ringside seat. Baseball had been the national pastime and dominated the American scene for the first half of the century. I was still a baseball guy but suddenly in 1958, football had stamped its mark on the nation's consciousness. Bert Bell was the rock upon which the NFL was built. His unique vision and style orchestrated the league's steady growth in post-World War II popularity, through the fifties, and culminated in the 1958 game. Bert was a Philly guy through and through. Since his roots were in Philadelphia, it was only natural that Bert located the league offices in Philadelphia. So Philadelphia can claim to be the birthplace of the Constitution, the Liberty Bell, and Bert Bell. As noted with the sudden death overtime rule, Bert was always the innovator. In 1942, when there was a shortage of players because young soldiers were fighting overseas, Bell and the Pittsburgh Rooney family temporarily merged their franchises. The Philadelphia Eagles and the Pittsburgh Steelers combined for several years and played as the "Steagles." Sadly, Bert died suddenly before seeing his vision completely realized. He died of a heart attack at Franklin Field in 1964. There were no defibrillators available on that fateful day, or Bert might have survived. After Bert died, the league owners retreated to find his replacement. They took the thirty-four ballots to elect a young Pete Rozelle. As I mentioned earlier, Pete was the perfect guy for the job. He was right out of central casting and he would step in to complete Bert's grand scheme. This sudden change of events directly affected me. Pete Rozelle's ascent into the Commissioner's job, and his moving the league offices to New York so that the league could be near Madison Avenue, paved the way for my eventual rise to Eagles' GM. I believe every single thing in life is connected. I can prove it. Hear my thesis in another context. Bert Bell was replaced by Pete Rozelle. Pete moved the league to New York. Pete Retzlaff took me to New York for a promotions meeting. From that I get bumped up to assistant General Manager. From there, Leonard Tose comes to know me and most importantly, like me. Pete Rozelle can't handle Leonard and Leonard didn't get along with Pete. Enter Jimmy Murray! You may not believe this, but I see it all of life as one continuous piece of string. Every event connects to another event. And when I look back, it hangs as a perfect tapestry. Some call it fate, some call it destiny. I call it Murray's rule. Every single event connects directly to another.

When you became part of the Philadelphia Eagles, you entered into a long, sacred tradition. Similar to the Vatican in Rome, you became part of a rich history. Though I didn't set out to get the job, I was pushed by Artie to expand my world and my good fortune continued from there. I didn't like being part of the painful GM decisions, like letting people go, but I'm privileged to have acquired some of the greatest, most treasured friendships because of the Eagles. And, one of the greatest blessings occurred when I hired Dick Vermeil as our head coach. As I mentioned a few chapters back, firing my friends like Mike McCormack or Eddie Khayat are sad memories. You can always hear rationalizations about firing a coach with clichés like, "it's just business," or "it's about winning." In the end, someone always takes the fall in an organization. And it's no fun being part of the firing of a coach. If you were to analyze things honestly, a coach usually is unsuccessful because the organization behind him fails him at some point. In Eddie Khayat's case, he wasn't ready to be a head coach when we hired him. He had played for us in the 1960s and '70s. Eddie was a popular player with our fans but we threw him into the job with no coaching experience. Then, we abandoned him when he had a 2-12 season. With Mike Mc-Cormack, we never gave him a good supporting cast. A coach is only as good as his players, coaches, facilities, and the amount of money the franchise controls. In the right circumstances, young coaches can become legends and in the wrong circumstances, even legends fail. Look at any season in the NFL. Each year you'll see a list of coaches on the hot

Mike McCormack, Philadelphia Eagles Coach from 1973-1975. He played for the great Paul Brown in Cleveland. Brown stated that McCormack was the best offensive lineman he ever coached. As a coach in Philadelphia he had a record of 16-25-1

seat. Sometimes a coach has a great run of luck and has a long winning string. Take a coach like Andy Reid of the Kansas City Chiefs or Bill Belichick with the New England Patriots. As great as they are, fans will only tolerate losing for a short time. Reid had an off-year or two with the Eagles and he was quickly removed after being one of the best coaches in franchise history. Belichick had some tough years before arriving at New England. The point is, even the great ones fall if they don't win. In other words, coaching is a big crap shoot. And, rest assured, there is no loyalty. We were at the very least, equally culpable as owners and management, as were the coaches, for the team's failure. But, power is what power is, and it's often ugly in its execution. I possessed a certain capacity to make peace between warring factions. I think of myself as a fat Gandhi. I like to work in the background of the madness, trying to keep a peaceful balance. But professional sports are an inexact madness!

ॐ

When we hired Dick Vermeil, it turned out to be the perfect marriage between an organization and its coach. After we fired Mike McCormack, Len looked at me and said, "Let's go hire a new coach." Len, never a patient fellow, wanted to hire someone right away, like 9 a.m. the next day. He felt he needed to redeem himself with the Philly fans for McCormack's failure. Without me in the office to slow him down, Len would have gotten a whim and made a hasty mistake. He would have called someone on the phone, most likely a legend in the league, and offered him the job without an interview. Actually, this is what he began to do. He threw out a few names to me as he picked up the phone to call his first choice.

I snapped at him and gave him a quick lecture on hiring.

"Leonard, listen to me. Even if you're going to call Jesus Christ, he's got to come back twice. Don't hire the bartender because you're bored or tired or impatient. Whoever we hire must come back twice. That's going to be our guiding principle. I'm going to get to know the candidates. I'm going to tell you what I think. AND I'm going to be honest and you're going to listen!"

My rant infuriated Leonard because Leonard was both tired and impatient and hated the sound of my "voice of reason" in his ear.

Leonard had listed a litany of legends on a piece of paper that sat on his desk.

"What do you mean?" he asked. "I've got Norm Van Brocklin at the top of my list! Bartender? Are you nuts? I know exactly what I'm doing."

Norm Van Brocklin, "The Dutchman," quarterbacked the only championship team in franchise history. He was, as they say, one tough son-of-a-bitch and he fit the profile for what we needed in a coach. On the field, we not only lacked talent, we lacked discipline. Leonard equated his players to himself when he was a young kid.

One day he seriously made the argument, "We've got all of these out-of-control kids. They need to go to Catholic school like I did."

Great. We would interview Sister Patrice, hire her, improve everyone's penmanship and win a title. Yet, Norm Van Brocklin was a perfect Mother Superior for undisciplined boys. There was no doubt that he could bring order to our chaos. Jack McKinney, a local sportswriter for the Philadelphia *Daily News,* was a frequent Leonard critic. Jack in his articles, loudly advocated for Van Brocklin. McKinney's support for Van Brocklin soon spread throughout the city, and everyone became convinced Norm should be our pick. Leonard always loved to create a certain dramatic atmosphere around most decisions he made. At heart, he was a showman and he loved playing the role of puppet master. He waited until Super Bowl week to begin the interview process. He knew that the press would be out in full force and fan interest would be intense.

"Let them speculate," he instructed, "it'll create a ton of interest."

We went to Florida for the Super Bowl and we stayed at the beautiful Doral Hotel. Len let the press corps know that we would be interviewing Van Brocklin while we were attending the pre-game festivities. We rented a posh suite for the interview and then, Van Brocklin walked in. No scratch that. Van Brocklin swaggered in! Actually Van Brocklin could swagger while swaggering. He had a cigarette dangling from his mouth and looked like that really cool kid from elementary school who made every other kid afraid. I understood immediately why the 1960 Eagles won the championship game, even though the 1960 team wasn't as good on paper as their opponents. The Eagles had what the Cleveland Browns and the Green Bay Packers didn't have, an X-factor. Van Brocklin had that presence that made champions, champions. It's funny,

Norm Van Brocklin (circa 1974)

the little things you notice in life. Some people just naturally possess some extra element. You can't put your finger on it but you sense it's just there. You just know in your gut. In Catholicism, we call it the "Holy Spirit." In theater, they call it presence. If you were in the room with me that day, you'd say too, there's something about this guy that was different. It was a great interview! Van Brocklin chain smoked Camels without filters throughout the entire hour. Talk about when men were men. Athletes chain smoking cigarettes without filters. Van Brocklin could smoke several on the sideline, go in the game, and direct an 80-yard march for the win. I called him Mr. Van Brocklin, never daring to call him "Dutch." He became very angry with me when I politely told him that as part of the process, we planned to interview several other candidates. He gave me a scary look. Momentarily, I choked on my words. After the interview, all of us knew he was the perfect fit for coach of the Eagles. After he had retired from football, Van Brocklin was given a promise by the NFL owners that he would always be taken care of, so to speak. For his contributions to the NFL, the owners promised he would always have some sort of income from the league. But that promise didn't materialize. Van Brocklin retired and nothing happened. Since he was one of our franchise greats, Leonard felt that the League's poor treatment of Van Brocklin brought some bad karma to our team. Leonard saw hiring Van Brocklin as a way to redeem the franchise and get a monkey off of our backs. Besides, Leonard was smitten with him. As soon as Van Brocklin left the interview, Len blurted out, "Number one, he's our guy." I had to remind Leonard of our agreement on two interviews.

I was determined to keep Leonard's hair trigger impulses out of the hiring process. I admired the former Kansas City Chiefs coach Hank Stram just about as much as anyone I had met in pro football. Stram was a championship caliber coach and he left a successful career with the Chiefs to become a television analyst. He was on the television during the days leading up to the Super Bowl game. Stram was a pal of announcer Al Michaels, and Al and I were great friends. I was leaving the Doral Hotel one day in Leonard's limosine when Al spotted me. He asked, "Murr, you have a limo? How about I get a ride to the stadium?" Al hopped in the car and I had the chance to ask him what he thought of Stram. Al believed that Hank Stram possessed one of the best football minds of all time. Without asking Leonard what he thought, I said to Al, "Tell Hank that Leonard would like to talk with him." Later Al arranged for me to talk with Hank and then we invited him out for dinner. Leonard and I took Hank to Joe's Stone Crabs, the famous Miami restaurant. Actually, Stram could dance as well as Fred Astaire and while we waited for supper, Hank got up and danced a few numbers with several attractive women. I asked Leonard, "How many teams could say that their coach could be in the movies but that he'd rather be the coach of the Eagles?" I loved Hank Stram and he was a great interviewee. I was even tempted to violate my own two interview rule that I had established with Leonard. During the interview, Hank let us know he already had an offer on the table from the New Orleans Saints. He was shopping, negotiating salary figures, playing off the Eagles and the Saints to see if he could wedge a better deal. He was committed to the Saints but he felt able to squeeze a better contract because we too, were in the mix for his services. From that point forward I became and stayed a Hank Stram fan. We remained friends for years and whenever we would show up in the same town, I would joke that, "You and me should go dancing! Then we'll find a great seafood place and settle for a dinner of soft shell crabs and pasta."

While we were staying at the Doral, we watched the Rose Bowl on New Year's Day. Coaching in the Rose Bowl that day was a young Dick Vermeil. The youthful, good looking Vermeil was coaching UCLA against that old-timer curmudgeon, Woody Hayes of Ohio State. Ohio State had walloped UCLA in an earlier game that season, and the Rose Bowl was to be a formality for Ohio State claiming the national championship. It was great theater with the underdog Bruins trying to knock off the heavily favored Buckeyes. Vermeil's team went out and pulled off the upset of the decade. In just a sixty minute football game, Dick Vermeil went from "No Name" to "Big Name." After the game, with cameras coming in for a close-up, Vermeil ran across the field, kissed his wife, and hugged his kids in a classic All-American Kodak moment. I could tell that Leonard was sufficiently impressed while watching the game on television. Leonard keyed in to Vermeil's youthful good looks and wholesome persona.

I shot a comment to him across the room, "I say put this guy on the list!"

At first Len reacted, "Hey, he only won by upset. He's not going on the list."

Later after doing some research, Len found out that Vermeil had coached with George Allen and the Los Angeles Rams. Len loved George Allen so Dick made our list...and now, Len coveted him!

Leonard really started to enjoy the stir he was creating in the Philadelphia press about who he would select as the next coach.

Each day there would be a new story, with new speculation about what Leonard was thinking. Len was having fun creating a "Casablanca" feel to the interview process. He suggested that we keep the interviews going and mentioned a few more of the usual NFL suspects, big names of the day within our reach. Don't forget, we were a doormat franchise with no draft picks. Though Leonard thought we were in control, the truth was, the head coach of the Eagles was not a coveted position. Allie Sherman, the great coach of the New York Giants, who was a first round pick of the Eagles in his playing days, had been recently fired by the Giants. I contacted him and he too, was an extremely qualified choice. Ironically, Allie was very similar to Vermeil. Both men were intense, specific, and paid great attention to detail. He would have been a great fit. With each interview, we became more confused. Sherman went to the top of our list but later changed his mind because he felt he wasn't ready to return to the grind of NFL coaching.

☙

Joe Paterno, legendary coach of Penn State

I don't remember specifically how we became interested in Joe Paterno, but the legendary "Joe Pa" got on the list. Had it worked out, it would have been like hiring God, himself. Now at the present moment, Joe Paterno has passed on, and everyone from here to

Mars knows the tragic story of his demise. But in 1976, Joe Paterno was the premier college football coach. Again, he was the perfect guy for the job because he was from Pennsylvania, and he was beloved in Philadelphia by both the media and the fans. He had almost taken the Steelers job the year before and the Patriots sent a plane to Happy Valley to pick him up for an interview. He sent the plane back. Leonard had me contact him and we arranged to meet in Washington, D.C. Paterno did not want any publicity around the meeting so Leonard booked a suite in the hotel where the Supreme Court Justices stayed.

"Think that'll be secure enough for him?" Leonard winked.

Paterno arrived with his brother and the four of us sat down to a six-hour interview. It was one of the most interesting interviews of my career. Joe Paterno was the consummate professor type. He was thoughtful, thorough, and keenly analytical. He had done his homework on the Eagles and he knew more about the personnel and our problems than I did as General Manager. We made small progress on day one and Joe suggested we reconvene the next day. The next morning, we waited for him in the dining room for breakfast. He walked in with a yellow legal pad on which he had written a list of his demands. There, singled spaced for what looked to be several pages, were all the things Joe would need to leave Penn State for the Eagles. He handed the list to Leonard and said, "Here's what I need." Leonard made speed reader Evelyn Wood look blind.

He glanced at the list and said sarcastically, "Sure Coach, anything else?"

Paterno turned white. I think Joe was on the fence about leaving Penn State. He was what I call "a leaner." The opportunity with us looked attractive so I imagine that he felt if he asked for too much, he wouldn't have to make a tough decision. He could save face if we made the decision for him. In the final analysis, Joe understood that he was a legend at Penn State and the life of an NFL coach was often a short ride to oblivion. But obviously, Joe underestimated Leonard.

Just to be on the safe side, I asked Paterno, "Excuse me Coach, can I take a look at the list?"

It was long and expensive with coaches, drafts, trades, money, facilities, scouting, on and on. If it had worked out, it would have been fantastic for the Eagles but then again, God works in mysterious ways. A week later, Joe declined our offer. He stayed at Penn State and at the age 84, he was a lock for the history books. Sadly, after the Sandusky scandal broke, Joe died and after his death the NCAA forced Penn State to vacate a sizeable number of wins. As I'm writing this, I can feel tears welling up inside of me. It is one of the saddest stories in sports history. I'll move on.

It was a cold Philly winter and Len was restless. After returning from Florida and interviewing several more candidates, we still hadn't hired a coach.

"Let's go to California and look for a coach," Len barked. "At least if we don't find someone, we'll be warm."

Len and I got on a plane for a quick getaway. Len was starting to get bored with the search just like I knew he would. He was half asleep when we interviewed Stanford's coach Mike White and another candidate by the name of Daryl Rodgers, who was a successful college coach at Arizona State. White had been tutored by the great John Ralston and Rodgers had ranked teams at several college stops. Neither coach excited Leonard. Eventually Rodgers ended up with the Detroit Lions. While in California, Leonard said, "Call that Vermeil guy from UCLA and get him over here." On that day, Vermeil was unavailable so we packed up and went home. Can you see Leonard's impulsivity? Quick trip to California, turn around, come back empty handed. The Philly press was getting restless for a decision and in particular, they were beating up on me as the primary culprit in the indecision. Jack McKinney was suggesting each day that I knew less than Leonard, and he had already established beyond a doubt, that Leonard knew nothing. At this point Leonard was just about flat out of gas with the search process. Our last candidate scheduled to interview was Joe Restic. Joe had coached in Canada where he won the Gray Cup. I didn't know much about Canadian football but the Gray Cup sounded suitably impressive. At one time, he coached at Villanova, so I knew Joe personally. Artie Mahan had great respect for him so naturally I did too. Restic was coaching at Harvard, proving that not only did he know football but he must have known a whole lot more. With urgency, I expressed to Leonard, "This is it, we've got to narrow this down and make our decision quickly." Restic was personable, smart, and very experienced.

As soon as he walked out of Leonard's office, Len said, "I really like this guy, let's hire him."

"No Leonard, we've got to bring back a guy two times," I reminded him.

Len and I then had a huge argument, complete with the full measure of Leonard "f-bombs."

"We agreed to work through the list. We agreed to take our time and find the right guy!" I pleaded.

"I'm the owner, goddamnit, what the hell am I listening to you for? I want Restic and I want him now!" Leonard insisted that before Restic left the building that Joe and I sit down with our controller Sidney Fortaller and talk contract numbers.

I protested, "The guy coaches Harvard. We don't have anyone close to Harvard grads in our locker room! We don't need brains, we need discipline!"

Thirty minutes later Restic came back to Leonard's office after coming to quick financial terms with Sidney. Joe and Leonard shook hands and Len asked, "Welcome aboard, anything else?" Restic replied, "Yes, there is one more thing. I'm going to have to run this by my wife because she really doesn't want to leave Harvard."

Leonard's nostrils flared as he asked, "Excuse me?"

"Yeah, I have to talk it over with my wife."

Restic walked out of the office. Leonard closed the door and waited until Restic was out of hearing distance. "Any (expletive) guy who had to talk to his wife before he takes a coaching job will never work for me! Get me a plane! We're going back to California to interview that Vermeil guy!" And naturally, Leonard then said, "And tell Restic he's fired!"

⁊❦

Sam Procopio was the travel agent who handled all of our travel arrangements for the Eagles. Though he wasn't officially a team employee, Sam was loved by everyone in our organization. Sam would often travel with us to away games so he and I became fast friends. Leonard liked Sam because Sam was always quick to satisfy Leonard's whims. In addition, Leonard trusted Sam as a friend. When Leonard said to me, "Get me a plane," he meant, get Sam to cover all of the arrangements and make sure Sam goes with us. Leonard liked traveling with an entourage of buddies. And certainly, Leonard didn't want to be alone with me in California. Remember, I didn't drink. Even though Sam tended to be on the nervous, high strung side, he was an oddly calming influence on Leonard.

Sam scheduled a flight for us that left on a Friday morning and clearly stated to Len and myself, "Look Jimmy, I have to be back by Tuesday. Promise me, we'll be back by Tuesday."

Leonard promised, "Relax. We'll be back by Tuesday."

Whenever we would travel to Los Angeles, Leonard insisted that we stay at the Beverly Hills Hotel.

Leonard handed Sam a fistful of cash and said, "Sam, remember, in L.A., I don't stay in rooms, I don't stay in suites, I only stay in bungalows."

The Beverly Hills Hotel had these very private bungalows that they usually reserved for big stars and dignitaries. Leonard loved rubbing elbows with the rich and famous. We landed in L.A., arrived at the Hotel, and the general manager of the hotel came to the registration desk to inform us that there were no available bungalows but that he would make sure we had rooms of compatible luxury.

Sam insisted, "But sir, we have to have a bungalow. Mr. Tose is the owner of the Philadelphia Eagles. He is a frequent guest and he always gets a bungalow when staying in Los Angeles."

"I'm sorry, there are no bungalows," the manager said.

Sam replied as he slipped the manager a few stiff Ben Franklins, "We have to have one."

The manager explained further after taking the bribe, "We're in a difficult spot. Itzhak Rabin, the Prime Minister of Israel is supposed to arrive soon and he wants a bungalow as well. His security requests that we keep the area free of guests. So you can understand, we're in a very sensitive position."

Sam perked up, "Mr. Tose is Jewish and an ardent supporter of Israel. In fact, I'm sure Mr. Rabin knows Leonard Tose."

Somehow the mention of Leonard's religious convictions changed the tone of the conversation causing the manager to say, "There is one bungalow and I suppose we might be able to squeeze you in, but only if you will be out by Tuesday."

Sam promised, "I have to be back in Philadelphia on Tuesday. Sure, give us the bungalow and I swear we'll be out first thing Tuesday."

The three of us parked ourselves inside Bungalow #9. Sam and I shared an Emperor's bed, while Leonard scowled, "I'm not leaving this (expletive) town without a coach!"

Leonard then barked at me, "Murray, call UCLA right now. Get him on the phone!"

I called UCLA's football office and asked to speak to Dick Vermeil.

"Dick? Jim Murray, Philadelphia Eagles…"

Before I could complete the sentence, Vermeil cut me off by saying, "Thanks, but no thanks." And then, he hung up. Stunned, I hung up too. Leonard barks, "Well, what?"

"He's not interested," I said.

"What do mean, he's not interested? I flew all the way out here for 'I'm not interested'?" (expletive, expletive, double, triple expletives)!

Dick knew that we were considering him but he was a California guy through and through. Moments later, the phone rang with an incoming call. Till this day, I don't know why but for some crazy reason, Vermeil called me right back.

"Jim, it's Dick again. Maybe we should talk a little bit."

And within five minutes he arrived from Westwood in a blue Mustang convertible. He knocked on the door of the bungalow and Sam answered it. He took one look at Sam and thought he was in a mob movie. I didn't ask why he reconsidered, I was just happy he did. Dick was a gentleman from the very first handshake. He too, was an extremely detail-oriented coach.

He began our conversation with, "Jimmy, can I ask you an honest question?"

"Sure," I said.

"Why should I come to Philadelphia?" he asked.

"What's that mean?" I asked.

"I come to Philly, the fans there are really tough, right? I'm not sure I want to relocate my family and then subject them to a bad situation."

I said, "Dick, let me tell you two things. Forget for a moment I'm the GM. Think of me as a fan, because I am one. First, our team is so bad that you will get a standing ovation if you win the coin toss." Then I turned into Jeremiah the Prophet. "Second, if you level with the fans, not only will they embrace you, you will move to Philly with your family, you will raise your family there, and you will become a household word."

My comments just served to confuse him more but in the long run I was right. Absolutely, unequivocally right. He did raise his family in Philadelphia (his kids were married at Villanova University's chapel) and to this day, he's an icon in Philly sports history. For many years, you'd find Dick doing local television ads and his picture was on every other bus in Philly endorsing Independence Blue Cross.

During his interview, he was perfectly honest with me. He had just won the Rose Bowl and he was in the middle of his recruiting season.

He reiterated his doubts asking, "Again, why should I come to Philly when I can win at UCLA year in and year out, without the huge pressures of the NFL?"

It was a great question and the facts were the facts. We stunk! He left saying he would think about the deal when he was on the road recruiting. Dick left the bungalow. Leonard was about to have a heart attack. Leonard wanted immediate gratification and he had ADD before anyone knew there was such a thing. Now, we were back to Mike White, the hippie coach at Stanford and Daryl Rodgers, both of whom would be difficult to sell to Philly fans. Tuesday approached and still we had no coach. Sam, who kept insisting that a cab was waiting for us, was pleading for us to leave.

Despite Sam's need to get home, Leonard stood firm. "I'm not leaving here without a coach!"

Sam protested, "I'm going to lose my job!"

Len told Sam that we were staying. He promised that if he found his coach then the Eagles would hire Sam full-time in the event he was fired from his job. Next, Leonard instructed Sam to go back to tell the hotel manager that we were staying another day. Sam nervously went back to the manager after he promised we'd be out by Tuesday. Leonard handed Sam another wad of bills to help our cause. I walked outside our bungalow and bumped into the great actor Orson Welles. Moments later I came across Gene Wilder, who made me laugh so much in Mel Brooks' *Young Frankenstein*. Despite not finding a coach, I was having a swell time hanging with celebrities galore. It was just like being back in my Malibu days.

Later that same night, we were awakened by a loud noise. Sam was a light sleeper. Immediately, he went to the window to peer through the blinds. When he looked out to a courtyard, he saw a full platoon of camouflaged Israeli soldiers, complete with Uzi machine guns. Rabin had a full regiment of armed guards. Were they looking for terrorists? Were they sweeping the area for bombs? Was Rabin missing? Sam was a nervous ninny and seeing soldiers with guns put him over the edge. He couldn't contain his fear another minute.

He jumped up on the bed and began screaming, "I'm Italian, I'm Italian! I'm not even Jewish!" I guess he thought he was defusing some tension, which it did. It was a funny, funny moment. I couldn't stop laughing but Sam was entirely consumed in fear. Leonard woke up and walked out of his room asking what the commotion was about.

After hearing what it was, Leonard said totally dead pan, "Sam, put a towel on your head!"

It turned out that Rabin was in another part of the hotel and the whole routine was just an ordinary security drill.

ॐ

The California trip managed to have a happy ending. We weren't shot by Israeli Security so that was a positive. Second and more importantly, Dick Vermeil took the job. It was an epic moment. A game changer! A franchise changer! A city changer! Philly and Vermeil was love at first sight and the start of our road to the Super Bowl. Dick turned out to be exactly what we hoped he would be.

From the first time we saw him flash across the television screen as the underdog coach who beat Ohio State, Dick was the epitome of the perfect hire. And as a coach, he was exactly as he presented himself during our interview. He was a teacher, a disciplinarian, and a full frontal assault. Dick had a game plan for everything from grocery shopping to draft day. I remember Dick being a list guy. Every single day of his life, he planned on having some type of success. He was Audie Murphy. He was Jimmy Cagney. He loved each and every one of his players and they loved him. He loved the community and they loved him back. He never drove anyone harder than he drove himself. His first act as coach was to hold a barbecue for the entire organization at his house. He spent the entire day grilling and making sure each and every person felt welcomed and at home as his guest. If an organization can ever hit a grand slam in football, we sure hit one when we hired Dick Vermeil.

Dick's opening session at his first training camp was a scene from a movie. First of all, he was like General Patton preparing to go into battle. He knew every detail of every phase of the organization. He knew instinctively if he had the troops or if he didn't. He used analytics before analytics were invented. I never met anyone more prepared for anything in my life. He had stacks of detailed notes and statistics on every single player on the team. After the first day, Dick confided to me, "We're not very good. We've got a long way to go. We've got to build." But to the players he was a cross between the movie character evangelist Elmer Gantry and the real evangelist Billy Graham. Dick was then and is now, a very emotional guy

Leonard Tose and Dick Vermeil.
Leonard with the ever-present cigarette and always with his hand in pocket,
Dick had movie star looks and the best move we ever made was to hire him.

who wears his heart on his sleeve. In the auditorium at camp, I
would sit in the back and just listen to him. I would watch the faces
of the players, who sat totally enraptured to the words of Dick's lessons about football but more importantly, about life. I had never
been around a coach who could instantly connect with everyone in
the room. Dick had the ability to get to the spot deep down inside
each player and he could motivate even the most disinterested
player in the league. He got the players to listen because he himself,
was a great listener. Every pastor or speechmaker should find a
copy of a Dick Vermeil talk and rip out a page and plagiarize liber-
ally. Dick had the respect of every single Eagles' employee because
he worked harder than any other person in the organization.

My job as the General Manager was sometimes hard to define but my skills were absolutely put to the test keeping the volatile Leonard Tose and the type-A Vermeil from sinking each other. To put it mildly, Leonard could be a very difficult person with whom to reason. Dick liked to be in complete control of his football team. One of my tasks was to diffuse Leonard whenever he had an irrational impulse or outburst. Also, I had to make sure that Dick had space to grow as an new NFL coach. Dick was an intensely loyal guy and no story exemplifies this better than one of our first drafts together. Anytime you sit in an administrative seat in professional sports, it's a poker game. There is lots of information at your fingertips but in the final analysis, many decisions come down to luck. This is particularly true when it comes to the NFL draft. It's very difficult to predict how a college player will perform as a professional. After our first year together, Dick dissected the team position by position as we prepared for the draft. He never minced words but at the same time he wasn't hurtful in his honest assessment of our team.

We sat down together and Dick was frank with me saying, "Jimmy, whatever went on before, it's a whole new page and I won't judge you on the past or anyone else on all of the mistakes that got us to where we are right now. We're awful but you and me have to prove ourselves now." Dick built a great staff with people whom he respected and they respected and believed in him. Initially, we didn't win many games and he predicted that. But Dick was in coaching for the long haul. He had a vision and the perseverance to see it through.

He instructed me on our first draft together, "Jimmy, we're going to have to be patient because we have to get better."

Dick Vermeil and Jimmy Murray
We were happy and I was skinnier!

We had no strategy because we had no draft picks. Though through his meticulous research, Dick had his eyes on a wide receiver from Clemson by the name of Perry Tuttle. Draft day came and I was as excited as an toddler on Christmas morning. I loved all of the draft days because the atmosphere is charged with hope. You are shaking all of the packages under the tree looking for buried treasure. In the draft room, every person in the room has fingers crossed, hoping to find that one player who might be the difference maker for the franchise. We belonged to a group called BLESTO. This was a group of teams who shared scouting information. There was a certain mystique on how to pick players, though no one every admitted it was mainly an inexact crap shoot. On the actual draft day, everyone calls around trying to make the perfect deal. You try moving up or down for the perfect pick, you trade, and you hope that what's done in April pays off in December during playoffs.

∽❧

As I mentioned, Dick's greatest asset was his loyalty to his players, friends, and colleagues. He's an old fashioned guy from the vineyards of the Napa Valley. I have always described Dick metaphorically saying, he didn't just plant seeds, he harvested the crop by hand as well. He just outworked everyone else. During one particular draft, we had let CBS Sports sit in our draft room as part of a behind-the-scenes look for fans. This was groundbreaking sports television giving viewers a inside view of the decision making process. Before the draft, Dick had confidentially mentioned to his former mentor and Buffalo Bills head coach Chuck Knox, that he liked Clemson's Perry Tuttle. Dick had worked for Knox when Chuck was the head coach of the Los Angeles Rams. Knox and the Bills had the pick one spot ahead of us and sure enough, Knox announced that the Bills would pick Tuttle. Moments after the announcement, the wind went out of our sails. We were on the clock and we only had minutes to recover and decide on a new strategy. The mood was manic hysteria. We were caught completely off guard by the Bills move to take Tuttle. Our room looked like the bumping cars ride at an amusement park. Our player personnel executive Carl Peterson and Dick sat stunned at losing Tuttle to Knox. While we were on the clock with everyone in panic mode, our veteran personnel guy, Herman Ball spoke up in a quiet voice.

Herman spoke and explained, "There's this other kid, he's not as quick as Tuttle but his name is Quick. That's got to be a good thing. He's decent and he went to North Carolina State. People have told me he can run after the catch."

With that little speech, Herman changed the course of two lives—Perry Tuttle and Mike Quick—and he changed the Eagles history book. Mike Quick went on to become a record setting receiver. He became a fan favorite and he is still in Philly today as the Eagles' play-by-play announcer with the great Merrill Reese on WIP sports radio. Does anyone know what happened to Perry Tuttle? He stopped in Buffalo for a cup of coffee and he never fulfilled Chuck Knox's expectations. The story speaks to the randomness of expert advice. There's a lot of money and time spent on preparing for the draft and when it comes down to it, the so-called experts frequently get it wrong. If you need further proof, recall the careers of two lower names from previous drafts, Bart Starr and Tom Brady. The experts didn't see the 200th and 199th picks as Hall of Famers. In the end,

Mike Quick

Merrill Reese, formerly WIP Sports Radio and now Eagles play-by-play announcer

no one can guarantee any future successes. No one wants to admit this, particularly people in the business, but sometimes it's in the hands of forces unknown to us. I sat in the draft room and thought that as GM, I was the only guy who had his hand in everything. Even though people criticized me for not being a "football guy," I knew the players like my kids. I was close with the coaches who coached the draft pick. And, I was the conscience of the man (Leonard) who paid for everything. I had deep knowledge of the Philly fans, their likes and dislikes, so I could tell with each draft pick that we selected whether or not they could survive in Philadelphia.

Dick used the draft to build a rock solid foundation for our football team. He had a knack for spotting talent and the translating to each player a belief and a confidence. Dick went with his gut and he was right more than he was wrong. Dick drafted one of his own UCLA players, Jerry Robinson. Robinson wasn't a big name but he had a great career with us. If they followed Dick, he would take them to the mountain top. One player in particular changed the face of the franchise. Dick came to me one day and suggested we try and find a way to deal for Ron Jaworski. Dick knew "Jaws" from his days with the Rams and he felt Ron had exactly what he was looking for in a quarterback. It turned out to be the perfect fit. Jaws was smart, tough, and humble. He had to be tough since our offensive line made the Maginot Line look like Swiss cheese. He was a great student of the game and he brought an incredible work ethic to the team. That type of leadership was infectious. Couple that with the fact that he had an instant rapport with Dick. Dick and Ron had that rare love for breaking down game film. Both were obsessive in their approaches to game preparation. Jaws and Dick proceeded to turn our fortunes around.

We did reach the summit of professional football, the Super Bowl on January 25, 1981. I remember it so well because it was the day the hostages were released from Iran. The hostages were taken dur-

Jimmy Murray, GM and Dick Vermeil, Head Coach
A MOMENT TO SAVOR FOREVER...THE EAGLES ARE GOING TO SUPER BOWL XV
We had just won the NFC Chapionship, beating arch-rivals the Dallas Cowboys 20-7.
That Marlboro sign in the back changed my life!

ing the Jimmy Carter presidency but they were not released until just after the Ronald Reagan inauguration. Unfortunately, the game didn't go as well for us as it did for Reagan. Our team peaked during the national anthem and by the time I reached the Super Box, we were down two scores to Jim Plunkett and the Oakland Raiders. But we got to the Super Bowl. It still bothers me today that we didn't get the victory but Dick and Ron got us to the game. Certainly, today I would love to own the memory of a Super Bowl win, but the years I spent with Dick Vermeil and Ron Jaworski were as great as any win. Today I frequently run into Jaws. Recently at a charity event I introduced him by saying, "Jaws pretends he likes me even though I gave him $112 million less than Donovan McNabb got from the Eagles." Though at the time, Jaws had a relatively great contract, there were no guarantees and no benchmark contracts. Like Dick, Ron became and intrinsic part of Philadelphia. He was a Catholic school kid from Lackawanna, New York by way of Youngstown State. He is and was always a down-to-earth, sincere gentleman. He was an intense competitor as evidenced by his 123 consecutive games played. He went on to become a national sports figure through ESPN and NFL Films but he had never forgotten where he came from. We were lucky to trade for Jaws and I was even luckier to get a great friend for life.

There is a great, funny story involving the great Eagles trainer Otho Davis and Dick which demonstrates Dick's obsession with detail. Dick was so meticulous that he couldn't stand even a crooked picture on the wall. Otho, who was elected to the Pro Football Hall of Fame as a trainer, died several years ago after battling cancer. While he was still alive and laying in hospital bed, Otho received a visit from Dick. Dick stayed with Otho for a while and then came out of the room with tears in his eyes. They were close, close friends.

Ron Jaworski and Jimmy Murray
"Jaws"is one of the nicest and toughest players you'll ever meet.
He had an amazing 123 consecutive starts as quarterback,
an NFL record he held for many years

Dick said, "You won't guess what happened in there. Otho could just about speak and I could barely hear him."

Otho had asked Dick to come closer because he had a secret he wanted to share with Dick.

Then Otho whispered to Dick, "Have you ever wondered who moved the pictures in your office?"

All trainers are pranksters and Otho was the king of the practical joke. Every time Otho would go into Dick's office, he would tilt a picture or two. Dick would walk into his office mumbling to himself, while straightening the picture, "Darn, this picture is crooked again." This scene repeated itself for years. For years, Dick could never figure out who was tampering with his picture. Previously, Dick had thought it was an office worker by the name of "Bow Wow" Wojeoewicz. Otho drove Dick loony for several years until, finally on his death bed, Otho whispered his confession to Dick. Through tears Dick, smiled and shook his head saying, "I don't think anyone has ever gotten me like that." Both Otho and Dick were two of the greatest guys I have ever met in sport or in life. Dick finally won a Super Bowl with the St. Louis Rams and I was thrilled for him and so was the rest of the football world. The simple fact is that Dick Vermeil represents the very best in sports.

Some of my greatest memories of Dick were when we didn't win. It never mattered what situation we were in, Dick always carried himself with professionalism and an infectious energy. After wins, Dick would be effusive in his praise for his players and after a loss, Dick would have all of his players hold hands in a post-game prayer. He was a master in building a common cause and he taught a reverence for team and togetherness. Once I got the game ball after a win in Green Bay. Even though I was the General Manager, I felt humbled to be singled out and thanked by Dick. What makes a great coach? There is no greatness in anything without authenticity. Dick knew the game of football as well as anyone who has ever coached the game. He connected with his players because he valued them as individuals as well as talented players. Sports can be cruel and this is especially true in the professional ranks. The head coach's job is to win and many times, coaches get caught up in the business of winning and tend to forget that players are individuals with feelings. Dick never took anyone for granted. He was straightforward, no nonsense, and always honest. He was completely dedicated to his team, so completely into his job that he eventually burnt out. In fact I think the words "burn out" were coined just to describe Dick. If he could have watched film for thirty hours a day, he would have. If you put as much of yourself into what you do as Dick regularly did, that intensity eventually catches up with you. After several successful years with the Eagles where he led the team to their first Super Bowl appearance in franchise history, he had to take time off from the game to re-group. What a coach, what a man! I am blessed that I was there with him.

CHAPTER 10

A Surprise Gift

"The worst prison would be a closed heart."

– POPE JOHN PAUL II

Please allow me to take a break from sports for a moment to talk about one of the most amazing chapters in my life. Out of the blue, Leonard called me into his office one morning and said, "Hey, you got a new head coach for your team."

"What? We're hiring another coach?" I asked.

"No, you nitwit! Your team, the Catholics, you got a new guy."

Leonard knew I was a devout Catholic and he was talking about the election of Pope John Paul II. This might sound strange but I'm actually a guy that gets excited about the election of a new Pope. I called my wife, Dianne, who is a convert, and told her the news.

"Hey, we got a new Pope," I said.

Dianne was watching the news coverage at home and she explained that the new Pope was "a little Polish guy who looks very nice." Immediately I turned on the television in Leonard's office to watch the coverage myself.

Leonard balked, "Why would anyone want to watch a Pope on television?"

I snapped back, "You're a Jewish guy who went to Notre Dame. You can't help it, you're affected!"

So the two of us together, watched the first non-Italian Pope in 400 years walk out on the balcony in St. Peter's Square. In one sentence Pope John Paul expressed the warmth and earthiness that would define his Papacy. Doing the Cicero thing he said, "I'm Polish, not Italian, so please, excuse the way I talk." He gave the perfect talk and suddenly he appeared more Italian than pasta. He even impressed Leonard forcing him to say, "Looks like you got a winner there."

Time passed and my wife was pregnant again. I had told her when she converted to Catholicism that the only things she would gain would be guilt and freckles. And, of course, marrying an Irishman, she had five kids. People often make a connection between Irish and lots of children. I wonder why? As we were preparing for the arrival of our fifth child, I said to Dianne one day, "If it's a boy, why don't we name him after the Pope? John Paul. Has a nice ring to it." Dianne just shook her head. It was January and it was the time of the Dallas-Pittsburgh Super Bowl game that was being played that year in Miami. As delivery date drew near, the doctors predicted that the baby might come early. Naturally with that news, I skipped the Super Bowl. Sure enough, the baby wanted to be delivered on the biggest day of the NFL season. We got to the hospital and the nurses and doctors started to quiz me.

"Do you want a boy or a girl?" they asked.

I gave the standard safe response. "I don't care, just as long as the baby is healthy."

"How about a name?" one of the nurses asked.

Half joking, half serious, I said, "If it's a girl, Dianne will name her. If it's a boy, I'm going to name him after the quarterback of the winning Super Bowl team."

I liked and respected the Dallas Cowboys quarterback Roger Staubach though I hated his team. Hate is a strong word for a football team but remember I'm from Philadelphia and we HATE the Cowboys. I immediately realized that calling my son Roger might haunt my child forever. I also loved Terry Bradshaw as a player and he happened to be a very funny guy as well. And on top of that, I was close to the Rooney family, who owned the Steelers. Secretly, I had to root for the Steelers to beat the Cowboys but it dawned on me that Terry Murray wasn't exactly a good name either. The doctors thought I was a little crazy with my name method and truthfully, I was beginning to agree. As soon as our son was born on January 21, Dianne and I looked at each other and both of us said in the same breath, "John Paul."

ॐ

Months later, Pope John Paul was traveling on his first pilgrimage as Pope to Mexico City. It was unfortunate that it wasn't the NFL exhibition season or I would have scheduled another pre-season game with the New Orleans Saints. But because our Archbishop in Philadelphia, John Cardinal Krol, was Polish like John Paul, the Pope decided to make a side trip to Philadelphia. It was a surprise announcement sending the entire Catholic population of Philadelphia into seventh heaven as they anticipated the first Papal visit ever to Pennsylvania. There was to be a huge outdoor procession and Mass on the Parkway Square in downtown Philly. I was very good friends with another influential Philadelphia Pole by the name of Ed Piszek. Ed owned Mrs. Paul's Foods, who made the famous Mrs. Paul's Fish Sticks. Ed was a frequent guest of mine at the Eagles games. As part of the Philadelphia Polish hierarchy and as a payback for my hospitality, Ed offered me two tickets to attend the Mass so that I could see the Pope up close and personal. I had made it a habit when I was GM not to accept any special favors from anyone, and as much as I wanted to see the Pope, I couldn't break from my established practice. Regrettably, I declined Ed's ticket offer. One week before the Pope's visit I was eating in a restaurant in South Philly. The Councilman of that particular Philadelphia district was a man by the name of Fran Rafferty. Fran, an old-time Philadelphia politician, was eating at the restaurant that same night. He stopped at my table and said, "Murr, I've got two silver tickets to see the Pope. I can't use them. Please, do me a favor and take them." Silver tickets? I had no choice. I had to renege on my "I can't be bought" policy.

ஜ௪

I was guaranteed a fairly good seat at the Mass. Anticipating the event got my imagination going and it was getting the best of me. Actually, I believe my minor league instincts took over. Wouldn't it be great, I thought, if I could get a picture of our baby (who we named after John Paul) with the actual Pope John Paul. But, that's an entirely crazy idea, don't you think?. Wouldn't I be too far away for something like that to happen? Not so fast. The day of the procession and Mass arrived. I decided to take matters into my own hands. I made a sign because in my heart of hearts, I was just a big fan rooting for my Pope. I made a huge poster that said, "I, TOO, AM NAMED JOHN PAUL IN YOUR HONOR, FOR HIS GLORY!" There was a sea of close to a million people on the Parkway that day. I was holding my John Paul while Dianne had our other four children. I got Dianne and the kids set up in one location and then I took the baby and my sign to where the silver ticket holders were sitting. I was standing with two friends I had brought along, Eddie Mahan and our team chaplain, Monsignor James Sharkey. I told them of my plan. I was going to get a picture of my John Paul with Pope John Paul.

Monsignor Sharkey said, "You're crazy, there are a million people here, you'll be lucky if you even see him from a mile away." Eddie Mahan (Artie's son) was our Eagles' team photographer so I prepped him on how I imagined the way things should go down. I was brimming with confidence. I was getting a picture with the Pope.

"Eddie, if I get close, and I'm going to get close, you have to get a picture of the baby and the Pope," I said in a voice reminiscent of Peter Graves in "Mission Impossible."

He politely said while humoring me, "Sure Murr, if you get close, I'll get the picture."

I quickly returned to check and make sure Dianne and the kids were in a safe spot. Then I made my way to the silver section. To give some further perspective, there were 20,000 silver ticket holders sitting behind 10,000 gold ticket holders. If I was a betting man, there was absolutely no chance of my scheme working. But then again, I'm a man of faith! No matter what the odds, I believe! Over my years, I had dealt with lots of stadium security during all types of sporting events. I had developed this special knack for identifying the sly undercover types. In this gargantuan crowd, I actually spotted the Secret Service agents. I don't know why, I can just spot them. One such agent was guarding the gold section. I walked over and introduced myself as if the Pope, himself, was expecting me. I was like Travis Bickle in "Taxi Driver." I approached the agent and he stayed totally in character acting if he were just a spectator.

I said to him as friendly as I could, "Hi, I'm Jim Murray, President and General Manager of the Philadelphia Eagles. I think we might have met before, maybe in New York?"

Believe it or not, it worked. My introduction relaxed him. I then asked, "What's the drill today?"

The agent spilled his guts and gave me the Pope's entire itinerary. "First, he's going to shake hands with Mayor Rizzo. Then he's going to bless some VIP's in the Cathedral. Then he'll get in his Popemobile and drive right past us here to the altar in Logan Circle." I had a chance. Slim. But I still believed I could get my John Paul in a frame with the world's top Catholic. Meanwhile, with crowds being what they are, I spotted Dianne with the kids. They had managed to get to the spot where I was, in the silver section. Luckily, Dianne had found me because our John Paul didn't care about the picture, the Pope, or anything else but mommy's milk. We were standing in the biggest crowd in Philadelphia history, and Dianne was doing her impersonation of "Our Lady of La Leche," breastfeeding our son in a shoulder-to-shoulder swarm. Several cloistered nuns appeared next to us. They hadn't been outside in public since the Kennedy administration and immediately they saw Dianne nursing and they became fixated on the whole scene. Suddenly, all they could concern themselves with was Dianne's comfort. I tell you, life's an audible. Here was my chance! Nuns! They had prime time gold seats. They insisted that Dianne, the kids, and me follow them through the crowd. Their Mother Superior, who easily could have been a holdover from the Gestapo, cleared a path to the front of the crowd better than Jerry Kramer leading a Packers sweep. We got stopped at about the fifth row. Nuns being nuns, they had enough food to camp out on the Parkway for a month. So, naturally they insisted that Dianne and the kids eat. Everyone had full stomachs as we waited for the Pope. All of this time, I was still not satisfied with my spot. I was still not in position A. I had gotten this far and I was not going to be denied. I went into my Marine Corps mode. "Sisters," I barked, "follow me. We are going to the front row!" Growing up Catholic I learned one thing. No Catholics ever questioned a nun and never an imposing Mother Superior. Next, I led a caravan of twelve people, including our photographer Eddie, to the front row by saying with great authority, "Step aside, the Sisters have to get in the front row." There we were, squeezed into the best seats of the entire event, and I had perfect timing. The Pope was just leaving the Cathedral. A priest friend of mine named Father Murray (no relation), recognized me and watched me masterfully pull off my hustle. I then decided to go all in and solicited Father Murray's help. I requested that if, in the event the Pope saw my sign and decided to come close, he would "Hold up the baby so Eddie can snap the photograph. Got it?" Affirming my wishes, Father Murray joined the plot!

From that moment on, God worked his magic. The Pope, left the Cathedral and much to the chagrin of the Secret Service, he pulled an improvisational moment. He skipped by the Pope-mobile and for whatever reason, he bolted right towards us. A zillion-to-one shot! He saw my sign, and he walked right to John Paul and then spent a full minute blessing our baby. It was exactly how I scripted it. Now, shake your head and nod with me, "Life's an Audible"...ya know, that should be title of this book!

The next day Eddie Mahan came into our offices with a look of utter dejection. "Murr, I blew the shot." He handed me a picture of the Pope's hand with a large Papal ring on it. It was like the photographer blowing the picture of the Marines' raising the flag at Iwo Jima. I didn't want to make Eddie feel bad, so I half-heartedly mumbled, "Don't worry about it Eddie, we got his hand." I walked over to Leonard and Dick Vermeil trying my best to hide my disappointment.

I said halfheartedly, "Can you believe it, in all of that crowd, we got this close to the Pope? Look, here's his hand, he's blessing my kid!"

Leonard and Dick thought I was nuts anyway, but now they were convinced seeing me almost in tears about Eddie missing the picture.

For the next two hours Eddie apologized like I was water boarding him saying, "Jimmy, I let you down. I'm so sorry. I don't know if you'll ever be able to forgive me."

We shook hands and Eddie walked out of the room. I closed my door and my eyes teared. Eddie waited a good five minutes and then knocked on my door.

"Jimmy, I forgot to show you this," he said as he pulled out the most incredible picture of the Pope and John Paul.

It looked like it was planned. A perfect shot, like it was a posed session at Sears. The sun was shining on the Pope's face at just the perfect angle. God's plan! Artie's kid set me up. Everyone in the office was in on the ruse. Everyone present in the room erupted in applause knowing what the picture meant to me. I was the happiest guy on earth. The picture became my cause celeb. I called it, "My Spiritual Super Bowl." It was everything to me. But, hold on, that isn't the end of the story!

The next year, we were playing Dallas on where else? *Monday Night Football.* The producer of MNF said to me before the game, "You got any more of those pictures of your kid with the Pope?" In the

A minor league baseball prank that I learned. It's all about the sizzle.
John Paul Murray and Jim Murray.

Here's that great shot by Edwin "Ed" Mahan...Pope John Paul II greets
John Paul Murray, October 13, 1979

3rd quarter of the game, our defensive tackle Carl Hairston got hurt. Carl always got hurt in the 3rd quarter of every game. If you had to bet, you could always win if you were to bet Carl would get hurt in the 3rd quarter. Carl was down on the ground writhing in pain when the "Voice of the World," Howard Cosell stepped in to fill some dead air time. ABC flashed the picture of Pope John Paul and my John Paul on national television. Cosell voiceover said, "This child, son of Eagles General Manager Jimmy Murray...Pope comes to Philadelphia, lays hands on this boy named for the man himself. Dandy Don, what a miracle story!"

Immediately after the broadcast, my phone rang off the hook for days.

I remember one friend saying, "Yo, baby pictures are one thing, showing them off on *Monday Night Football* is something else." The picture started to take its own little journey causing other events to happen.

Enter Tom Fox. Who was Tom Fox? Tom Fox was a reporter for the *Philadelphia Inquirer* who knew the city inside and out, in particular the neighborhoods and the Catholic parishes. I used to call him, "Philly to the 9th power." Tom called me the next day and asked, "Murr, you got any more of those pictures?"

"For what?" I asked.

Tom explained, "I want to give one to Ed Piszek."

Weeks later, Ed Piszek called me and told me he was holding a picture of the Pope and my John Paul while standing in the Vatican. Ed's company Mrs.Paul's Foods, sold frozen fishcakes and he must have sold a million fish cakes in Poland to get his own private audience with the Pope. I had vaguely been introduced to Ed Piszek but he and I would later become great friends.

He returned from Rome and told me he had shown my picture to the Pope. The Pope smiled when he was shown the picture and said, "Yes, I remember this. A wonderful moment!" Ed invited me to his office in Philadelphia to pick up a signed picture of the Pope holding up my picture. Two weeks later, I got another call from Ed.

"Jimmy, Cardinal Krol wants you to go to Alaska with us to meet the Pope," he said.

"Excuse me? Why?" I asked.

Ed explained, "The Pope is coming to Alaska from the Philippines and we've been invited to be part of the welcoming delegation for the United States and the Cardinal wants you to take part."

"In February? In Alaska?"

"We'll fly in a private jet," said Piszek.

I don't like flying on big jets, so I was even more terrified to fly on a small one. The next day I saw Cardinal Krol at a funeral in Philadelphia.

"See you tomorrow in Alaska?" he asked me as we passed one another.

"You're not going on the toy plane with us?" I asked him. I wanted to have him traveling with me for obvious safety reasons. "IN CASE OF PLANE CRASH, MAKE SURE YOU'RE TRAVELING WITH A CARDINAL!"

The Cardinal laughed and said, "I'm going with President Reagan on Air Force One, the real deal!"

I then said half-jokingly, half serious, "Then I had better go to confession."

The jet we were to board was parked at an old hangar at the Philadelphia Airport. The hangar itself was run down making me more nervous. We boarded the plane. It was an ecumenical plane ride. The plane was owned by Bob Levy, a Jew. On board were Levy, Sixers' owner Fitz Dixon, a Protestant, Piszek, author James Michener, and a reporter by the name of Larry Kane, who was also Jewish. As a bonus, there was another Cardinal on board with us. Stan "The Man" Musial stepped on the plane. Talk about the bonus of all bonuses. My idol! Musial was a friend of Piszek and also Polish through and through. I started thinking, "Hey if this plane goes down, I'm dying in some great company." After Musial took his seat, I walked over to him and promised that I would bend his ear all the way to Anchorage. And I did.

I always try and think ahead and anticipate opportunity. Just for the heck of it, I took an Eagles jersey, with the # 1 pasted on the front and back. I thought that I would bring it with me to Alaska, just in case I might get a second chance to meet the Pope. We arrived in Anchorage and I was extremely disappointed that we weren't greeted by Eskimos on dog sleds. Surprisingly, Anchorage looked just like Philadelphia in the winter, cold with scattered patches of dirty snow. Air Force One had landed just moments before. The big shots were shuffling off the plane onto the tarmac. Hundreds of movers-and-shakers were gathered for a reception in advance of the Pope's arrival. The reception required a ticket and Larry Kane suggested we should find a way into the reception, because as a reporter, he was on the prowl for a story. I explained to Larry about the ticket manager's creed. Every important event that has ever occurred requires a ticket. Larry needed his story and I needed food. We had to crash the event. There was a small Irish priest collecting tickets by the door. Larry tried to face guard this priest with his press credentials. The priest wouldn't budge. No one without a ticket was getting admission. He was a dogmatic old timer, who guarded the door like a Doberman Pincher. Later, I found out that the priest was a local guy. He was stationed at a church in Anchorage after spending years in Hawaii. That explained why he was angry. Larry wasn't getting anywhere with him, so I decided to take over.

I began, "Father, I know this is a ticketed event, and I know we don't have tickets. We're part of a Polish delegation from Philadelphia. I understand that my friend and I can't enter but there are two people you must let in, Mr. Piszek and Mr. Stan Musial."

"The baseball player, Stan Musial? Are we talking about the baseball player?" he exclaimed.

"Yes, Father," I said, " The two of us don't matter but please, could you take care of my friends?"

My strategy worked like a charm. The old guy softened immediately. "You folks just come right in. Stan Musial doesn't need a ticket." All of us strutted into the reception. Larry couldn't believe that I was able to buffalo the priest with no tickets. Later, Larry said to me, "Murr, I want you to do the color play by play when the Pope arrives at the airport. It would be great to pipe that back to Philadelphia with you on camera with me."

Afterwards, everyone was gathered at the airport to await the Papal jet. Larry and I were doing the play by play with me droning on and on in my formal reporter tone. "Here comes the Holy Father, the 232nd successor to St. Peter…" Truthfully, I was having the time of my life. The Pope arrived and he stepped off the plane. As usual, the Pope drifted away from his entourage to mingle with the common people. He loved crowds and it was Philadelphia all over again. He bee-lined right to me. I took out a pair of rosaries from my pocket. Being the overly emotional person I am, I had tears streaming down my face. He looked at me as if he remembered me and then beamed a wide smile. I could have put my hand out for a handshake but I was too caught up in the moment. What else could happen? My life was complete. Wow! But I was still holding the television microphone, forgetting the whole time I was supposed to be offering comments to the television viewers back home. Larry picked up for me while I blubbered.

From the airport, we followed the Pope to an outdoor venue where he would say Mass for a huge throng of Alaskans. I spotted Cardinal Krol, ran up to him, and I handed him the Eagles jersey that I had been carrying around.

"Your Eminence," I asked, "if it becomes appropriate, would you pass this on to our Holy Father? And seeing it is the anniversary of my father's death, could you please say a special prayer for him?"

The Cardinal responded, "I'll go one better. I'll concelebrate the Mass and with the Holy Father, I'll offer a special prayer during the Mass in memory of your father." Maybe not for anyone else, but for me there was no greater gift for me than having the boss of all bosses say a prayer for my Dad. I imagine that my father was tickled pink in his grave. We stood in the cold, arctic air on a beautiful, sunny, Alaskan afternoon, while the Pope said the Mass. Right after the Mass, the Pope was scheduled to return immediately to the airport and quickly depart for the next stop on his tour. He climbed into the Popemobile and then it began to snow. Larry Kane, his cameraman Phil Carroll, and I were shivering at this point. As we stood there with chattering teeth, a large bus pulled up to transport all of the VIP's back to the airport for one last goodbye ceremony. There is one more thing I learned over my years in sport and that is that security diminishes towards the end of an event. I said to Larry and Phil, "What do you say we get on the VIP bus?" Without a hiccup, we got on the bus, right under the Secret Service noses. When the bus arrived at the airport, everyone flooded off. There were a thousand photographers capturing the Pope mugging on a dogsled. Cardinal Krol happened to be standing near me and I was hoping he was still holding the Eagles jersey that I had given him earlier. He walked towards me and said, "Jimmy, follow me!" I followed him like A.J. Foyt following Richard Petty in the Indy 500. A Secret Service agent put his hand in front of me to stop me. I smugly said, "I'm with my Cardinal." Krol walked us right to the steps going up to the Pope's plane. The Pope stood at the bottom of the stairs and recited a script in broken English to the assembled crowd. "Bless you, thank you Mr. Reagan, and all the cardinals and bishops." He shook the hand of every single person lined up. Yet, Cardinal Krol was the last man to say goodbye to him. Pope John Paul hugged Krol because of the Polish thing, while I stood a few feet off to the side. Krol was conscious of exactly where I stood. He turned to me and then I heard him say to the Pope, "Holy Father, I want you to meet Jimmy Murray, my good friend." I shook the Pope's hand and then I started talking a hundred miles a minute.

"Holy Father, I am so honored, I named my son after you and you blessed him," I babbled. I went on and on for several moments like a broken record. I was able to hand him the Eagles jersey, which I hope he wore on weekends and vacation or whenever he watched football on television! Pope John Paul blessed me and then pinched my cheek. Phil and Larry caught the whole thing for television. All told, a trip with Stan Musial, the Cardinal and Archbishop of Philadelphia, and a blessing by the Pope. That's a fairly complete day. It should have been finished now, right? Nope! Not even close!

The moment the Pope was back on his plane, Mr. Piszek came up to me and said, "Jimmy, I'm taking you to Rome." Piszek was what I call a "made" Polish Catholic. He had been invited by the Pope's Secretary for a private visit to the Vatican. He and the Pope were friends for years and they had a sort of high school buddy relationship. I flew back to Philadelphia where I told my wife of my good fortune. I can't honestly say she was excited about the idea of me now going to Rome, but she knew how excited I was. Being the

A meeting in Philadelphia of Cardinal Krol (holding John Paul Murray), James Michener, Ed Piszek, Steve Van Buren, Jim Crowley, and Tom Fox

great wife that she is, she encouraged me to go. I had never been to Rome. After the Alaska trip, I was set for life. I could die fulfilled for having shaken hands and being blessed by a Pope. Little did I know, things were just warming up.

ॐ

We arrived in Rome a few weeks later, Ed Piszek, Stan Musial, James Michener, and me. How's this for a lineup: a Hall of Fame baseball player, a Pulitzer Prize-winning author, a billionaire, and me? I was out of my league. We stayed at the famous Hotel Alcovy, which was directly across from the Vatican. I knew nothing of the plans for the trip. I was just happy to be along for the ride. Mr. Piszek told me to rest up for a bit because later he would have a big surprise for us. Several hours later, we were introduced to Mimmo Del Vecchio. Mimmo was Mr. Piszek's private limosine driver during his frequent trips to Rome. Being with Mimmo was like having an all-access pass to Disney. Everywhere we went, people knew Mimmo, and in turn, gave us the red carpet treatment. Piszek instructed Mimmo to drive our Mercedes to St. Peter's Square where, he informed us, we were to have a private Mass with the Pope.

"Just for us?" I asked.

Yes, just us. Monsignor Jevich, the Pope's secretary had set the whole thing up with Piszek when we were in Alaska. When we arrived in Rome, we found out that Jevich had left for vacation. In Europe, vacation means vacation. Jevich was completely inaccessible. He was in remote hiding with no phone and no contact with the outside world. Monsignor Jevich, a Pole himself, was the gatekeeper to the Pope. With no Jevich in town, there would be no audience and no private mass. Needless to say, we were all very disappointed except little Jimmy Murray from Brooklyn Street. I had still made it to Rome. The disappointment waned as Mimmo gave us some great history lessons as we toured the Catacombs and the Appian Way. Even without the private Mass, I was a kid in the candy store. Later, we were able to meet another secretary high up in the Vatican food chain. His name was Bishop Mgumbo, and he was from Africa. He apologized profusely because we were unable to meet the Pope in Rome. He informed us that the Pope was resting in his villa at Castel

Gandolfo. However, Mgumbo, surprisingly, gave us the green light to drive out to the villa. He didn't promise we would get in but he suggested, "Why not drive out and see what happens." We arrived outside the city at the Pope's residence and there was another Bishop on duty. He was not at all pleased when we showed up unannounced.

It was a similar scene to the one of Dorothy trying to see the Wizard. "Friday, come back Friday," said the priest. "The Pope will offer a Mass for the Polish people who are visting on Friday."

That could have easily be a couple of million visitors. Now I was disappointed. We were so close. We decided that we would take our chances and stay around for a few days. We would hang out for a few days, try and see the Pope, and then head back to Rome. We toured the area with Mimmo. We ate like Roman emperors and we had a grand time. Friday arrived. We went back to the villa. We were ushered to first row seats in a small chapel. The chapel was filled with a large number of Polish pilgrims and four of us, out of place, uninvited Americans. The Pope entered the Chapel and he was beaming being among his Polish guests. He said the Mass. After he finished, he walked down the aisle, stopping to warmly greet everyone in the Chapel. Afterwards, a Monsignor walked in and asked, "Is there a Mr. Piszek here?" Later, the Monsignor asked us to follow him, which we did. He took us up a narrow, winding staircase. As we walked up, the Pope was coming down the same staircase. He had taken off his vestments. The Pope gave Piszek a bear hug of recognition. Ed asked the Pope, "Where's Jevich? Is this a good time for us to see you?" The Pope assured us, "Don't worry, don't worry, welcome, welcome!" For the next hour the Pope posed for pictures with Mimmo, Stan, Jim, and me. He sat and spoke with us in his courtyard just as if we were hanging out at a playground in my old neighborhood. It was a surreal moment.

&*

Later, we were invited to a concert given by young Polish children, where they sang and danced in native costumes. I watched the Pope keep time to the accordion, his red shoes and white socks tapping enthusiastically. He brought up each and every child performer for a blessing and hugged each one. It was a moving moment. I witnessed first hand why he appealed to everyone, both young and old. He had universal attraction as he reached out and touched everyone. It was a sacred experience, profound in its simplicity.

The following Monday we were invited back for our original official visit because Father Jevich had returned. He had no idea we had already visited the previous week. We didn't tell him otherwise. He invited us to a private chapel for our promised private Mass with the Holy Father. This time, there were several world renowned politicos in attendance and I got to shake hands with the Austrian chancellor during the "kiss of peace." Needless to say, he didn't recognize me. I was sure he wasn't an Eagles follower. After Mass, Jevich invited us to have private breakfast with the Pope. Breakfast with the Pope? No. I couldn't believe it. We would be breaking bread with the successor to St. Peter. Jevich led us to a cozy room with tables set for dining. The only people in the room were Ed, Stan, Jim, Jevich, and Bishop Mgumbo. No one else joining us? Wait, we were having a real private breakfast with a real superstar? Pope John Paul walked into the room dressed in a white cassock. Immediately, he walked over to Ed and again hugged him like they were old college roommates from Warsaw. Ed sensed my excitement and turned right away to me and re-introduced me.

Ed said, "Holy Father, I want you to meet my friend, the world's greatest communicator, Jim Murray."

I might have imagined this, but the Pope seemed to remember me from our previous meetings in Philadelphia and Alaska. It had to be my imagination because I'm sure he met a thousand short, fat guys a day.

Jim Murray, Pope John Paul II, Ed Piszek, Stan Musial,
Domenico "Mimmo" Del Vecchio (our driver)

I said, "Holy Father, Ed exaggerates. You speak one hundred languages, I speak Philly."

He laughed and then said, "Let's sit and eat together." A twenty-minute breakfast turned into a two-hour love fest. At one point during the breakfast, Ed turned to me and asked me to explain to the Pope about the Ronald McDonald House in Philadelphia. I gave the Pope an abbreviated version of the founding, and told a few stories about some of the families and how the house helps those in a difficult time. He was visibly moved. He asked me many thoughtful questions about the house and he prophetically said, "That's an idea that could go around the world." I was feeling my oats. The conversation was relaxed and loose. I then said, "Holy Father, do you know who you are?"

"Who am I, Jim?" he asked with a smile.

"You're the head coach of the world," I shot back.

He laughed aloud for several moments and replied, "That's a tough job!"

The two hours went by much too quickly. I didn't want to leave. I thought about asking him if he wanted to hang out with us later but that would have been greedy of me. As we were leaving, he hugged each one of us. I was so moved, so emotional that my whole body shook. He was the only thing he was capable of being, himself. He was beatific. From a Mass to pictures to breakfast with the Pope, the altar boy from Our Mother of Sorrows Church had traveled to the very top of the mountain. My own personal Super Bowl victory. I was humbled. I thought back to all of the people who helped me on my journey. They should have been here with me, sharing in this great moment. Why me? Why did I have such good fortune? I had encountered a saint face to face. Relaxed, he had invited me to be myself. As we stood in the doorway about to leave, I thought about the amazing hand of God. Here was a Polish actor turned coal miner turned political resistor turned Pope, who at his core was nothing more than a humble servant to his flock. At his center, he was a simple priest trying to do God's work. The dream ended. We left. I knew this high would never be repeated. It was an extraordinary gift!

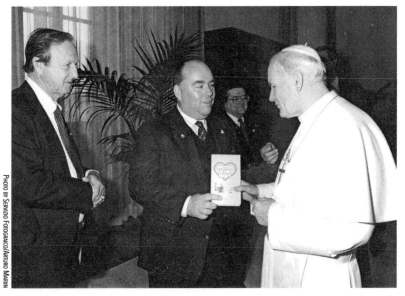

Stan "The Man" Musial (the other cardinal from St. Louis!); Jim Murray giving copy of Journey to the Heart (a history of the Ronald McDonald Houses) to Pope John Paul II

CHAPTER 11

A Momentary Break in the Action

"Ends are not bad things, they just mean that something else is about to begin.

— C. JOY BELL

I have known few people more interesting than Leonard Hyman Tose. He appeared larger than life in one moment, and then hopelessly lost in another. Like everything in life, the good and the bad exist side by side…each fighting for expression. Leonard eventually broke my heart by firing me but he was a one-of-a-kind character, whom I loved dearly, despite the rocky years we shared together. I'll talk about the firing later but first, I would rather recount one story about Leonard that is my all-time favorite and demonstrates how I was Abbott to his Costello.

❧

We were sitting in a bar of the Polo Lounge in the Beverly Hills Hotel during the same week that we interviewed Dick Vermeil for our head coaching vacancy. A long-legged, blonde beauty walked into the room and caught the eye of every man in the room, but in particular, she dazzled Leonard. Leonard could fall in and out of love every five minutes. For some reason that habit seems easier to develop when you have lots of money. Actually at this point in his life, he had squandered so much money that his wealth existed more in his imagination than on paper. He still carried on like the playboy he was in his younger years. In any case, on this day, Leonard became infatuated by this model/actress/cover girl (she qualified for all three). Naturally, Leonard turned to me to act as his advance man and arrange a rendezvous later that evening. He instructed me to go over to her table, introduce myself, and inform her that there was a very important person who wanted to meet her. He expected that I return promptly with the woman in tow, while he waited at the bar downing several scotches. Always obedient to Leonard's commands, I walked over introduced myself to the girl.

I said, "Hello, my name is Jim Murray and I am the General Manager of the Philadelphia Eagles."

She was polite but clearly my introduction did not impress her. It was clear that she wasn't interested in what maybe seemed to her, an overture from a short, round guy.

Then I said, "Our owner, Mr. Leonard Tose, sitting across the bar, would very much like you to join him so that he can buy you a drink."

That's another thing that I've learned over the course of my life. No matter what the circumstances, no one ever, turns down a free drink. This especially holds true in Beverly Hills. Immediately, she stood up and we walked back to where Leonard was sitting at the bar. Leonard loved women and he was an excellent knave of hearts, even in situations like these, where it was clear that he was old enough to be the girl's grandfather. With me, Len could be quick tempered, demanding, and at times, demeaning. With women he possessed an instant Rudolf Valentino charm. With my assigned task completed, Leonard quickly dismissed me. I took his cue and left the newly acquainted love birds to coo together. Sam Procopio and I walked across the room and sat down at another table. We ate a wonderful meal, while Leonard worked harder to secure the blonde than he did securing the Eagles. Eventually the woman excused herself for a restroom break while Leonard hurried over to our table.

"She likes a place called 'The Magic Castle.' Find out about it!" he commanded.

Again, this was a huge part of my being an NFL executive, playing the dutiful gopher for the obnoxious owner. I went to the hotel concierge and I asked him if he knew anything about a place called the "Magic Castle." He said he hadn't but that he would research the place for me. I asked him that if possible, could he find the place and make a reservation for Mr. Leonard Tose and his party. Back at the bar, Leonard was restless.

Upon returning, Leonard quizzed me, "What did you find out?"

"I'm working on it." I said.

"Well work fast, I already told her that we're going there."

A small bell hop with a high pitched voice, reminiscent of an old 1940's movie character, walked in and announced, "Phone call for Mr. Murray!"

I had always dreamed of that scene in my head, where I would be paged in a big Hollywood Hotel, just like Cary Grant. The concierge had found out that the "Magic Castle" was a private club in the Hollywood Hills and it was run by professional magicians. The maitre'd at the Magic Castle called me on the phone. He informed me that they required membership in order to make a reservation. I dropped Leonard's name and occupation and promised to pay any membership fees on site. He agreed to give us a reservation for later that evening. Later on, we walked into the Magic Castle and I was suitably impressed. I love magicians and magic shows. I became very disappointed later in my life when a reality television show took audiences behind the scenes of magicians. The show gave away all of the secrets of how any trick works. It killed my fascination because magic was always my favorite form of entertainment. Inside the Magic Castle I was captivated by the entire atmosphere. By the time we arrived, Leonard and his girlfriend had invited some tagalongs. Our party size stood at twelve people. The maitre'd was a very serious, scary-looking Boris Karloff type fellow. After a series of magicians performed a dozen or so warm up tricks, we were led upstairs to a special place they called, "The Séance Room." The room was impressive. Whoever conceived of the idea, thought of every detail. The atmosphere was such that you really felt that it was possible to contact the dead. All of us sat down at a large round table in the middle of the room. Naturally the séance didn't take place right away. We had to order dinner and drinks, which was really what kept the magicians in business. No one from the other side would consider talking to us until we ordered four or five rounds of cocktails. Leonard, a lifelong Scotch drinker, asked for an entire bottle of Johnny Walker Black for himself. This was on top of the six or so glasses he drank at the hotel. Everyone was laughing loudly and having a great time. I sat calculating in my head how much this little excursion was going to cost the Eagles' front office. The dishes were cleared from the table and the séance was about to begin. A white haired guy, right from central casting, prepared the table for our trip to the nether world. He insisted that the table be absolutely cleared of any material objects.

He began, "We must be in a total spiritual state to be accepted into their world."

I was totally hooked. I even had a list of people I wanted to talk with. Leonard yawned and placed his scotch between his legs. As Ed Sullivan used to say every Sunday night on CBS, "This is going to be a really big show." The lights were turned out, and the medium instructed us in a low whisper, "Now we will all hold hands." Our psychic tour guide began speaking aloud like Dracula begging for a neck.

"Harry, Harry, we are here," he whispered.

There were a few chuckles from our party and immediately he shushed everyone, annoyed that we weren't fully cooperating.

Again he asked, "Harry, Harry, can you hear me?"

The floor dropped suddenly from under our feet. I don't know how they did it but I was buying in. It was better than any illusion I had ever experienced on the Atlantic City boardwalk. Somehow they had installed some type of hydraulic mechanism that caused the floor to drop. Every one quickly sat up and took notice.

"Harry, Harry, do you have a message?"

There was complete silence. The tension was so thick that each of us were drenched in sweat. I started to feel Harry's presence. Whoever Harry was, I was convinced he was in the room. The action continued moving towards the big moment. Something big was about to happen, the climax to the entire event.

Once more, the magician asked, "Harry, Harry, what is your message?"

I was sure Harry was just about to say something when Leonard shouted out, "Yeah, my balls are freezing!"

His scotch on the rocks was literally, scotch on the rocks. With that, Leonard had killed the charade. Totally pie-eyed, Leonard was doubled over, laughing at himself. Boris Karloff became so angry, he ran out of the room, and he never came back. Immediately the manager of the place came up and asked us to leave. Holding me accountable for Leonard, he told me that we would never be allowed to return. To make matters worse, he added that we could forget about a membership. Actually I felt bad about the whole episode. After all, I was hooked in to the idea. I was really holding out to talk to some of my dead relatives. Disappointed, I found the angry actor on our way out of the place. I apologized and then gave him a thousand dollars for his pain and suffering. Since then, I have wondered many times over the years, exactly what was Harry's message to us? No matter what it was, this was a typical Leonard moment. And one of the many ones that I'll never forget.

ॐ

We came back from California with a coach and a ton of laughs. Life is a version of the facts as you saw and remembered them. I have great memories of Leonard Hyman Tose, even though he eventually fired me in an underhanded and public way. He never called me into his office and fired me in person. I guess that means I'm naïve thinking that there is a proper way to fire people. But, that really bothered me. I was kicked off the cliff one day when I picked up the morning paper. The announcement of my firing made the front page of the *Philadelphia Inquirer* on my wife's birthday. Actually, I received a bigger headline than the Preakness, which ran on the same day. That was a consolation of sorts.

MURRAY OUSTED AS EAGLES GM!

Public humiliation! It was the first time in my life when I felt there was no place to hide. Believe me, in that situation, you want a place to hide. I learned that being let go from a high profile job is a long, lonely, painful road to walk. The highs were the highest of highs but oh, that low of being fired was the lowest of the lows. Nonetheless, despite the untimely end, my years with Leonard were the most fascinating of my life. He broke my heart but I can still say that my life was better because of my experiences with him. My breakthrough with the Eagles was the Marlboro presentation in

New York, when Pete Retzlaff jumpstarted my career by placing me a few notches higher in the organization. From that day forward, I refused to be Leonard's puppet. Leonard could always count on me to be respectful, loyal, and understanding. I knew the boundaries of our relationship. He owned the team. It was his ball, and he let me play with him for a time. But, I always operated in the same manner that I did with my first job in college, when I was the lowly manager of the Villanova baseball team. I always felt and I made it my practice to look everyone straight in the eye and be true to myself and my values. I never looked up or down, but straight on. Just like my Dad and Artie taught me. Certainly, if I was one of the Seven Dwarfs, I wouldn't be "Bashful." I was one of the few people in Leonard's life that could go toe to toe with him. Rich and powerful people naturally can become insular. Often, they get surrounded by subservient people and lose touch with the common folk. That may be a gross generalization but I think it was true in Leonard's case. He was used to raising his voice, snapping his fingers, and watching every underling jump at his every command. That was Leonard's world that I walked into one day. Despite being brash, cocky, and self-indulgent, he could also be an introspective guy. Few people ever got to see that side of him. Initially it surprised me that he was much deeper emotionally and spiritually than people knew. He never intentionally sought out my counsel but nonetheless our relationship forced a number of closed door sessions throughout the years. He used to explode at least once a day. He would have major blow-ups sometimes several times per week. I was there standing close by to do damage control. I was in the IED (improvised explosive device) business before the army. Unlike everyone else in the organization who would run for cover, I would let him vent and then calmly bring him back to earth whenever he went on a tirade. That was my skill. That was my strong suite in its entirety, and most likely the reason Leonard kept me around. How's that translate into a job skill on a résumé? 1971-1984: Calmed down a millionaire. But in the end, I had gotten very close to him. I have always said he was like Dr. Pepper. Misunderstood! He flaunted the rich boy persona, flashed lots of money, and chased beautiful women. I never did or could. Owning the Eagles was the high point in his life. He was the prodigal son to his father. His older brother, Louis, was much more like his father. Louis took to the family business while Len took to the high life. Sadly, Louis died young. Len was the polar opposite of Louis. He lived in the New Yorker, spent lots of his father's money as the Playboy of the Western World. When Louis died, Leonard came home and out of necessity, committed to the family business. He loved his father dearly, though he was never sure if he could please him. He and I had long talks about our respective upbringings. Though he grew up in a family with money, he didn't escape the experience without scars. At times I would tease him calling him "poor little rich boy." Early in his schooling his father had sent him to a military school in Virginia. Len used to tell me that his years there were the loneliest he remembered. He served in the U.S. Army, where he was stationed in Puerto Rico. Not bad. I never did get to Puerto Rico after my baseball academy days. And then, Len was a Jewish kid, who went to Notre Dame and he did well there. Ironically, one of the things he was most proud of were his years at a Catholic school. We had our share of laughs about that, too. Leonard contributed great sums of money to ND football and coaches, alumni, and staff. Everyone in South Bend loved him. Whenever I would travel to Notre Dame with him, he was treated like a celebrity. I used to kid him that he would have looked really spiffy dressed with a Roman collar and that the school's fussing over him was just a ruse to get him ordained to the priesthood. Leonard would have made a great priest, that is, if priests were allowed to drink heavily, curse loudly, and cavort with wild women. Cardinal O'Hara, who was Archbishop in Philadelphia, was the one time chaplain for the Notre Dame football team. O'Hara loved Tose and Tose loved him back. Once when Leonard was having some marital difficulties with his first wife, the Cardinal called Len and ask, "Can't you work it out?"

Len turned to me and asked, "How do these guys know these things about my private life?" "Because," I said, "you're not private about anything."

Leonard relished being a public figure and everything he did somehow got reported in the newspapers.

I explained to Leonard that Cardinal O'Hara "just wanted you to be happy and he's just concerned about your wife as well. That's his job."

Catholics were a mystery to Len. He couldn't figure us out even though he was a huge contributor to a Catholic institution. It's difficult for anyone close to Notre Dame not to get caught up in the school's lure. Whenever I visit the campus today, I always stop by the famous grotto and say a prayer to Len telling him, "Len, after all the help you gave the Catholics, I hope it helped."

᠗

Though Len was a proud ND alum, he got kicked out of the school for shooting craps in his dormitory. Eventually, after some begging by his father, the school let him back in and all was forgiven. Surely, the stream of checks from his Dad never hurt his cause. Years later, he got furious with me after a draft when we didn't pick Joe Theismann. Theismann was a great college quarterback at Notre Dame but that year, we had more pressing needs on the offensive line and we passed on Joe. We picked Jerry Sizemore, a big tackle from Texas to solidify our line. Leonard immediately walked into the draft room, screamed and ranted and insisted that we make a trade for Theismann. He left our draft room and then the first person he saw afterwards was Don Shula, the coach of the Miami Dolphins. Shula knew how to draft better than anyone, and he would sooner give up his first born than make a deal with us for Theismann. Leonard was extremely disappointed. Eventually he came to understand our thinking on Sizemore but he had such a fierce loyalty to Notre Dame that he couldn't bring himself to forgive us for passing on a fellow "golden domer."

᠗

Let me wander off the topic of Leonard for a minute to tell a great Joe Theismann tale. To this day, Joe is one of my favorite professional athletes of all time. Even though Theismann was a high draft pick, he began his career by signing with the Toronto Argonauts of the Canadian Football League. After several great years in Canada, Joe came back to the States and became a successful NFL quarterback. One time, we were opening a Ronald McDonald House in

Washington, D.C. As part of the festivities, we were attending a gala at the Kennedy Center hosted by then First Lady Barbara Bush. That same year, our placekicker was Mark Mosley, who we traded to the Washington Redskins. What a mistake we made with that trade! After the trade, Mosley beat us a hundred times and he winked at me each and every time I would run into him. Mosley was with us when we opened the first house in Philadelphia and he stayed involved with our cause even after we shipped him to Washington. The Bush family had lost a child to leukemia and as George was Vice-President to President Reagan, they lived in the Vice President house at the Naval Observatory. Barbara Bush had invited us out to their house for a pre-gala reception. Mosley and I were driving out together in his car, and he stopped to pick up his teammate Joe Theismann. Theismann, who was and is a "chatty Cathy," badgered me for the entire ride about not drafting him. "You didn't pick me because I'm small. What, you hate small people?" he joked.

I said, "Joe, look at me, I'm 5' 7". You should be down on your knees thanking me. If I drafted you, you would have never gotten to the Redskins and made it to a Super Bowl. You would have been booed on a losing Philly team. Just try and tell me that God wasn't watching out for you!" We laughed the entire evening about it and I really enjoyed Joe's company. Maybe Leonard was right, we should have drafted him. Later that year Dan Fouts, who was the quarterback for the San Diego Chargers, was named the winner of the Maxwell Award for the top NFL player. The awards dinner was to be held in Philadelphia. At the same time, because of my involvement with the Ronald McDonald House, I received a letter from a woman in New Mexico. Her son was a huge Dan Fouts fan and asked me if I could please get Dan to talk to her critically ill son. Fouts couldn't make the dinner because he had undergone some post-season surgery. Joe Theismann was sitting at a nearby table at the dinner. I told Joe about the letter and the mother's request.

"How about it, Joe? Can you do a big favor for me and just say hi to the kid?" I asked.

"But I'm not Dan Fouts," he said.

"But you're Joe Theismann!" I protested.

Then Joe left the dinner, went into a room in the hotel and talked to this boy for the rest of the evening. He missed the entire dinner. Later, the mom wrote a beautiful letter to me expressing her gratitude to me for having Theismann pinch hit for Fouts. From that time forward, Joe owned me. Joe had a great post-football career as a football analyst for ABC. He is a great guy and yes, Leonard, you were right, we should have drafted him!

Alright, let's get back to Leonard. Leonard Tose possessed many great qualities that I believe he picked up from his Notre Dame days. He loved tradition. He particularly enjoyed when a large crowd of us would pile on a train for a trip from Philly to South Bend for a big Irish football weekend. I wasn't his illegitimate son but I was close enough. Since he had two daughters and many women in his life (did I mention Leonard loved women?), I was a buddy, a pal, and a guy he trusted. If something important was to happen, he always wanted me close by. Once, he needed to have open heart surgery. He insisted that we find the best physician money could buy. We did. We searched and discovered that the best doctor for the surgery was a Dr. Denton Cooley from Houston, Texas. Leonard had a hard time keeping secrets, in fact the truth was, he couldn't keep even one. In this case, it would have been big news for the papers that the Eagles owner was having serious surgery. Within the organization, we agreed that it would best to keep the operation out of the press. It was a total valve replacement before total valve replacement was a routine procedure. I'm sure it is still not routine today but it was a scary undertaking in the 1970s. Leonard smoked a pack of cigarettes a minute and drank a bottle of booze every hour. By anyone's measure, he was not a healthy horse. I didn't want a ton of distractions for our team and I wanted to keep everyone calm, so I flew to Houston with Leonard. We were playing the New York Giants that Sunday at the Meadowlands in New Jersey. Leonard and I arrived at the hospital in Houston and Dr. Cooley's partner, Dr. Carfagnon walked into Leonard's room. Dr. Carfagnon became my favorite doctor of all-time when he told me it was alright to be fat. That was my favorite medical advice of my entire life. Next, Dr. Cooley walked in with a posse of interns. Leonard began to get a worried look on his face. He was rightfully scared.

"Are you going to do me or are they going to do me?" Len asked pointing to the young interns.

Cooley, as cool as he could, said, "I'm going to cut you and do you, skin to skin."

Len replied, "Just wanted to make sure I've got the starting quarterback."

Once Leonard relaxed and was confident in Dr. Cooley, he dismissed me to go back to New York for the Giants game. I returned to New York and on game day took my seat in the press box. At halftime, I went to a public phone and called Houston long distance. There was no cable television back then but somehow the game was carried on radio in Houston. I gave Leonard a briefing on the game, hung up and returned to my seat. Toward the end of the game, with less than a minute to go, the Giants had the lead. I left the press box and went down to stand on the sidelines, thinking to myself, "Oh no, we've lost another one." I had better start thinking of excuses for the post-game interview questions. The Giants had the ball for one last play. We had no timeouts. The only thing the Giants had to do to seal the win was to have their quarterback, Joe Pisarcik, take a knee and let time on the clock expire. For some reason unknown to man to this day, the Giants chose to run a play. Pisarcik handed the ball off to fullback Larry Csonka. The exchange was botched and the ball came out of Csonka's hands. It bounced on the ground like an Alka-Seltzer tablet, and came right up to our guy, Herman Edwards. Edwards grasped the ball and then ran 80 yards the other way for a touchdown. The "Miracle at the Meadowlands" was born. If that same play happened in Kansas City, no one would have heard about it. But, because it was New York, Herm became a legend. I stood on the sideline jumping up and down in disbelief as the whole play unfolded before my eyes in slow motion. After the game I called Leonard to tell him. He had been listening to the game on the radio and he became so angry that we were losing that he cursed and prematurely turned off his radio. Leonard, the team owner, missed the greatest play in Eagles' history. A few years later, we signed Joe Pisarcik as our backup quarterback, after he was cut by the Giants. The first day he arrived in camp, I asked him, "Are you Catholic?" He looked at me like I was crazy.

"Why?" he asked.

I said, "All you had to do was genuflect and there would be no 'Miracle of the Meadowlands.'" That one moment, that one bad fumble affected the Giants for many years to come. Soon after, the Giants' coach was fired and the franchise fell into a funk for quite some time. Sometimes crazy things happen when you mess with karma. It was certainly true in this case until the Giants later hired Bill Parcells, who was able to break the curse and restore glory to the New York Giants.

✽

The doctors in Houston gave me some good news about Leonard's condition. Because of his bad health habits, Leonard had the fight of his life and the surgery had been long and tough, but we succeeded from letting it become a media event back home. After a few initial rough days, Len recovered from his surgery and returned home to Philadelphia. Things were never dull with Leonard. As soon as he was up and about, he returned to smoking, drinking, and gambling as if the Martians had invaded Camden, New Jersey! He picked up where he left off before the surgery and then he needed me more than ever to dampen his urges. Ironically, I ended up losing my job trying to dampen Leonard's vices. Leonard was a compulsive gambler and this was to lead to his eventual demise. Every casino from the Vegas strip to the Atlantic City boardwalk welcomed us with their best red carpet treatment. We had favored status at any casino we entered. I used to say that Leonard was the "first Jewish Arab." Resorts, Caesars, Playboy, he was one of the most favored high rollers at every stop and got along with anyone he met in a casino. On one winter's night, there was huge snowstorm. We were working late in the office and we were just about getting ready to wrap up and go home.

"I'm going to the casino," Len announced.

"In this snowstorm?" I asked.

"What snowstorm?"

"Well I'm not going," I protested.

"You're going!" he commanded.

It was my regular custom to give in to Leonard's commands, so as usual, I caved. We drove three hours from Philadelphia to Atlantic City in a driving blizzard, putting ourselves in grave danger only to satisfy Leonard's craving. Fortunately, we arrived at the first casino safely. I had this crazy notion that maybe I could set some limits for Leonard and by doing so, help him out, maybe even moderate some of his appetites. He was gambling so frequently and heavily that our banking partners began to take notice. They were becoming noticeably worried about their loans to the organization.

We entered the hotel and I said jokingly to Leonard, "How about if you win $50,000 here, we leave."

Leonard chuckled and said, "How about if you just keep quiet?"

I tried harder to convince him saying, "Can't we walk out satisfied with reasonable success?" Because of the snowstorm, we arrived to an empty casino. Our arrival made their night. We were the only idiots in the tri-state area who were dumb enough to venture out in such horrible conditions.

Here was a completely empty casino and in walked high-roller Leonard Tose. I'm pretty sure the management recognized that one Leonard Tose could provide them more revenue than ten buses full of senior citizen slot players. The overzealous staff escorted Leonard to the high stakes table where they plowed him full of free scotch for the next thirty hands of blackjack. Casino managers were never happy to see me tagging along. The pit bosses would call me Jimminy Cricket, because like the Disney character, I was chirpy. And like Jimminy Cricket, I had a conscience. Leonard played for thirty minutes at a $1,000 per hand. He was a terrible black jack player. With all of the different wagers and presses he'd go after, he would regularly lose a hundred grand in several minutes. The casinos would always bring in their best dealer when Leonard showed up. They would have a hand-picked dealer ready, and it was a dealer who was mechanical and fast. Faster than Richard Petty! Actually it was overkill on the casino's part, since Leonard was significantly slowed down by the liquor. It didn't take much effort to wrestle money from Leonard. But, on this particular night, Leonard was up $65,000. I don't remember too many times when Leonard played in the black.

I announced to Len, "We made our number! Let's go home!"

Len just laughed at me. "I'm hot! We're staying!"

So then we left the first casino. We walked a block through the snow, and entered a second casino. Lightning struck twice. He gathered up another $50,000. That made $115,000. Not nearly enough for Leonard. We went off to a third casino, and unbelievably, he won another 50g's. I felt great! For one of the few times, we weren't borrowing with markers as was our normal habit. I was firm and successful imposing a rigid curfew on Leonard. Uncharacteristically he would occasionally obey a rule I set down. I could be firm with him whenever he took me along because I didn't have the stamina to gamble throughout the night. My rule was that he had to stop gambling at 2 am on weekdays and 4 am on the weekends. Had that not been the rule, I'm sure he would have lost the Eagles much sooner than he did. Finally, we ended up at the Playboy Hotel and Casino where we were escorted to the top floor penthouse suite.

Let me if I may, try to re-create the picture for you. This was the point where things were entirely out of control. When we walked into the lobby of the Playboy Hotel, Len insisted that Sam Procopio and I buy a few new suits. Again, it was at two o'clock in the morning, not a great time for a suit fitting. Who gets tailored by a small Chinese guy named Ling for a custom-made suit in the middle of the night? But this was a typical experience with Leonard. When Len felt good, he wanted everyone around him to feel good. How? By buying whatever you wanted, whenever you wanted. Of course, on the flip side, when things were bad, they were very bad. The penthouse suite at the Hotel though, was spectacular. It had a pinball machine in the living room, a great big one with lights and sounds. As a kid who grew up in the city, I loved pinball! Naturally, I stayed up all night and played a thousand games of pinball. I didn't even care if I "tilted." Sam fell asleep on the couch despite the constant ringing of the machine. Being a restless guy, Len was unaffected due to his borderline insomnia. He sat up, drank more scotch, and smoked a carton of cigarettes. He enjoyed watching me have fun on the pinball machine. The sun started to come up and I walked to the window to take in the view of Atlantic City from the 32nd floor. As I looked down on the beach from our window, I could see a homeless man laying face down in the snow. This was an extraordinarily strange sight from atop the penthouse. Nonetheless, this image of a poor homeless guy hit me! There's something wrong with this picture! I was totally out of sorts. Here I was, involved in this all night gambling splurge while this other reality was happening only several feet from the casino. I called Leonard's attention to the window and had him look down to see the man in the snow.

"Len, look down here on the beach. Look at this poor soul," I said.

Len walked over to the window and looked down.

"We up here in the penthouse and he's face down in the snow… doesn't seem right now does it?" I asked.

My conscience always made Leonard uncomfortable. In fact, Leonard could get infuriated with me whenever I brought his attention to the real world. He thought that I was too much of a softie and that I had a "savior" complex.

"You love to spoil my fun, don't you?" he chastised. "For Christ's sake, if you feel so bad, why don't you go down and sleep with him?"

"Maybe I will," I shot back.

Next Leonard took out a wad of cash from his pocket. He instructed our limo driver, Johnny Fitch, to "take this goddamn money down to that guy on the beach, wake him up, hand it to him, and get this goddamn Murray off my back!"

Johnny complied, took the money and got on the elevator and went down to the beach. We looked out the window as John walked out to the guy. He shook the guy, woke him up, and gave him a $100 bill. The guy stood up, hugged John, took the money and then ran off. As you can see, Len had a huge heart. No matter what the situation, Len always shared the wealth. Sometimes he did so willingly, sometimes reluctantly.

Afterwards he said to me, "You know, if we stay over another night, guess what? He'll be back there tomorrow, same spot, same situation. You just can't fix everything, Jimmy. And for God's sake I wish you'd stop trying, especially when you're around me."

But, that's my nature. I always wanted to try to right wrongs and even today, that's still my nature. I'm an optimist. I think I can fix everything. We did stay one more night. Len had another lucky night at the casino. He played $10,000 a hand with a private dealer. Yes, you read that correctly...$10,000 a hand! I don't know where you come from but from where I come from, they call that a serious addiction. I tried with all my energy to rouse him away from the table but as he continued to win, he anchored himself to the table. I couldn't pry him away with a crowbar. At the end of the evening we left the casino again. We went back to the penthouse. Sure enough, the next day, we looked down on the beach, and just as Len predicted, the homeless guy was back on the beach. However, the second night there was a second guy laying face down as well. Len belly laughed.

"Didn't I tell you? Of course I did!" he shouted. But, then he quieted down and he became a bit philosophical saying, "It's a good thing that two people had a good time with my money. Don't you think? I hope they did anyway."

We left the snowbound excursion $200,000 in the black. That was one of the few trips, if not the only one, that we ever took a bite out of the casinos. And, we took hundreds of trips. This trip was so good that we were able to pay off a nice chunk of Leonard's marker at the Sands Casino. We (Leonard) owed the Sands a million and some change. Most of our trips ended with us leaving with time stamped slips that recorded the money we borrowed. But on the way home that day, we stopped at the Sands and surprised the Sands management with a payment. Esther Sylvester, the General Counsel for the Sands, gladly brought two professional counters into her office while Len had me stack several piles of hundreds on her desk. I watched these guy quickly flip through the piles. I thought to myself, this was more money than my father had made throughout his whole life. If Leonard gave me anything, he sure as heck gave me perspective.

≈

On the way out of Atlantic City, Len was high from his great card playing fortune. He said to Sam and me, "Hey, I want to do something for you guys!"

Sam was driving when Len instructed him to pull over to a Chrysler dealership. Like a stern schoolteacher Len said, "Pick out a car, both of you."

I laughed and said, "Yeah, sure."

Len insisted, "No, get a convertible."

"What?"

He said, "I want you two guys to each get a car."

"I was happy with the suit," I quipped.

Even though Len's winnings were burning a hole in his pocket, I knew that we had huge financial problems back at the Eagles' office. Sam didn't know the details of Leonard situation and so he gladly obliged hopping into the convertible Len picked out for him. Leonard paid cash for the car and Sam drove that car for years, in fact until his death. This was a stereotypical Leonard move. But it was one highlight among too many lowlights.

ॐ

Back in Philadelphia, the banks were closing in on us due to Len's gambling issues. We were constantly strapped for cash and soon we were back on a fairly consistent losing streak with the casinos. Len's habit of ignoring reality continued but every once in a while, a light bulb would go off in his head. The light bulb flickered and said, "Hey, I'm carelessly blowing my family fortune." Sadly though, Len never followed up on that first idea with a second thought like, "maybe I ought to stop gambling!" Len's solution was always that there was a bigger prize waiting just around the bend. The gambler's dream.

One day he said to me, "Get in the car, we're going down to AC."

"No!" I said.

"Yes," he barked. "We're going to visit Steve Wynn and sell him a stadium box."

A young Steve Wynn was and still is today, a very sharp, bright guy. Len had the idea that we could sell him a box in centerfield in Veterans Stadium for the unheard of sum of $2,000,000. We needed the cash desperately but Len had overlooked one small detail. We didn't own that box or any other one for that matter. The banks owned everything. We had no assets. I told Leonard that he wasn't going to Atlantic City but that I would go call on Steve Wynn, which I did. Len backed off and let me go. I remember going into Wynn's office and he greeted me like I was a long lost friend. He was a warm, friendly guy just like in his television commercials. After I introduced myself as Leonard Tose's representative, Wynn said, "I don't know your owner but I love him. He's exactly what my father was, a compulsive gambler!"

Wynn went on to give me a brief history of his family and told me that when his father died, he owed $168,000 in gambling debts. The young Steve Wynn went on to pay off every cent of the debt he inherited from his dad. He then said to me, "I don't want Len Tose in my casino but I'd love to meet him."

He concluded our meeting by telling me, "I'm the only casino owner who supports the Institute for Pathological Gambling." Then he handed me a card with the name of a Dr. Robert Custer. Custer was a doctor in Washington, D.C. As I left, he said he'd give me a half million for a block of seats at all of the Eagles games. Later, Sam Procopio broke the news to Leonard that we didn't get the two million.

Leonard screamed when he heard the news. "I'll never step into that son of bitch's casino again," he said slamming his fist on his desk, along with a long string of nouns not suitable for family reading. I laughed out loud thinking how ridiculous and out of touch Leonard's thinking had become. He actually believed Wynn would miss his casino business. From that moment forward, he hated Wynn with a passion and he never even met him.

Even though it may have seemed that I was aiding and abetting Leonard's demise, I was actively trying to man the lifeboats on the Titanic's deck. I had this dear friend, Walter "Corky" Devlin, who also had similar issues with the sauce and gambling. Corky had been the first round pick of the NBA Philadelphia Warriors in 1954. He was a big, talented guard who in a few games actually beat up on the legendary Bob Cousy. But Corky's vices got the better of him, too. His drinking and gambling eventually led him to attempt suicide. Through my relationship and interaction with Corky and his problems, I had remembered that he was helped by a psychiatrist also from Washington, D.C. It turned out that the same Dr. Custer that Steve Wynn had recommended had helped Corky as well. Immediately, I hopped on a train to D.C. where I became familiar with

Custer's storefront counseling office called the "Institute for Pathological Gambling." There were two terrific doctors who staffed the Institute. Custer and his partner Dr. Garr. Custer had brought Corky back from the brink of self-destruction. Literally, Dr. Custer brought Corky back from the edge of a bridge moments before he was going to jump. Then he was able to help him find sobriety. I explained to Custer my motives for helping Leonard. Custer promised me at the conclusion of our meeting that "we're going to send someone up to see your friend." Corky showed up at our offices on Christmas Eve at my asking. Corky thought he was there to help one of our players. By this time, we were in critical financial trouble and there was no sign of Len curbing his gambling. Day by day, he lost more control. I made a decision that I knew would likely cost me my job. I confronted Leonard and tried to get him to put a seat belt on his appetites. There was no way Len was going to receive or appreciate any overture from me. To him, I had no business entering his personal space, despite the fact that his ship was sinking. As they say, he was not in the place where he needed to be to begin the healing. He was not in the least receptive to my helping attitude or message. He had no intention of looking in the mirror or within himself. He was never an introspective person and he was not about to start. And conquering addiction is all about introspection. I don't drink but it was clear that Len had to start understanding that he had dug a large hole for himself. He was personally drowning and so were the rest of us with the franchise. I explained to Corky that I had reservations about confronting Leonard. Corky told me that if I was really Leonard's friend, it was crucial that I take some kind of action. Meanwhile back at the ranch, I was juggling bank loans and keeping a few inquisitive bankers at arm's length. One morning two young bank officers resembling Ken and Barbie showed up in my office. They expressed their concern.

"Does Mr. Tose gamble heavily?" Ken asked.

I didn't entirely lie when I said, "Occasionally."

Next Dr. Custer himself, came to Philadelphia to meet Leonard. Custer had held a large psychiatric position in the Veterans Administration and he had written a definitive medical textbook on compulsive gambling. I was sure he could make a breakthrough with Leonard as he had with Corky. I asked Custer that if it were possible, could he meet Leonard alone and leave me out of the conversation. I explained to Custer that Leonard hung out regularly in a Philadelphia bar and that might be the best place to confront him. At the same time I told Leonard there was a possibility that someone might talk to him about "some things." Custer went to the bar and met Leonard.

The next day, I met with Custer to get the play by play report.

Custer began, "It didn't go well."

"No?"I asked.

He then explained, "I met your guy, just where you told me he would be. Jimmy, I've been in this business a long, long time. I've heard every line, and I've seen it all. Then, I met your guy. He was magnificently dressed. Leonard had a scotch in one hand and a cigarette in the other. I introduced myself as Dr. Custer. Leonard looked me straight in the eye and asked, 'Yeah, so what the hell are you here for?' Then I told him, 'People are concerned about your compulsive gambling.'

Then Len delivered the punch line of all punch lines. Leonard said with a straight face,

"Compulsive gambling? Hell, I gave up drinking and smoking, what makes you think I can't give up gambling?"

Leonard stumped the veteran addiction expert, Dr. Custer.

Custer, exasperated, next said to me, "Like I said, I've been in this business all my life. I know more about compulsive gambling than anyone in the country. I wrote the book for God's sake. And your friend? Well, he needs a boatload of shrinks!"

☙

Over the next few days, Leonard said little to me. The meeting between Custer and Leonard signaled the beginning of the unwinding of our relationship. I had broken a sacred boundary and it would cost me significantly. Soon after, Len's gambling just got worse and then the banks started calling in all of our loans. I was called into the NFL League Office and our house of cards fell quickly. Next, Leonard fired me without telling me to my face. I read about it in the morning edition of the paper. It was the toughest day of my life. Not because I had lost the job. I knew I would find another one. But, the rift between us and the finality of our relationship was very painful. Despite our ups and downs, Len was like a brother to me. When you're close to a brother, you give your all to the relationship. And, a breakup between close friends hurts every part of your being.

Len and I had ridden to the top of the wave for quite a spell. Then, we crashed, burned, and hit rock bottom. I became a statistic of one.

≈§

Afterwards, I had to fight in court for the rest my contract. I never had to go to court for a personal matter but here I was sitting in a room with my former close friend where we reenacted the "Gunfight at the OK Corral." Previously, I had been given a small percentage ownership in the team but there was no money left in the franchise. Even if there were, Leonard had cut me at the knees. The saddest part of the end was that we no longer talked. It was like one of us had died. I wouldn't say I became depressed but I can only describe my feelings at the time as very, very sad. A year or so later, Leonard was forced to sell the Eagles in a fire sale to Norman Braman. Braman was a successful car dealer from Florida. Leonard declared bankruptcy and then he suddenly found himself alone and isolated. The thousands and thousands of people that he had helped for those many years suddenly were nowhere to be found. We didn't talk for a long, long time. One day, we met accidentally at a mutual friend's wake. He ignored me while he stood in line. That really got to me.

I walked over to him and said, "Yo, we're both going die like this guy one day. I don't want to go to your funeral and wish that I had talked things out with you."

That broke the ice. The thaw between us began. We reconnected several times after that. Len could never bring himself to say he was sorry and we never did recapture our former closeness, but I was there when he died. One of his last days of his life while he lay in Jefferson Hospital, I caught a look from him. Call me corny but I felt God was in the room. Through our silence, we spoke volumes. We said a lot without saying a thing. It seemed like we both got it at the same time, non-verbal cues so to speak.

I told Leonard, "I love you." He died shortly thereafter.

Leonard Tose, Playboy of the Western World, Philadelphia and suburbs. He had one addiction above all others. He was generous. And, I was lucky to be his altar boy. If allowed, I would have carved this epitaph on his grave, "Leonard Tose: He never turned anyone down." Throughout our years together, letters would come from all over the world and Len's response was always, "Send them a check." Just a few days ago while I was thinking of him for this book, someone recognized me and then relayed a story about Len. This man was down and out at one point in time and had sent a note to Len. In his note he talked about not having money to buy his son a birthday present. Len personally sent him season tickets and a note that said, "I hope your son enjoys football." Leonard was a truck driver at heart. I used to call him the "purple-collared Jew." That's a blue collar guy with really good shoes! There would have never been a Ronald McDonald House without Leonard Tose. Though he hurt me when he unceremoniously fired me and he got to my Irish core, I loved him dearly. To this day, when I think of Len, I smile and I let a tear run down my cheek.

CHAPTER 12

My Vocation Realized

"Cry. Forgive. Learn. Move on. Let your tears water the seeds of your future happiness."

— STEVE MARABOLI

Sometimes the grass looks greener and sometimes it turns out to be AstroTurf. In other words, things are not always what they appear to be. And sometimes when life throws you the toughest curveball, and your eyesight is poor, hopelessness produces some very dark clouds. I was used as an instrument to build the first Ronald McDonald House because circumstances helped me recognize a need that was obvious. Here I was, at the pinnacle of my working career in professional sports and then suddenly, I was pushed overboard by Leonard and the sinking ship called the Philadelphia Eagles. Initially, I was in shock. Not just about the loss of the job, but the loss of my friendship with Leonard. As I mentioned, we were buddies, friends, brothers. Fortunately, as I was treading water, I was quickly rescued by the good ship, the HMS McDonald. Leaving the greatest job I ever had, in the way that I did, was shocking. I can't lie, it was extremely depressing. Even for an optimist like myself, it was a deep fall and one that I wasn't ready for, or quick to recover from. Luckily for me, my years with the Eagles were paralleled with my involvement with the rapidly expanding charity called the Ronald McDonald House. Being out of sports for the first time in my adult life had a big downside. But, the huge upside was that I was able to give all of my time to what I discovered was my real passion and my true vocation. I was able to devote myself fully to the expansion of this beautiful concept of helping families in need, who were battling the dreaded cancer. It was God's timing not mine. This tiny idea that began in Philadelphia was about to grow exponentially throughout the United States and then, the world. I was able to use my contacts to make inroads in every NFL city. There is now a Ronald McDonald House associated with each and every NFL franchise. In 2012, we opened a new house in Charlotte, North Carolina with the support of the Carolina Panthers. Isn't that amazing? Every team in the NFL—32 teams—have an affiliated house and a group of players and executives who made it happen. That's what I call the power of sport for good!

In 2011, I was in Pittsburgh for the opening of their new house. Actually, it was a new house that replaced the original house, and it is three times the size of the first one. The great thing about the Ronald McDonald Houses is that each house develops its own identity depending on the geography and culture of the location. In the case of the Pittsburgh house, it was built as an addition to an elder-care facility for nuns, which in turn was located on the grounds of the local hospital. So, not only did they triple the size of the original house, they made it easier for the parents of the children visiting to be on the same grounds as the hospital. A perfect fit! I have two specific memories of the Pittsburgh opening. First, the Pittsburgh Steelers' quarterback Ben Roethlisberger made an appearance despite having just lost a big game to Cincinnati. In addition, he was banged up pretty bad in a game that had playoff implications. As a former General Manager, I was impressed that he showed up under these circumstances. He had had a bad run of off-the-field incidents where his reputation was sullied quite significantly. But here he was, at the opening, and there couldn't have been a nicer guy than Ben. It wasn't just one of those quick appearances and then off to another commitment. "Big Ben" stayed and spent quality time with each and every child and their families. He not only signed autographs but he asked questions about their situations. Again, the Ronald McDonald House brings out the best in everyone.

As if I needed more to fuel my love for the concept, I met an old friend of mine by the name of Joe Gordon at the same opening. Joe was on the Board of Directors for the house and he informed me, "Murr, guess what? We still meet in the Steelers' offices." That fact made my heart sing! The mustard seed that we planted in Philadelphia had mushroomed into a national movement. That never stops amazing me. But, the fact that the Board of Directors still meets in the Steelers' office, the "shrine of the Rooney family," proves the power of the idea. The connections between the teams and the houses are not superficial but go deep within the NFL organizations. The Rooney family is an NFL legend. In particular, Art Rooney Sr. was one of the greatest men I have ever met. Mr. Rooney was a real character—a throwback guy who was as decent a human being as anyone could know. The family is very much like my own, Irish Catholics. They're gracious, generous, and patient and they have been this way throughout the team's history. The Steelers lost consistently for forty years and though today the team is known for Super Bowl prosperity, it wasn't always that way. Win or lose, the Rooneys always gained respect from the entire NFL for their class behavior and loyalty. One time I brought my friend, Jim Delagatti to meet Art Rooney Sr.

Jim had created the "Big Mac" and when I introduced them, I said, "Mr. Rooney, meet Jim Delligatti! He founded the Big Mac."

Art Rooney and his son, Dan Rooney.
Art Rooney said "Yes" to picking Terry Bradshaw #1 (see blackboard),
but Dan also said "Yes" to sponsoring the RMH in Pittsburgh...two great moves!

Mr. Rooney responded, "Jimmy, I own the team and Jim has the box next to mine and it's twice the size of mine. So everyone knows what's important, food over football!"

Mr. Rooney and Jim epitomized the great people I met on my Ronald McDonald House journey because they are/were both understated in their success. Neither man needed attention showered on him. Each was just a solid citizen doing good works every chance they got. Opening the second Pittsburgh house brought me full circle back to my first experience. Pittsburgh, like Philadelphia, like Chicago, and like many other cities since, recognized a need, brought a huge community effort to bear, not just to fix a problem, but to relieve the suffering of others. Again, it's a beautiful thing to witness the power of good when it is in full bloom.

After I left the Eagles, I was on defense financially. As anyone knows when they get the sudden pink slip, your life gets turned upside down. I had a family and I didn't have much in the way of security. On top of that, I was frozen out of my one percent ownership of the team. When you are fired from a professional sports team, there is no severance, buy out, or parting compensation. It put me in a bad way. The truth is, I've never been good with my own money. For most of my career, I've been good for many others but never for myself. The post-Eagle shock hurt emotionally for sure, it hurt much more financially. I wasn't exactly the Wizard of Wall Street and I had never prepared for unemployment. Soon after I was let go, a friend of mine and a McDonald's owner-operator, Frank Quinn, had the idea to start an LPGA (Ladies' Professional Golf Association) tournament. Knowing I was having a tough stretch, Frank reached out to me in two ways.

One day he said to me, "Murr, you should get a McDonald's franchise."

What? Besides the fact that I would have eaten all of the profits, I wasn't interested in getting into the food business. I didn't have the necessary capital to buy a franchise and my attraction to the McDonald's Corporation had always been strictly in terms of the Ronald McDonald Houses. Though unemployed for the first time in my married life, there was an upside. I was a free agent and I reported to no one. Even if I had the money to buy a franchise, I'm not sure I was owner material. At first, I was extremely unsettled being unemployed. I searched deep within myself and asked that very scary question, "What is it exactly that I do?" What could I tell potential employers? Today the question is framed as, "What's your skill set?" Back in those days and still today, I couldn't tell you if I have a "skill set." With all of the jobs that I previously held, the only constant was that I tried to build a family or team atmosphere wherever I went. How does that translate to a résumé? My skill set, so to speak, was making people feel good about themselves and the organization that they were part of. That's not exactly "marketable" stuff. But I believe that is extremely important in an organization. I like to think that I was a good leader. I treated everyone well and I wanted the best for every single person in the organization. Even today, that's still my strongest suit. But I can't define exactly what I do. I had my own company which I called "Trinity International." People would ask, "Why do you call it Trinity International?" and

I'd say, "Because it's a mystery!" I don't know, nor does anyone else, what it is I do!

ॐ

Since its inception, I have always worked on the Ronald McDonald House project. Since leaving the Eagles, I have traveled the world over, witnessing the power of prayer and God's spirit. When it comes to the success of the "Ronald Houses" all credit goes to God. However, there is one aspect of the Ronald McDonald House concept for which I would like to claim personal credit. Soon after we opened the second house in Chicago, I pushed for the idea that each house is an individual entity and should be treated as such. I didn't feel the idea should be corporatized with layers and layers of bureaucracy. I envisioned each house as its own parish or neighborhood, exactly like the place I came from. That's the Philadelphia boy coming out in me. I felt and still feel strongly that each house in every city reflect the local character and values of the particular city's inhabitants. I was the first President of the Ronald McDonald House Advisory Board. We enjoyed great corporate support and McDonald's ruling structure gave great leeway to develop independently. We met regularly in the board room of McDonald's headquarters, with lumpy me at the helm. I had no portfolio and no qualifications for the job. I brought nothing to the table but a pure heart and a love for the work of the houses. We had so many wonderful people involved at the time that it morphed into the International Advisory Board and more houses took root.

ॐ

After the second house opened in Chicago, right in the corporate headquarters backyard, McDonald's President Ed Rensi embraced the idea with full force. Ed put the full energy of McDonald's Corporation behind the idea and only a mega-corporation could have pulled off the expansion that would eventually take place. For the first few years after I left football, I was on the road constantly for the cause. I was too busy to feel bad about being out of football. My wife, Dianne, became a widow to my new calling. Taking the Ronald McDonald Houses national and international was a high-demand, full-time endeavor. We had to shop for prospective locations, and then organize the local operators. Closing deals gave me two hundred years of experience every twelve months. I traveled and talked

Ed Rensi, President of McDonalds Corporation and huge supporter of both Ronald McDonald Houses and the LPGA

all over the country, much like St. Paul did in Syria, but without the horse. And, lucky for me, the good folks of McDonalds kept me around and their consulting fee helped keep me in the game and on my feet.

⧉

Today, I'll stop sometimes where we built the first house at 4230 Spruce Street in Philadelphia. I still see the image of Len Tose, Bill Bergey, Harold Carmichael, Tom Brookshier, Audrey Evans, Ed Rensi and John Canuso. I can vividly see all of the original folks from the first house standing on the front porch. I love reliving the initial days of the first house and, though the house is now the Lubbovich House, I'm pushing to make it a National Historic Landmark. I admit I may be a bit obsessed, but I believe the Ronald McDonald House is a national treasure and should be honored as such. Particularly, I love the fact that the first house was born in Philadelphia. I'm Philly through and through. When I go to see the Liberty Bell or Independence Hall, I make comparisons to the Ronald Houses. One time I took my daughter Amy for a carriage ride around Olde City Philadelphia. I had the image of the ordinary people who founded this great country of ours. Farmers, printers, and kite flyers. The men who drew up our Constitution created the basis for so many other democracies that have sprung up around the world. That's extraordinary! And, when I look at the 300+ Ronald McDonald Houses, as different as they are, they all share one core value, "How can we help somebody in need?" The second great revolutionary idea born in the City of Brotherly Love! Though our sports fans take a beating in the national media, no one can argue with the origin of a great Philly idea.

A simple notion of putting parents of sick children together to share a meal and some accommodations is as powerful in its simplicity as democracy's "one-man, one-vote." Maybe I'm stretching a comparison but the fact remains, the original Ronald McDonald House concept remains today a giant step for mankind.

ॐ

Frank Quinn, bless his heart, got me involved in the McDonald's LPGA tournament. Working on the tournament was like working for the third secret of Fatima. Ladies' golf was about as publicized at the time as Mary's appearance to the three small children in Portugal. It was a great challenge, not only to tell people how great

Herb Lotman, Ed Rensi, Jim Murray, and CBS broadcaster Pat Summerall July 17, 1983 McDonalds L.P.G.A. Kids Classic check for $500,000 to the Ronald McDonald Houses

the sport was, but to be present during the seminal years before it exploded nationally. Herbie Lotman, who was a butcher turned McDonald's supplier, and Frank Quinn initially came up with the idea that we could raise money for the Houses through women's golf. Herbie, one of the truly great characters I've known in my life, was from a small meat purveyor in a little borough outside of Philadelphia named Folcroft. He grew into the biggest meat supplier in the world, all with just a handshake. Sadly, Herbie recently passed. He was one my best friends and I miss him terribly. Herbie could have easily negotiated a nuclear disarmament treaty with the Russians and sealed it with just a handshake. Herbie's first inclination was to host an LPGA event for charity. He hooked up with Frank Quinn and then the they called me. I was not a golfer and I didn't know much about men's or women's golf and I didn't have the time to learn. As an aside, I will tell you this. I have been around a lot of athletes in my lifetime but the women of the LPGA are some of the best athletes in the world. As people, the women golfers were even better. What started as phone call from Herbie and Frank turned into a 29-year job for me. I remember Herbie's initial attempt to broker a deal with the LPGA commissioner. Then he had to get CBS to televise the local Philadelphia event. The commissioner was pessimistic about the prospects of a tournament in Philly. He couldn't envision it being successful.

"I'm the commissioner," he said, "and I know you're going to lose $300 grand, that's just the facts of women's golf."

Herbie replied to his skepticism with a wry, "We'll just see about that."

❧

For the first 6 years, we held the tournament at the White Manor Country Club. We made $300,000 annually for each tournament. After that, we moved the event to the DuPont Club in Delaware and then after another eight years, we moved it again to Bulle Rock in Maryland. All told, over the years we made $47 million for the Ronald McDonald Charities. That is an out-of-this-world figure for a sport that wasn't known or promoted. Certainly, we would never be in the same sphere as the Super Bowl or the Final Four, but $47 million is a lot of cash. Once again, the McDonald's infrastructure, Frank Quinn, and Herbie "the handshake guy" conspired to succeed where angels feared to tread. Herbie was a true genius. He hired the right people and he always led by example. Everyone associated with the tournament, including the McDonald's executives, rolled up their sleeves with the hundreds of volunteers to make each tournament successful. I remember the very first year. The legendary Betsy Rawls showed up to string up the boundary ropes. Betsy won 55 tournaments in her career and had career winnings of $302,664. That would be equivalent to one purse today. Regardless of her being the tour's big star at the time, she pitched in like the rest of us to get the idea off the ground. The McDonald's tourney did so much to grow women's golf and the LPGA Championship ultimately grew out of our humble little beginning. Later, we became an international event. I was a marketing guy from the start and it was a great platform for me to rediscover my creative juices. It fed my sports appetite as well as anything I had done previously. I loved looking for angles to promote a sport which no one knew or cared about.

୨୫

I have to brag about one unforgettable stroke of genius that came to me. In the annals of sports marketing, I think this may be one of the most original ideas of all time. While helping to get the tournament off the ground, I came up with one crazy promotional idea. Laura Davies, a tremendous player and a wonderful woman, was at the center of my plan. Davies should be in the LPGA Hall of Fame, but for some crazy reason she hasn't yet made it in. Seems that there are some convoluted rules set by the LPGA that have kept her out, much to everyone's chagrin. If you've ever seen Laura Davies, you can tell just by looking at her that she can hit the ball a country mile...and there lay the secret of my genius scheme! I came up with the idea that we would try to break the Guinness Book record for the longest drive. I had Laura Davies hitting a driver but how could she break the record? The Guinness Book record for longest drive was 515 yards by Mike Austin in 1974. You might be asking yourself, as did everyone else at the time, how could Laura Davies drive a golf ball that far? Not to be sexist, but aren't all of the long drive records held by men? Rsemember what they say in the real estate business, "location, location, location!" I asked the question, "Do we have to have Laura hit a ball on a golf course to get the record?" I followed with, "What if we took Laura Davies to the Philadelphia International Airport and let her hit a ball down a runway?" Who said anything about hitting on grass? I figured that if Laura smacked a ball with a driver and it hit the runway, we could establish a 500-yard drive. And, if I could pull that off, it would be one of the great marketing stunts of all time. I'd be right up there with famed Bill Veeck, my old pal from Maryland.

For the stunt to succeed, I had to get the press out in big numbers. If I could do that, I would excite an entire city about a golf tournament and a sport that no one knew or cared about. There was a childhood friend of mine with the common name of John Smith. John held a fairly big job at the airport and we had kept in touch over the years. I asked John, "Do me a favor... I need a runway for an afternoon." Then I proceeded to tell him about the stunt.

"Are you out of your mind?" he asked.

Of course I was. But I convinced him that it would be great press for everyone, including the airport. By some miracle, John was able to pull the right strings to clear a runway for just one hour.

He nervously called me saying, "Jimmy, you got to get in, do your bit, and get the hell out of there. You are going to get one shot!"

That's all I needed, one shot. I contacted every press outlet that I could think of and explained my plan to anyone who would listen. Naturally every sports reporter in the tri-state area of Pennsylvania, Delaware, and New Jersey was instantly curious. And to make it easier for them to cover the story, I hired a bus to take all of the reporters out to the airport runway to see this historic event. It was a P.T. Barnum moment. Yes, again, God has a sense of humor! Everyone gathered near Runway 10. Davies stepped up to a tee'd ball. I was hoping for the ball to land somewhere across the Delaware River into South Jersey. What I hadn't figured on was Davies' driving style. Her unique swing put a slight glich in my plan. She habitually hit her driver with an extremely high trajectory. She was a long driver but she hit an extremely high altitude ball. I had anticipated that I needed a line drive hitter. In addition, I didn't take into consideration that runways are marked with ruts in the asphalt from impact landings of the jumbo jets. Davies took a huge swing and then hit a ball that might have easily brought rain. It was long but it was just as high. The only record that we had a chance to break was for the highest bounce by a golf ball off of asphalt. Sadly, this isn't listed in the Guinness Book. Her ball eventually did come down, but then hit a rut, and bounced a hundred feet in the air. The ball shot off sideways into a marsh. Needless to say, we didn't break any records. Oh, but what a visual! The picture of Davies hitting a golf ball on a runway at an airport went around the world. Who cared about a stupid record? Mission accomplished! Everyone knew about our tournament. Sometimes, God blesses you with failure. There was no time where this was more evident than the day of my airport idea. Afterwards, we had record crowds at the tournament all because of my nutty idea.

Another time, I had another crazy scheme where I put a million bucks on a putting green at the DuPont Country Club. I called it "Green on Green." I hired an armored Brinks truck to show up at the putting green. With the television cameras rolling I laid out a whole million bucks in cash on the practice green. Next, we took all of the big players present at the tournament and had them putt through the money. I even got the Governor of Delaware, Tom Carper, to attend and take a few putts. The McDonald's tourney reignited my old baseball marketing gene. It was like being back in the South, trying to fill minor league stadiums. I guess that after all was said and done, I did have a skill. I could come up with these insane promotional plans to publicize an event. I didn't think too much of it at the time but $47 million dollars later? I'm proud to say, I played a small role in the evolution of a tournament, that initially, no one gave it a nickel's chance at success. Both the LPGA and CBS didn't think we'd last a year. And of course, the ultimate winners were the children and families served by the Ronald McDonald House. Leonard let me go, but God made sure I landed on my feet.

Laura Davies, our mighty-hitting LPGA Champion helps to load $1 million onto the green for my "Green on Green" promo! (The armored delivery truck is seen over her shoulder.)

CHAPTER 13

Me and The King of Pop

*"The most exciting place to discover talent
is within your self."*

– ASHLEIGH BRILLIANT

Admittedly, I've been around for a long time and I've spent quite a few pages in this book dropping names from years gone by. Here's a great story about my time working with the legendary Michael Jackson on his 1984 "Victory Tour." Although Michael Jackson died in 2009, I'm confident that this is one of my biggest name drops. Since I'm an old-timer, I hope this helps me with the younger demographic. Maybe the younger readers will feel that I have some credibility because of my relationship with Michael Jackson. Few people know that Michael Jackson played one of the largest, albeit accidental roles in the history of the National Football League. Though he never played a down, Jackson influenced the NFL in a most unusual way. And I was there to witness the whole episode.

ॐ

Soon after I was let go by the Eagles, I received a call from Chuck Sullivan. Who was Chuck Sullivan? Chuck's father Bill Sr. owned the New England Patriots in the 1980s. Chuck was the Vice-President of his father's team and we had gotten to know each other during years of league meetings. In addition to working for his father, Chuck had a fairly successful legal practice after he graduated from Harvard Law School.

One day, he called me out of the blue and said, "Jimmy, I need your help and I think I can help you too. We're going to promote the Michael Jackson Victory Tour."

The Sullivan family owned Foxboro Stadium where the Jackson tour was to begin. While I was working for the Eagles, Leonard frequently had me call Chuck, since Chuck had excellent connections in the financial world. On Leonard's behalf, I often sought his counsel. Though I knew the name of the Jackson Five, I knew almost nothing about Michael Jackson. Again, this was the pre-Michael Jackson of plastic surgery and Neverland fame. Jackson was at the top of his popularity and he was about to launch a national tour with a series of shows beginning in Foxboro, Massachusetts. Unknown to me, Jackson's people approached the Sullivans about using their stadium. The Victory Tour was to mark the last time that Jackson and his four brothers would play together. Michael had begun his own solo career where he proved rather quickly, that he could move to the top of the pop world without his family hanging on his coattails. Jackson's camp planned a nationwide tour of 50 cities. Entertainment industry insiders predicted that it would be the biggest musical event in pop history. Chuck Sullivan agreed to begin the tour in Foxboro and then he applied to the local government officials for the necessary licenses and permits. Legend has it that the Foxboro Board of Selectmen refused the permits on the grounds that the concert would bring an "unknown element" to the town. Sullivan repeatedly asked the "Selectmen" for permission but he was ultimately denied clearance to hold any concerts in his stadium. Even today, people still debate what exactly the Board meant by the term "unknown element." I always figured it was either one of two things. First, it could have been a classic case of racism, since the Jacksons were African-Americans. But, then again, I would be quick to discount that theory since Jackson had a most diverse fan base. He was extremely popular with teens, both white and black. And, all of the parents and grandparents would have to escort their youngsters to the concerts. It seemed to me that every kid in the country hounded their parents to take them to a Jackson concert. The second reason suggested for the Selectmen's stonewalling was the fact that Sullivan Stadium had a reputation for having poor security during football games. Like the old Veteran's Stadium in Philadelphia, drunk, misbehaving fans were the rule, not the exception. Whatever the reason, Chuck was not going to get his way in his own stadium. Depending on whose account you want to believe, one thing was certain. Though Chuck couldn't get the dates approved in Foxboro, he managed to work his way into the role of the tour's primary promoter.

Chuck Sullivan and the Jacksons forged a loose partnership and to

this day, I still don't understand how and why. Most likely it was because Chuck and his family had sufficient capital and collateral to
bankroll the entire tour. When Chuck finally called me to be involved, the tour was slated to open in Kansas City's Arrowhead Stadium on July 4th. My conversation with Chuck was basically one
sided. With Chuck doing all of the talking, he said, "Jimmy, I need
some people like you on my team." Looking at the situation now, I
still shake my head on how I came to be involved. Chuck knew nothing of promoting concerts, particular a mega-tour like Jackson's.
Jackson's camp was equally unsuited for the job since there existed
factions, sub-factions, and a ton of family squabbles. I believe that
the Jackson camp saw some type of benefit in having an NFL insider
working with them. They believed or at least it was my impression
that they felt that Chuck's connections were going to make it easier
to score large stadium venues in NFL cities. My experience with
Chuck was that though he was a good-hearted guy, promoting a
concert tour is night-and-day different than running a football team.
To further complicate things, football people and music people come
from different planets. Their respective cultures don't easily mesh.
The Jackson camp was filled with an assortment of characters that
I had only seen in movies. Agents, musicians, and various hangers-
on made it impossible to form a unified organization. I believe
Chuck wanted me and a few other familiar faces, to protect his interests. He wasn't feeling secure about his involvement.

Chuck called me on the phone and said, "Jimmy, drive out and meet
me in Kansas City and just be there, help me get things going."

My friend Walter "Corky" Devlin, my unemployed former NBA player friend, decided to take the ride with me from Philadelphia to KC. I bought a car, a gray and red van, and christened it the "Woody Hayes," in honor of the legendary Ohio State football coach. We arrived at a hotel where there were throngs of Jackson's people housed and working. Chuck met me in the lobby, pulled me aside and said in his thick Boston accent, "Jimmy, I waaant ya ta meeeet the Raverand Aaaaal Shaaaaptin." I had never heard of Al Sharpton. He wasn't dressed like a minister so naturally I asked, "You're a reverend? What kind?" One of the unique characteristics of Philadelphia Catholics is to ask upon meeting someone, "What parish are you from?" I followed this ritual when I met Sharpton for the first time.

"Reverend Sharpton, what parish are you from?" I asked.

Without missing a beat Al Sharpton said, "Jimmy, my parish is ag-itation!"

Reverend Al was a funny, friendly guy and he and I developed a great relationship from that moment forward. What was clear though, from the first day of my arrival, was that the Tour was a modern Tower of Babel. There were more disagreements than there were at Versailles. The concert at Arrowhead did not go smoothly with both Sullivan and the Jacksons pointing fingers at one another. This distrust would continue on until the very last concert and even beyond. Security, unions, concession splits, you name it, there was a fight. There was constant bickering over every detail of every day. There were too many chiefs in the presence of too few Indians. One problem that no one planned on was the size of the stage which Jackson

At a press conference for the Michael Jackson Victory tour. This was when Michael was at the peak of his powers...imagine that, pitching a celebrity as President!

needed to perform. Since Jackson's signature talent was dancing, the stage took up a significant amount of space. This was space that we couldn't seat paying customers. We were losing about twenty-five percent of ticket sales just due to the size of the stage. Chuck was frustrated early on and it was abundantly clear to me that he was in over his head. Quickly, I understood that my role with the tour was going to duplicate my role with the Eagles. Again, I was to play the role of the "Fat Gandhi." From its inception, the tour had money and personnel problems. Also, there was no clear leadership voice for what was to happen next. Improvisation is too structured a word to describe the situation in which I found myself. The only real benefit I received from my involvement was that I insisted that throughout the tour, every kid and family from a Ronald McDonald House got into any of our concerts for free. That, I guaranteed.

ॐ

Even at the beginning of Jackson's solo career in 1984, Michael was larger than life. Friends have asked me throughout the years, "What was he really like?" I respond honestly. He and I didn't have a lot of face to face time, at least not enough for me to have an informed opinion. Surely, hindsight is 20/20 and volumes of media scrutiny have been written about him since. To me, he seemed like a very pleasant young guy. If pressed to give my real impression, I would have described him as a guy alone in the crowd. He seemed surrounded by everyone yet attached to no one. My personal five-by-five physical dimensions kept me from pursuing a dance career so I was never schooled in the finer points of choreography. I can tell you this. Michael Jackson was an AMAZING performer. A truly magical talent! He had a special gift and an energy like no other. To witness 70,000 people go insane when he "moonwalked" across the stage was something to this day, I have never forgotten. He was adored!

ॐ

I dealt with his handlers but I still had plenty of time to watch him make millions of people happy. Naturally, Michael wanted to play the nation's biggest venue, Madison Square Garden in New York City. From the moment we stepped foot in the "Big Apple," we, as a tour trying to turn a profit, were doomed. No one involved had planned or considered union negotiations before arriving in any town. Everyone, including Chuck, believed that we would arrive, set up shop, sell out the Garden, and make money. Immediately, we had big trade union problems. Chuck was trying to put out so many internal fires that he had me negotiate with the unions. Their demands were so great that we had to give in or not run the shows at all. In the end, we put on three sell-out shows but lost a ton of money because we had to overpay the unions. On the second night in New York, Chuck came running up to me, out of breath.

"Jimmy, pardon me, we need two tickets for Barbara Walters and her guest. What should I do?"

I snapped back, "Chuck, you put up $40 million dollars for the tour and you're asking me for two tickets and it's a crisis? Do you sense a problem here?"

Let me tell you, that when scalpers are outside getting a $1,000 per ticket and the boss can't find two tickets, you've got serious issues. We did end up seating the famous television reporter Barbara "Wah-Wah" Walters.

ॐ

On the last night in New York, I was sitting in what they called the "Ambience Room." This was a private celebrity perk. Many of the special guests were ushered back stage where they received the VIP treatment. For me, I got to rub elbows with the likes of Chevy Chase, Bill Murray, and Dan Akroyd. I was keenly aware that we had lost our shirts big-time in New York. We were pulling out after three shows dripping red ink. Our next stop was Knoxville, Tennessee, where we had already pre-sold out the University's stadium with 70,000 tickets. According to my calculations, Knoxville was going to be the first stop where we would make money since we weren't dealing with any city-slicker unions. While in the "Ambience Room," a security guy came in and informed me that we're not going to Knoxville. That afternoon, someone had walked into a McDonald's restaurant in Knoxville, pulled out a gun and then opened fire on the patrons, killing several people. Later police received a threat saying, "If you think San Diego was bad, come to Knoxville!" This was in reference to an earlier mass shooting in California. Chuck needed Knoxville badly to stay afloat. After New York, things began to spiral out of control quickly. As you might imagine, an already loose confederation fragments fairly quickly when the losses began to pile up. Chuck's ship was sinking faster than the S.S. Minnow. The next day we were in the lobby of the Waldorf-Astoria, when Michael walked in with a gorgeous movie star actress and young Gary Coleman, from the television sitcom, "Diff'rent Strokes." There was an entourage of about 200 people following him. Looking back on it now, Jackson was probably supporting a small state with his fame and star attraction. Distrust between the Sullivan and Jackson sides was running at peak levels. Finally, we were cleared to play Knoxville. In Knoxville, security was so tight that MJ was brought to the stadium in a Brinks truck. 70,000 screaming fans had no idea what was going on behind the scenes. Chuck lost a ton of money in Knoxville too. There were just too many contracts, too many quick hands in the pot, and Chuck's too little experience in the fast world of rock and roll.

In Philadelphia, we packed the old JFK Stadium in South Philadelphia with 100,000 fans. It was the first show where the sun peeked through Chuck's clouds. But bad luck followed Chuck like a bad penny. A huge storm came through town with very dangerous lightening, forcing the cancellation of the show. It was going to be a catastrophic loss if the concert didn't happen. As disappointment permeated the tour offices, I suggested to Chuck that we give everyone a rain check. Everyone in the office thought we should refund all of the ticket money. People said that I was crazy proposing such a "ridiculous" solution to the cancelled show. They said that I was naïve thinking that people would readily accept a rain check.

One lawyer insisted that "people want their money back now and we should just give it back to save problems later." I had a baseball background and I knew Philly and I especially knew its people. I recommended that we give the people a rescheduled event and then couple that with an interactive return policy.

My exact words were, "In a situation like this you need to give the people a place to vent and then the confidence that you're going to do everything in your power to exceed their expectations."

The fans were disappointed and they wanted immediate justice. Facility wise, we were not set up to do a massive refund for 100,000 people. But I was able to engage two old friends of mine, who were also Philly legends, Dave Zinkoff and Rich Ianelli. Dave was the great public address announcer for the Philadelphia Sixers for years and years. Dave and Richie also owned a ticket agency in the Sheraton Hotel in downtown Philadelphia. There was no such thing as the internet or instantaneous communication. We did it the old fashioned way. We set up phone lines in their office where people could call for information and they could scream and rant as well. Then we announced a new concert date for the next week. When the concert happened a week later, we only lost 120 seats. 99,880 showed up and we fully recovered in Philadelphia. For the first time on the entire tour, we finally turned a profit.

Photo by Edwin Mahan

100,000 fans watched Michael Jackson, onstage at Philadelphia's JFK Stadium, at the peak of his artisic powers...he was an AMAZING performer!

"You look like hell!" I said. "And you'd better go see a doctor."

Chuck blew me off with "after we get this L.A. deal done."

I'm no doctor but I knew that something drastic was going on with Chuck. I immediately put Chuck in a car and rushed him to Cedars-Sinai Medical Center.

I ran into the Emergency Room screaming, "See this guy right this minute!"

Fifteen minutes after I got Chuck signed in, I went to speak with him in his little emergency cubicle. "Jimmy, they think I may have already had a heart attack, so you had better call my father."

I left the hospital promising Chuck that I would secure the L.A. dates and that he had nothing to worry about. Easier said than done! By this time on the tour, the Jacksons had brought in the legendary boxing promoter Don King to manage their end of the business. At this point, everyone was at each other's throats and all I was trying to do was cut some of Chuck's losses. In L.A., the entertainment capital of the world, things were even more vicious. Now we had big Beverly Hills lawyers and agents stepping in for the Jacksons, and only me representing Chuck...seemingly unfair for Chuck. We all gathered in a conference room. If I'm not mistaken, there was even one of Frank Sinatra's lawyers present. We needed extra dates desperately and without them, Chuck would lose his entire investment. As I mentioned, Chuck had bad luck and he ended up requiring open heart surgery. Now the entire L.A. business was left up to me. At the meeting, I was introduced as the representative for both Chuck Sullivan and Leonard Tose, as if I was an actual lawyer. Luckily we were able to secure the Stadium and for a brief second things were looking up.

ℝ

It was decided at our super meeting that we would hold a huge press conference announcing the L.A. dates. The press conference was held in a downtown hotel with a big balcony overlooking the podium. Chuck was recovering from surgery so I was the lone representative for his side. I stood on the hotel balcony witnessing the entire legal and entertainment assembly. Don King finally showed up an hour late. He set the stage in classic Don King fashion by blaming the whole fiasco of the tour on Chuck. He blamed Chuck for just about everything else that was wrong with the world including the Vietnam War and several natural catastrophes. King referred to Chuck as "Charley the Tuna." We called him "the man with the hair." Somehow, King managed to declare martial law and then imposed himself as the new tour promoter. Corky Devlin and I stood listening to King until even he ran out of rant. In all my years of watching Don King, it was one of the few moments he had talked so much that he actually ran out of words. I left the room momentarily and called Chuck on the phone.

"How we doing?" he asked.

I replied, "At the moment you're responsible for all failures of the western world including the crash of the Hindenburg."

Everything came to a nightmare halt but Chuck lay in bed hoping that I could protect his interests. I called Chuck again later in the day and I had to inform him of the Don King mutiny that had taken place.

I said to Chuck, "I can handle the whole thing if you need me to. I can approach all of the tour problems in one of two ways, the Marine Corps way or the Gandhi way."

After I hung up I went back to the room where King was holding court. He spotted me as I re-entered and then he yelled, "Hey, there's Chuck's guy right there."

With that, all eyes turned towards me and the room went dead silent. I stood tall and shouted back to King, "Don, I just spoke with Chuck on the phone. I've got a message from Chuck, two words!"

With that everyone gasped thinking that I was about to utter a string of profanities. Instead I said, "Chuck said Thank you!" That was it. "Thank you" was Chuck and my concession phrase to King and the entire Jackson entourage.

Initially, Chuck became involved because the tour wanted to start in Foxboro. He got pulled into just one date and local politics suck-ered punched him. The Victory Tour turned into a colossal defeat for Chuck. It bankrupted him and his family. Reports of his losses were anywhere from $25 to $40 million. The tour grossed a total of $75 million but because of all the money grabbing, bad luck, and general mismanagement, the episode put the entire Sullivan family into bankruptcy. To make matters worse, Chuck went through a nasty divorce after the tour. The family was forced to sell the Patri-ots because of this money pit called the Victory Tour. The entire Chuck Sullivan-Michael Jackson chapter paved the way for eventual succession of ownership to Robert Kraft. Since then, the Patriots have become synonymous with a premier NFL franchise. With Super Bowls, Bill Belichick and Tom Brady, they have become one of the richest, most valuable teams in all of sports. And to think, none of it would have ever happened if not for Michael Jackson. I'm not sure that New Englanders ever sufficiently thanked Michael Jackson for inadvertently changing their football fortunes.

❦

It was reported that for years after the tour, Chuck wrote to Jackson repeatedly asking for the superstar to bail out his family financially. And as everyone knows, life can be very cruel. Jackson, too, went from the apex of the entertainment industry to a very sad death. In the end, he too went bankrupt exactly like Chuck. For me, it turned into a lesson for the ages, both in terms of business management and in terms of human relations. Sometimes, when you're close to high-stakes big money, you learn that the flip side of success is worse than not having anything at all. I came back from the whole experience having made very little money for the year I had worked. But, I was still a very rich man. I had my beautiful, faithful family.

CHAPTER 14

McMoments

"Happiness is not something ready made.
It comes from your own actions."

— 14TH DALAI LAMA

I have spent the greatest years of my life in the service of this magic
place called the Ronald McDonald House. Way back in 1974, when
Dr. Audrey Evans asked me about helping her fund her "island
rooms" and her subsequent idea that we rent a YMCA for the parents of suffering children, I said, "You need a house!" Dr. Evans, a
genius, had the foresight to create a place for families who each
shared a similar problem, children diagnosed with a fatal disease
and limited resources. Out of her very simple utterance, "Put people together that have the same problem," grew a most amazing
charity that keeps hope alive for those who might be struggling to
find some. If a young child undergoing chemotherapy, who has lost
his or her hair, sees another child experiencing the same condition,

an air of mutual support and understanding circulates. Even with the threat of fatality, parents lean on one another. Just like in my old neighborhood on the front step where we congregated. Everyone needs a place where they feel that no matter what life throws in your path, there is a blanket of love that you can count on. I have been blessed for the last forty years witnessing some of the most beautiful moments possible in the human experience. All because a feisty Welsh doctor with great intelligence, but more importantly a bottomless heart, had a revolutionary but elementary impulse to help others in need.

It is both easy and difficult for me to write about my experiences with the Ronald McDonald Houses. Easy because I've had thousands and thousands of the most intimate, wonderful experiences that still live in my heart. Even though I've been officially declared an old timer, the memories are vivid and close to the touch. Difficult because I've met so many wonderful people who have contributed so much to Dr. Evans' idea. To acknowledge the thousands of people who have helped to grow this idea would take a multivolume encyclopedia. The McDonald's Corporation is famous for adding the "Mc" in front of just about every word in the language. There are McMuffins, McRibs, McFlurries. As I sit here today, reflecting on all the years of my involvement, I'd like to share some of my great McMoments. What's a McMoment? It's a gift! It's something that finds you when you're not looking. It's God touching you on the shoulder and whispering, "Pay attention, you'll find me here."

I'll begin with just yesterday. I was walking out of the Philadelphia Ronald McDonald Houses and I ran smack into a young family walking in. The couple was from Dallas, Texas and they were pushing a three-year old in a stroller. Over one eye, the little boy was wearing a patch that immediately caught my attention. I stopped to welcome them and like I do with all families, I asked about their medical situation. The boy had neuroblastoma.

His mother explained, "He has cancer in the eye and he's being treated at the Wills Eye Hospital."

I assured them that it was one of the best eye centers in the country. What struck me was the energy and optimism exuding from the parents who stood face to face with this terrible diagnosis.

The mom then said, "I believe that the Doctor can save his eye and will save his life."

We hugged, I wished them luck, said a small prayer with them, and went off to a meeting. Throughout the meeting, I thought about this book and what I wanted to convey. This woman communicated to me in just a few minutes, the essence of my experience with the scores of families I've met through my career with the Houses. Hope! Ronald McDonald Houses give hope. AND families get hope for nothing. It's a gift from the thousands of volunteers, personnel, and supporters of the charity. This is what I've seen over and over again each and every day of my life. God gave me eyes to see this beautiful side of our humanity and I believe this is what is meant by the presence of Spirit. Here I was yesterday, in a McMoment!

God tapped me and said, "Listen, Jimmy, I'm present!"

Sometimes, I can't see through my own problems but whenever I go into a Ronald McDonald House, I have an out-of-body experience. I feel God's presence in a very real way in my life and his call to me to help my neighbor.

⁊❧

Let me tell you about a great player in this ever unfolding Ronald McDonald story and a guy who has given me many McMoments. Dr. Bill Cromie is a doctor from upstate New York. In his younger days, Bill was a naval officer, number one in his medical school class, and a surgeon at the Children's Hospital of Philadelphia. I met Bill through Dr. Evans when he was on staff at CHOP. Bill was always an innovator and a cutting edge researcher when it came to cancer treatment for kids. He was a pivotal force in the opening of the Albany, New York house. Why do I mention Bill Cromie? I speak about Bill because he represents to me the definition of a hero. I would have only met Bill because of the RMH. Hero is a word that gets tossed around a lot, but Bill is a hero in the strictest definition. What's my definition of a hero? To me, it's a person who does ordinary things for others in an extraordinary way. Bill goes a step farther and does extraordinary things in an ordinary way. He runs an oncology unit. To picture Bill, think Jimmy Cagney with a stethoscope. He's short, enthusiastic, well-organized—the last I'm not. What amazes me about Bill is that no matter what the project, be it a serious medical procedure or just painting a room in one of the houses, he attacks any task as if it's his last day on earth. As a sports guy, I love that energy. He's spent his life battling cancer as a researcher and practitioner. When we opened the second house in

Chicago, Bill was there advising and consulting on his own time and dime. Eventually Bill was part of the national and international advisory boards for the Ronald McDonald Houses. In his personal life, Bill had some tough pitches thrown his way. He lost his son, Jack, so he knows well the issues of the people he serves. Never distant, always present, sincere, Bill is a guy you could meet for thirty seconds and feel that you have known for thirty years. Recently Bill was diagnosed with cancer. He went to the Cleveland Clinic where they gave him five years to live. Recently I visited Bill in Albany and he's bursting with life. He works in a soup kitchen helping out someone every day of his life. He keeps a full schedule and still commits to the house, always putting others first. A real hero! I've watched him handle his latest setback, refusing to be beaten by a disease that he's dedicated his life to defeat. Here's a doctor who knows the score of a cancer diagnosis but still fights the fight, still lives every moment to the fullest, with a smile on his face…a most special guy I've had the privilege to know. Bill has taught me many things by his example but key to me is that Bill is always present in the present. I've found that's something we really need to work on as human beings. Be present in the present! The cell phones rings, our knees jerk, it must be urgent. Bill has shown me what's possible, what can be accomplished if we become present to God and present to one another. McMoment!

※

The guiding philosophy of the RMH as set down by Dr. Evans a long time ago is "one child, one family, one community." A great story that drives this home is the story of a family named the Taylors.

Thirty-one years ago, Mary and Rick Taylor showed up at Children's Hospital in Philadelphia with conjoined twins. Carol worked for me at the Eagles offices and if you worked for me you had to volunteer at the House. It just so happened that on that day, Carol was working the phones at the House. Rick Taylor had called the House earlier and was somehow left with the impression that only families of cancer victims were welcomed to stay at the house. After listening to Rick's situation on the phone, Carol called me and said, "I need you to come over immediately and meet this guy." I dropped what I was doing and met Rick Taylor. He was a young, good-looking 27-year old and there were two things about him that impressed me in our first few minutes of talking. First, I was stunned by the complexity of his twins' case and his detailed knowledge of what the surgeons at CHOP proposed. Second, I could feel the enormous strength emanating from a relatively new parent. He seemed to have wisdom well beyond his years. I promised that I and all of the resources of the House would be behind him through the biggest challenge in his young life. The twins Emily and Claire, though conjoined, both had their own hearts so doctors were optimistic that they could be separated. Regardless, it was to be an extremely risky and complicated operation and an extremely tough time for a young couple with their first born children. They were from a small town in Wisconsin called Portage. Here they were in the big city all alone to face this Herculean challenge. For some reason, their resolve and strength affected me to the point where I felt they needed someone to go the distance with them. I invited the Taylors to stay at my home with our family during the whole process. We opened up a steady line of communication to Mary and

Rick's families in Portage. The operation was set for June 18th and it was a typical Philadelphia summer day…hot and humid. The operation lasted all day and into the night. At 9 o'clock that evening we had a powerful thunderstorm blow through town that knocked out power. Everything in the hospital went dark. My Irish says that it was all very symbolic. It was the darkest moment, yet we were all together. The hospital generator kicked in and the operation continued. At midnight the doctors brought out Emily. She had lost a leg in the separation surgery but she was perfect just standing there, witnessing the joy of that precious scene is a sight that still plays daily in my head. Mary held Emily and then this perfect couple stood up and went to wait for Claire. And the next McMoment? It was the Super Bowl, World Series, Olympic Gold all rolled into one. At 4 a.m., the entire medical staff from the operating room pushed Claire through the doors to a waiting throng. Imagine this if you can. An operating team comprised of Protestants, Catholics, Jew, Hindus, and probably a few Atheists, came out as one pushing a gurney after performing this miraculous surgery. The last guy out of the operating room was one of the doctors and he punched the air with his fist like Rocky Balboa. What an honor it was to be there to witness this magnificence. There it was, my out-of-body experience. What was once impossible became possible. Two little girls separated physically by this amazing team, all working as one to perform this incredible feat. After staying up all night, exhausted, I told Mary and Rick that I would drive them to the Ronald McDonald House. I dropped them off and each of them hugged me and Rick said, "You're a part of our family forever." Driving up Walnut Street, I cried all the way home until the sun rose in full light. I became a part of the Taylor family and a year or so later they called and asked my wife, Dianne and myself, to be the Godparents for their newborn son, Ian. If NFL Films could do a highlight reel of my life, being part of the courage and faith of the Taylors gets top billing. Huge McMoment!

         ❦

Can I top the Taylor story? I can't. But there was a sequel to the Taylor movie. A few years later, a writer published a story in *Reader's Digest* magazine. He had read a "Dear Abby" column where a parent had written to Abby asking, "Where can I stay if my child needs medical care and I have no money?" The short version is that the writer wrote a terrific story about the RMH and the story went international (we didn't have the internet so I can't say viral). In the article the author had told of the Taylor's experience in Philadelphia. A couple in Ireland, who happened to have the same exact medical problem as the Taylors, read the article. Mary and Liam Holton had twin girls Katie and Eilish, who were also connected. Mother Mary called the Taylors in Portage for no other reason than to share experiences. The Irish twins were going through the same surgery as the Taylor girls and Mary was seeking the Taylor's advice. Soon after surgery Katie died but Eilish survived. Through some conversations with the Taylors I heard the story and I felt I needed to respond. The next thing you know, I was on a plane to Ireland, ostensibly to open a new Ronald McDonald House, but I just felt like I needed to meet them. I just wanted to let them know that I cared. I didn't know what to bring them so I bought a statue of the Blessed Mother. When I arrived at their home I found a big typical Irish family. Liam was one of 18 children so immediately I got to meet just about everyone in the town. Liam and I seemed like we had known each other in a previous life but I knew that was just God's way of working. I handed Liam the statue and quietly he asked me to get in his car. Immediately he drove me out to Katie's grave and placed the statue on it. We stood in silence for several minutes and then Liam broke the quiet with an apology. "Jim, I don't know how to tell you this but we're one of the two towns in Ireland that doesn't have a pub." I said, "Well Liam, I don't know how to tell you this, but I'm the only Irish guy in the world who doesn't drink." What possessed me to get on a plane, go three thousand miles to offer my condolences to a family I never met? Who knows, the Spirit? Later, the Holton family came to the United States for a visit. The BBC was following them and filming a documentary about their story. In a strange coincidental twist, Eilish had to be fitted for a prothesis in Wisconsin. The Taylors, the Murrays and the Holtons met up in Portage, Wisconsin. It was the perfect ending to a perfect story. The Taylors live in a converted Lutheran Church and naturally they're Green Bay Packer fans. With BBC cameras rolling, we sat close to the warm fireplace on a snowy day with one of the Taylor twins playing Christmas carols on the piano. I looked out the window and Eilish was making a snowman. I looked up to God, winked, and prayed quietly, "God, you work in amazing ways!" Forget wealth, forget riches, and forget money. The chance of these two families coming together was a zillion-to-one shot but here we were, sharing in the love God intended for us. I thought of all the people in the world who had been touched by these two families' hardships. Doctors, nurses, scrubbers, kitchen help, housekeepers, and a very portly former NFL general manager were all changed for the better. A mosaic! A Mc-Moment!

☙

There are so many beautiful stories about the Ronald McDonald House and not enough paper or time to tell them. But my statistic as a sports guy is always one. One child, one family, one community responding! Though the litany of saints involved is lengthy, I'm smiling right now just thinking about the saints I've known and walked with. No one goes through life undefeated and I have no end to the stories of how people react to the ultimate adversity. When one of us gets that word, that ourselves or someone we love is going to die, it's a Joe Frazier knockout punch. A good friend of mine Father Don Burt counseled me once saying,

"Sometimes there's nothing more that can be done and you're left with only faith. You hope there is a God and you hope He loves you enough to allow you to cope with your loved one's or your own illness."

Though we're all going to die someday, the death of a child is something that we can never reconcile. Recently, I went down to the House, which I often do, to give a tour to a senior citizen group. A guy in the crowd recognized me from my days with the Eagles. I was giving my long-winded history of the House when Susan Campbell, the House Manager arrived with a family. I finished my talk, said my goodbyes to the seniors and then stepped quietly into the background, watching Susan welcome this family. They were

Asian and spoke broken English but the father's name was Leonard, which grabbed my attention immediately. That would be fun, to see Leonard reincarnated as an Asian owner. Leonard had two perfectly, beautiful children. Their journey brought them to RMH because their little girl, Gabriella Joy, was being treated at CHOP. The two children immediately got swept away in the activity of the House, playing games with the other kids. You could tell that the parents were ecstatic at how their two children were fully enjoying the House and the other children. I found out later from Susan that Gabriella Joy was one of those cases where the odds were off the board. The Doctors had exhausted all options, nothing could be done. I was moved so deeply by the parents' response to the whole environment. They were perfect parents with perfect kids, and, exactly the picture of the phrase I love to overuse, "central casting." Both parents talked about the great care they received at CHOP and the love shown to them by RMH. I stopped in a week later to check on Gabriella Joy. She had passed on. Sadly, I have been at the Houses far too many times when a parent comes to the reception desk to turn in their key after their child has died. There's no way to sugar coat it. It's the worst time we face. But the hope lives in watching the volunteers in these ultimate moments. No matter how many times you've witnessed it, participated, hugged, no matter how good you may be with words, there are no words. I watched Gabriella's parents. I felt their gratitude for all of those who were with them on this journey, and now they were going home. Life forever changed. No, we can't change the inevitable but the volunteers are going to do their absolute best to comfort a stranger in need. A McMoment that we can all work to create!

Susan called me yesterday. They got a gift in my name from a guy named Steve. Apparently I had visited Steve a few years back and brought him an Eagles jersey. I can't remember the exact visit though his wife Leigh said I made Steve laugh. Leigh gave a generous donation to the House. It wasn't his donation that made me feel good, it was the idea that God gives all of us these incredible opportunities to witness the power of simple love. I've had more than most. This same scenario has played over and over in my life. My point is that it goes back to my parents and what they taught me. A sincere heart is God's idea. RMH is one of the pure things in life. Few things are what they seem to be. We're so cynical that we have a hard time believing in the train schedule. Yet, here is a place that deals with children going to heaven way too soon. But, the work is simple yet so profound. All of these life-changing people do nothing more than open their hearts to the love that exists inside each one of us, and they say yes to that love. You can't quantify it, but I've gazed upon the smiles of a sea of children's faces, who until the moment of their death, found smiles in a crazy fictional character named Ronald. The Taylors, the Holtons...stories that don't end. I've been up close and personal with miracles. Am I blessed? You bet I am, with McMoments!

CHAPTER 15

Celebrity McMoments

*"It's not how much we give but
how much love we put into giving."*

– MOTHER TERESA

In keeping with my spirit of name dropping, I would be remiss if I didn't tell a couple of tales about some celebrities who too, were drawn into the Ronald McDonald House mystique. During the Michael Jackson Victory Tour, I made sure that every kid from a Ronald McDonald House could get into a concert for free. We were in the Meadowlands in New Jersey for a concert where a little boy and a little girl from the New York House wanted to see Jackson perform. The Victory Tour had few rules but there was one strict one. Only Jimmy Murray could escort the McDonald's kids backstage, no one else, not even the parents. Every stadium or venue had an "Ambience Room" where celebrities would congregate, drink, and fraternize with Michael. Naturally, it was every child's wish to shake the hand of the biggest pop star in American history. The mother of the two children met me and we were to walk backstage to the Ambience Room, meet Michael, shake his hand, and get an autographed picture. The little girl, who was about 10 years old, was the shyest girl I had ever encountered. No matter what, she would not let go of her mother's hand. Even the promise of "you want to go backstage and meet Michael?" didn't faze her. She was holding on to mom like a life raft. Though it was a very strict security policy, I decided to break it. I would bring the child backstage with her mother. Of course, a zealous security guard stopped us and forbid the mother's entrance. I pulled the guard aside and apprised him of the situation. "Sorry, no exceptions," he replied. I then asked him if he had ever heard of the 17-inch rule. The 17-inch rule comes from my good friend, Father Mickey Genovese. "There's seventeen inches between the brain and the heart...when in doubt start at the heart." That little ditty actually softened up the guard and the mother and child passed into the Ambience Room. Still, her hand had a stranglehold on Mom. Into the room came the famous puppeteer, Jim Henson. He drew a hand puppet of Kermit from his coat. He sensed the little girl's shyness and immediately began playing to calm her fear. "Hey Mom, it's Kermit!" Her eyes wide opened, she let go of her mother. Henson walked her over to meet Michael and the trio joyously bonded as one. I wish I had had the chance to thank Jim Henson but I never did. Here was a big name entertainer who was not looking for a photo opportunity. Henson's heart was as pure as they come. It seemed like his whole life's work was to make the little child relax. I always loved "Sesame Street" but from that moment forward, Jim Henson became one of my all-time favorite people. I watched Sesame Street regularly from then on, with an even deeper appreciation of his diverse gifts. He knew how to translate feelings so that a minor miracle could take place. Miracles are usually small moments. But, it was one of the only highlights of the Victory Tour for me. A celebrity McMoment!

ॐ

Another great story involves the greatest basketball player of all-time, Michael Jordan (don't get mad at me Wilt Chamberlain fans…okay *one* of the greatest of all-time). We were at a charity golf tournament that Michael was hosting to support the Charlotte, North Carolina House. Michael Jordan is bigger than life itself but always finds time to help others. He has been a big RMH supporter and his golf tournament is a first-class event. This particular year, there was a dinner and an auction afterwards. I was lucky enough to sit at Michael's table. As the dinner got started, there were still two empty seats at our table. Moments into the dinner, a RMH volunteer walked two small boys to our table. Both boys were as cute as cute gets but one, Carlton, had Eddie Murphy wit. For an 8-year-old, he was funny enough to host an HBO comedy special. Michael instantly bonded with Carlton. Throughout the dinner, Carlton and Michael bantered back and forth like they were teammates in a locker room.

"Carlton, eat your peas."

"Michael, I don't tell you how to shoot a jumper so don't tell me how to eat."

After dinner the auction began. Things, particularly any Michael Jordan items, were flying off the stage fast, furious, and expensive. It was an old-fashioned North Carolina auction complete with one of those rapid-fire tobacco auctioneers. The pace was quick when a Michael Jordan autographed NBA championship ball was introduced. The auctioneer started the bidding at $500. Immediately Carlton raised his hand. The auctioneer yelled, "$500, we've got $500, do I hear…" There were no bids against Carlton and the ball was "sold to the little man in pajamas at table one." The second item was a custom set of Michael Jordan golf clubs. Bidding began at $2500. Once again Carlton raises his hand. The bidding continues with hands going up and Carlton matches every bid. He saw everyone raising hands and assumed anyone who raised a hand got a prize. Michael looked over and asked, "Hey Carlton, you got four grand?" Tears began to stream down Carlton's face when he realized that his hand raising cost money. Michael picked up Carlton, put him on his knee and just held him. No cameras catching a child bald from chemotherapy being cradled by one of the best athletes in the world. Later Jordan continued to visit for several years before Carlton left us for heaven. This was a big time NBA McMoment.

One last celebrity story before I move on involved Jayne Kennedy. Jayne was an NFL announcer, a Miss America type, and one of the most beautiful woman on the planet since Cleopatra. She was one of the first NFL female announcers and she was as nice as she was pretty. We were attending the 30th anniversary of the New York House. The New York House was unique in that it was the New York

House. It was what you would expect a New York House to be. It is the biggest and best of them all. In addition, it had a chapel and it had its own chaplain, a woman by the name of Reverend Frei. Her husband was the head of the Westminster Dog Show so the crowd for the anniversary gala was the "Who's Who" of New York society. I was late as usual, but I finally arrived at this red carpet glitzy affair. I sneaked into the foyer where a crowd was gathered. A small boy with an obvious bald head ran across the room into his grandmother's arms. Again, it was one of those joyful moments that we rarely notice but one that grabbed my attention. Just watching them interact made me begin to blubber with tears. I began bawling so I tiptoed off to the Chapel. I was to speak at the event and I always like to meditate and pray before I talk about the RMH. I usually try and remember all of the kids I've met and all of the kids I will meet. I came back to the room and a doctor from Sloan-Kettering spoke before me.

He said, "When this house opened thirty years ago, 5% of the children made it. Now we have an 85% cure rate for childhood cancer."

As he spoke the little boy looked across the room at me and our eyes met. I winked thinking of all the kids that have gone before and the thought that this boy had a better than average shot of continuing to hug his grandmother. It gave me chills. After the festivities I went over to Jayne Kennedy who was standing with my old pal, Pete Rozelle. Jayne asked that I show her around the house. We walked into the basement which was actually a Toyland to the tenth power. Again, being New York, the house playroom was like FAO Schwartz. As we watched the kids play, it was apparent that all of these kids were different. They represented cultures from all over the world, Asian, African, European, South American. Jayne watched the scene as if she was opening up a diamond on Christmas morning. "Look at this," she exclaimed. "See what's happening? This is how God wanted the world to be. Every kid regardless of where he or she comes from can talk to one another. They talk the universal language of play. Why is it that we can't talk to one another as adults but these kids get it?" Jayne took my hand and whispered, "I'm utterly humbled."

I've said too many times to count that the greatest moment in life is to watch a child sleeping. A child's sleeping face is a gift. God speaks to me when I watch a child sleep. I'm transformed like no other time. It's Michelangelo, the Louvre, and heaven all at once. So much of God's best work went into the simplicity of a sleeping child. RMH is, at its core, a spiritual experience. I believe it came from, and is sustained, by a higher power. It is as simple as kids just being kids. God's Happy Meal served to us daily.

CHAPTER 16

Some Rare Editorializing

*"You can't stop the future. You can't rewind the past.
The only way to learn the secret...is to press Play."*

— JAY ASHER

Sports is show business. And in sports, all of the rules of the Harvard Business School get violated. Every sports agent starts out with the same, "It's not about the money," to which I always replied, "No, it's about the cash." Over my life, sports have changed dramatically in scale and importance. Today, we are a nation of sports junkies. Leonard Tose bought the Eagles for $16 million. Today a bad short-stop with a .188 batting average gets that much. Recently Albert Pujols and his agent were insulted at a $192 million offer from the Anaheim Angels. Who, fifty years ago, would have predicted this? Money has changed everything as it always does. The intricacies of the salary caps, collective bargaining, free agency make sports a very technical complicated business. Every "i" needs to be dotted and every "t" crossed. The stakes are higher now because so many people are supported by and rely on our national obsession with sports.

When I was the General Manager for the Eagles, Jim Solano was the agent for at least half of our players. Jim was smart and he was present at every practice. He would buy the players their bubble gum and he understood before anyone else the importance of pampering your clients. He did their taxes, he bought their cars, and he took care of his players like family. Jim was a pre-cursor to what takes place today. The film "Jerry Maguire" did a great job documenting how crazy the football world has become. I don't think it was over-exaggerated. Sometimes I feel the pendulum has swung too far out of balance. But that might be my age talking. There have been many changes for the better. Pete Retzlaff, my old boss, organized the Players Union and it was a prophetic move on his part. Thank goodness the players have an important voice in the NFL's affairs. The revelations about sports concussions are a great example of the constant need for a counter balance to protect players. The unions have been vital in promoting player safety.

Writing this book has forced me to reminisce about the old days. It's been fun going back over the past few decades seemingly looking at greener grass. My Dad raised me and harped about the "old days" when things were "better than today" and now I tend to do the same. We tend to romanticize or inflate how good things used to be. But, sometimes our memories trick us. Sometimes our memories are like AstroTurf, things are not what we think they were. One thing is true, life was simpler. When the Eagles played in the 1950 NFL Championship, their star running back rode a trolley car to old Shibe Park. It snowed that day and the players cleaned the field with shovels. Football for the players was a second job. All professional athletes worked in the off-season. They smoked and drank and no one trained at all, never mind the 365-day programs of today. It was a different world. Mr. Rooney bought the Steelers for $2500. One thing is certain and undeniable. The old timers paid their dues. They built the foundation for today's athletes. They struggled and paved the way for the next generation to capitalize in a huge way. In other words, the athletes of my generation lived the "sorrowful mysteries" so that the athletes today could live the "glorious mysteries."

᠁

Another marker of change is guaranteed contracts. If a player got hurt in 1950, that was it. You got hurt and that was it. Nowadays, your family is taken care of to the grave. Who pays? Ultimately the fans pay. I don't want to sound like I'm bitter or pressing sour grapes but change doesn't always bring improvement. All of us know that television dominates. The Dodgers, the Clippers, and the Eagles are now billion-dollar franchises. Owners blackmail cities to build stadiums and politicians create tax breaks for billionaires to keep teams from relocating. Things are out of whack but yet there is still magic in sports. We, I, still root for the underdog. We still love to root for the guy who earns his way. We love the Vince Papale "Invincible" long shot. We are an underdog society and we don't like guys who make too much, particularly when they don't perform. The door swings both ways and the players can benefit and they can be bitten by the same process. Sports leagues today are not fair systems. That is why there is so much litigation. We need lawyers because big money and corruption have become regular fixtures. Cheating by coaches and players is well established because again, the stakes are high. I am not naïve. It wasn't perfect in my day but it wasn't as extreme as today. When I was GM, we had a marvelous tight end, Keith Krepfle. One year Keith had a string of bad games where he dropped a few easy passes. He came to my office with his contract and said, "I'm getting paid too much. I'm not earning what you're paying me." I immediately ripped up his contract and gave him a raise. I said, "Keith, this is the first and last time this will ever happen in sports." Compare that to players today who sign a contract, have a productive year and then want to renegotiate a contract that they've already signed. I'm not sure the system can survive if people can't be trusted at their word or signature.

Technology has changed sports as well. The live fan experience is getting so expensive that families have to ransom their first born to see a game. The home television experience is such a heightened one that you are no longer watching a game but you are participating in orchestrated theater. Announcers are front and center and the most minimal, mundane things are news. 24/7 sport programming has saturated our homes with detailed dissections of everything from player private lives to concession hot dog ingredients. To me, the soul of sports is a live audience. If you remove the fan, you kill the game. I think we have to be careful. Even though owners rely on television for their revenue, the live drama is still what drives the games. Sports are community events. They are a common denominator, a microcosm of life. It takes the plumber, the doctor, the lawyer, the waitress to come together to cheer for "our team." We're proud when our team wins and we grieve together when our team loses. That's important for us to remember and even more important for us to preserve. It's not that I'm against Facebook, SportsCenter, or the hundreds of other changes I've lived through, it's just that nowadays there is so much noise and distraction that we miss the simple things. Sport is not a narcotic but a medium that adds joy to our lives. Sports can make us feel better. What did the soldiers do when they took a break in Afghanistan? They watched football. I don't want to debate old school/new school values but I think it's important that we respect the past. One of my reasons for writing this book is to celebrate those who came before me. I've learned everything from my elders and I want to pay homage to them.

⧉

Without over-editorializing, I do think we, as a society need to reflect on where we've been and where we're going. Parents today are in a frenzy trying to keep up in a world of hyper-organized, commercialized kids' sports. Collectively, we need to read, think, and discuss the real purpose of sports. I've heard it a million times. *Sports are supposed to be fun.* We know that today we're living on the extreme side of the scale and that has its costs. Kids are oftentimes victims of out-of-control parents, who corrupt the kids' games treating them like the pros. What I've always tried to remember is that being part of a team is one of the great joys of being alive. Throughout my sports journey the great memories come from the friends I've made for life. Sports aren't pure and sports aren't fair. But once in awhile, a great player is discovered and the essence of the human spirit is revealed. We cling to the hope that we find in sports. Who can forget the hope we felt in the classic victory of the underdog when we watched the USA hockey team win Olympic gold in 1980...and need I mention the "Underdog" Philadelphia Eagles who won Super Bowl LII? We've seen countless examples of sport uniting political rivals for temporary moments of cooperation as happens every 4 years in World Cup soccer.

☙

I wasn't a great athlete. I wasn't a great football mind. I wasn't talented nor did I play in any memorable, important games. But sports changed my life. From stickball, through Art Mahan, through getting fired by Leonard Tose, I grew through my involvement with sports. I was changed by being part of a team. It is only a game. Did you do your best? We hear this but it doesn't always sink in. Sports bring joyful moments to all of us. They can also bring heartbreak. Ask Bill Buckner, who after making an error that cost the Boston Red Sox the World Series said, "Buried as remembered." Sometimes I feel that loyalty is missing in our world, particularly in sports. It's what have you done for me lately or else we'll show you the door.

CHAPTER 17

Everything Starts in Philly

(and how the Eagles Fly for Leukemia has helped to save the world)

PHEW. Finally, I am nearing the end of this tome. It has been a lot of fun remembering so many great people and stories and most importantly, reflecting on my blessed life. As I mentioned early on, the dash (–) is your life. My dash started with the great fortune to be born to exceptional parents who started me off on the right foot. My consistent thesis throughout this book has been, "There are no accidents," and my life proves that life is one continuous thread of events that in hindsight connect seamlessly. Another theme I like to echo is that all great things start in Philly! The Declaration of Independence, the Constitution, scrapple, cheesesteaks, hoagies, Goldenberg's Peanut Chews? Come on, that's some heady stuff. But, the greatest Philly original is the Ronald McDonald House.

ह

The exercise of writing this book forced me to relive my cherished experiences and then realize it just went too fast. A great friend of mine used to say, "It had to be great because it went so fast." And

359

it seems just yesterday that Dr. Audrey Evans asked the question, "Jimmy, do you know what life is like for families with a hospitalized child?" Her follow up was, "What if they're from out of town and they have to stay here for a week?" Our conversation about sick children and the great seeds planted by Stan Lane and Fred Hill grew into the great worldwide Ronald McDonald House network. My first exposure to the problem came when Stan Lane held a fashion show in South Jersey for his neighbors, the Hills. That event set off a chain reaction involving Leonard Tose, who by decree, deputized me to involve the Eagles organization. From that point on, I can only say that the evolution was a revolution. Rather than fighting against Britain, Philadelphians got together and fought childhood cancer...and we've been doing it in a big way ever since. Imagine the mustard seed of the first Philly house growing into more than 360 houses worldwide. That's astounding. And after all this time, the same people who were there at the beginning are still committed to the idea as if we just started yesterday.

The Eagles Fly for Leukemia is doing the same amazing work that they began in 1971. In fact, after all of these years, Stan Lane is still actively involved in the charity. Their current president Steve Kelly has led the organization for the past several years and the only way to describe their work is "consistent greatness." Steve and I became great friends over the years and I thought it would be a great idea to finish up with the amazing work going on today that continues to grow from Stan Lane's fashion show.

I had the chance to sit down with Steve recently and talk about not only the past but how this great history continues to work the same magic moving forward. Steve is a successful entrepreneur who got involved with the Eagles Fly for Leukemia (EFL) and just like most of us who get started with something worthwhile, it's an accident. According to Steve, he was invited to a few golf outings to support EFL and through this he was introduced to some of the children who benefit from the charity. One day, Steve had a similar "a-ha" moment to mine when he discovered that one of the children he had come to know at several of the golf events had passed away. For anyone, the death of a child will smack you hard in the face. Steve used the experience to further commit his time and resources to EFL by becoming the president in 2004. He is still the president and he has a vision for continued guidance of the organization to maintain their status as a "game changer" in the field of treating pediatric cancer.

When I first met Audrey Evans, the mortality rate for children with cancer was 90%. Today, Steve reported to me that the *cure rate* is around 90%. This reversal could only have happened with the commitment and dedication of thousands and thousands of bright, generous souls. One of the great stories that has come out of EFL is the incredible work of Dr. Stephan Grupp and his cutting-edge research in cancer immunotherapy. Dr. Grupp's work can only be described by me (the guy who flunked biology three times) as science fiction. What was unthinkable a mere 20 years ago, is now commonplace. Dr. Grupp treats the most difficult cases of childhood cancers through his Stem Cell Laboratory. You must have at least a Master's Degree in science just to read the titles of his research articles but the key point is that Dr. Grupp and others like him are delivering the fruits from a long line of patient farmers and growers. From what I could understand from Steve's layman's explanation to me is that Dr. Grupp built on some medical science started at the University of Pennsylvania, where a Dr. Karl June laid the foundation of an idea to use the immune system to fight cancer. This was a whole new concept from previous treatments. Dr. Grupp ran with the idea and worked on the research at Children's Hospital of Philadelphia.

"In 2007, we (EFL) bought Dr. Grupp $30,000 worth of lab mice," Steve explained. "That doesn't sound like much," Steve chuckled, "but at the time we didn't think a world class researcher should be panhandling for laboratory animals." EFL was able to help Dr. Grupp with some radical new ideas well before they were proven to work. His research continued to develop over the next several years until the first patient, Emily Whitehead was cured with this new therapy.

Emily Whitehead's story is a powerful one and it reaffirms the power of community and the idea that there are no accidents. Emily was ill in a hospital in Hershey, Pennsylvania when doctors told her parents that Emily should be taken home and placed in hospice care. The parents made one last-ditch attempt to save Emily by calling Children's Hospital of Philadelphia. She became Dr. Grupp's first patient. Barely surviving the first treatment, Emily was eventually cured of her cancer and today (2019) is a healthy teenager. "I witnessed a miracle from mice to a cure," beamed Steve. And if you connect the dots as I like to do, you begin to see that one of the pre-eminent cancer trials started in Philly with the continued thread of EFL.

Golf tournaments, car washes, local events gave Dr. Grupp his start and today there are 17 sites around the world focusing on perfecting this therapy. Miracles happening in Philly? "An acorn turning into a mighty oak," is how Steve described it to me. The very simple act of funding some mice turns into an international effort to alleviate a punishing disease.

⧉

But that's not the end of the story. The story goes on with new challenges and there's still more to do. EFL continues to be relevant, just as RMH is still relevant because there are still families that suffer from the traumatic news that their child is ill. EFL, like RMH, is there for the family as well as the patient. Steve Kelly asked me the same question that Audrey Evans posed back in 1974. "Do you know what some families go through when they get the news that their child has cancer?" Months and months, maybe years of treatment completely consume a family both emotionally and financially. "Certainly we're about the research but we can never forget the ripple effect cancer can have on the family," Steve explained. He continued, "We try and help with the mundane things that can really distract the parents from the care of their child...a rent check, a cell phone bill, insurance, any support we can offer lets them focus on what's most important...getting their child well." Again, person to person, neighbor to neighbor, like Stan Lane helping his neighbor Fred Hill. That simple person-to-person, neighbor-to-neighbor habit—begun in 1971 with Kim Hill's diagnosis—continues today.

⧉

A lot of people in a charity such as EFL might stop and congratulate themselves after 50 years of success. Steve cautioned me that you can't stop to think *"We've got this thing beat…*because *there's still so much that needs to be done."* Steve is a leader. He understands that great visions must continue to be re-visited, re-evaluted, and re-invented. Steve pointed out that the practical side of all the research and findings is that we have to make these amazing medical advances both accessible and affordable to the most people we reasonably can. It's not useful to make great discoveries that are out of reach for the average person. Steve drove home an important point, "Charities like EFL or RMH are always relevant because at their core they're here to serve anyone in need. Certainly, we'd eventually like to be out of business but until that day we still need to be concerned for our neighbor and vigilant in our service."

On the right are Fred & Fran Hill with their daughter Kim, who was a catalyst for the formation of the EAGLES FLY FOR LEUKEMIA…in turn, Leonard Tose, owner of the Philadephia Eagles, made a huge commitment to Dr. Audrey Evans of CHOP…this seed created the world's first Ronald McDonald House in Philadelphia. Here, on the steps of that house are Ronald McDonald, Jimmy Murray and Audrey Evans, M.D., cofounders of the Ronald McDonald House.

☙

From the first impulse of Stan Lane to the deep passion of Audrey Evans and Laurie Naiman to the numerous Ronald McDonald Houses, and today with the research of Steve Grupp, the thread is long and continues. And, all of it is driven by our best trait—love. Every single person that I've come into contact with through this journey has been pure in their motivation to serve the children. And this is the point of my whole life story. It started with what looked like an accident. It was! Just a random moment where Leonard Tose ordered me to get the Eagles involved. It might have died on the vine. But, it didn't! The seed grew and grew and continues to grow. Why? Because we are driven to serve each other. Because we have the capacity to feel and empathize. We can see and feel another's pain and then take an action. And when we do this as a community, miracles happen. So a miracle happened in Philly. And the miracle spread. Just like independence, just like freedom. A germ of an idea started and grew. It never stops. So as I come to an end, and I mean that literally, I can see the clubhouse from here. I've reached old age but I've never been more optimisitic in the power of good people coming together with purpose and love. To any young people reading and to old people as well, life is tough, yes, but life is great. All of us have a part to play. I hope after reading this, you are inspired to play your part well.

The stories on the following pages provide perfect illustrations of how "Sports Can Do Good for our World"

It all started in Philadelphia!

Jimmy Murray launched what will soon be a 50-year-old relationship between the NFL and Ronald McDonald House Charities. His vision is the reason that so many have a strong connection to the mission of the House, and is why I have personally been involved with Ronald McDonald House Charities in three cities during my time with the NFL, and continue to be involved in my retirement.

—TIM CONNOLLY, RETIRED NFL EXECUTIVE
KANSAS CITY CHIEFS,
JACKSONVILLE JAGUARS
& GREEN BAY PACKERS

CHAPTER 18

The NFL and
Ronald McDonald Houses

Many from the NFL—owners and players
—gave the world an enduring gift that
will forever be a source of pride,
a legacy that will endure.

We thank those Ronald McDonald Houses who were kind enough to provide stories and photographs for this chapter. Where possible, we show pictures of the original houses which were usually large, renovated "neighborhood" homes. We have generally listed club owners who were in charge when the commitments were made to support their team's local "House."

With the worldwide success of Ronald McDonald House Charities™ newer, modern facilities—which cater to larger groups of families-in-need—are being constructed in many cities. For example, in the Fall of 2018, the newest Philadephia Ronald McDonald House will have accomodations for 50+ children and their families.

#1 supported by **THE PHILADELPHIA EAGLES**
- LEONARD TOSE, OWNER

4032 SPRUCE STREET,
PHILADELPHIA, PA

The following account is excerpted from the website of the Philadelphia RMHC:

Co-Founder, Dr. Audrey Evans, was working as a pediatric oncologist at the Children's Hospital of Philadelphia and saw the need for families to have a supportive place to stay while their children were in treatment; she had a vision for a home away from home, similar to a YMCA.

At the same time, the Philadelphia Eagles were fundraising in support of player Fred and his wife Fran Hill's daughter, Kim, who was battling childhood leukemia. Thanks to Leonard Tose, then owner of the Philadelphia Eagles, the team received his undivided support to continue raising funds to help benefit local area hospitals.

Stan Lane, neighbor to the Hill family, formed Eagles Fly for Leukemia, to organize fundraising efforts to benefit Kim Hill. For over forty years, Mr. Lane has been a strong proponent for leukemia research and oncology families.

Co-Founder and then General Manager of the Philadelphia Eagles, Jimmy Murray, approached Dr. Lawrence Naiman at St. Christopher's Hospital for Children with proceeds raised by the Eagles. However, Dr. Naiman directed Jimmy to Dr. Evans; stating that she had a greater need for the proceeds.

The first proceeds from the Eagles went towards creating two positive pressure rooms at The Children's Hospital of Philadelphia and then Dr. Evans told Jimmy of her vision for a house.

Jimmy approached Don Tuckerman and Stanley Elkman of Elkman Advertising and came up with an idea that a quarter from every McDonald's Shamrock Shake sold in the Philadelphia region would go towards the purchase of a House located by Dr. Audrey Evans.

Thanks to Ed Rensi, President of the McDonald's Region. He said yes to this proposal and agreed to provide funds from the sale of Shamrock Shakes if McDonald's could name the House.

On October 15, 1974, the world's first Ronald McDonald House was born and now serves as the model for over 365 Houses in 43 countries.

Opposite Page: **The Opening of the World's First Ronald McDonald House**
Front row: Dr. Audrey Evans, Richard Wood (Chairman of CHOP and Chairman of Wawa, Inc.), Leonard Tose, Harold Carmichael (Eagles' Wide Receiver), John Canuso, Second Row: Tom Brookshier; Ray Kroc (Founder of McDonalds), Frank Rizzo (Mayor of Philadelphia) Bill Bergey (Eagles' Middle Linebacker)...the signature on the $100,000 check from Eagles Fly for Leukemia is "Leonard H. Tose"

#2 NFL-supported **THE CHICAGO BEARS**

- George Halas, Owner

Two "Opening Day" visitors, Charlie Marino, Sy Oliven[1], Dr. Edward Baum (April, 1977)

(In front of Chicago's first Ronald McDonald House in Lincoln Park)z

For more than 40 years, we have supported children and families through our Ronald McDonald House®, Ronald McDonald Family Room®, and Ronald McDonald Care Mobile® programs. Ronald McDonald House Charities of Chicagoland & Northwest Indiana® (RMHC-CNI) is an independent not-for-profit 501(c)(3) organization whose mission is to care for families of children with complex medical needs by providing comfort, compassion, and a sense of community.

Each night, we keep 153 families close to the care and resources they need because of the comfort, compassion and community at our five area Ronald McDonald Houses and three Ronald McDonald Family Rooms. Allowing families to stay close to their child in the hospital supports the child's health and well-being while saving our families hotel and food costs.

---

[1] Sy Oliven was a very special contributor to our house. Charlie Marino remembers him as follows: "His name is Sy Oliven. He was a key volunteer parent in opening the Deming Street RMH. Sy was an experienced construction expediter and was employed by Walter Heller and Company at the time. He used his many contacts in the building trades to obtain donations of labor and materials needed for the House renovation. Also, as a volunteer, Sy managed the project, and was at the House to supervise the work every day on his way to work and on his way home.

"Dr. Baum, Bill Chunowitz and I were very dependent on Sy and dozens of other parent-volunteers to get the House renovated, furnished and ready for the opening on April 28, 1977. Sy's inspiration was his daughter, Mona, who survived cancer as a child. After Sy's death, Mona donated a memorial roof tile in Sy's name at the Grand Avenue RMH."

Our Ronald McDonald Houses are located near Advocate Children's Hospital, Ann & Robert H. Lurie Children's Hospital of Chicago, Loyola University Medical Center, Northwestern Medicine Central DuPage Hospital , and UChicago Medicine Comer Children's Hospital

For Charlie Marino, the dream of a Ronald McDonald House to serve Children's Memorial Hospital began in 1975, after his daughter, Gage, was diagnosed with non-Hodgkin's lymphoma and leukemia. The Marinos' spent stressful weeks at her bedside in the intensive care unit and saw many other parents in similar situations. After Gage's recovery, the Marinos' began thinking about the need for a place where parents could find comfort and be close to their children in the hospital. The Marinos' shared their idea with Children's Memorial Hospital pediatric oncologist Dr. Edward Baum and consulted with the Philadelphia Ronald McDonald House for counsel and insight into opening a house in Chicago. In February 1976, they made a presentation to the McDonald's Owner/Operators of Chicagoland and Northwest Indiana. Compelled by the opportunity to play a vital role in helping families during their hours of greatest need, the McDonald's Owner/Operators enthusiastically joined the effort. In April 1977, the Marinos' dream was realized as the 18-room house in the Lincoln Park neighborhood opened its doors to grateful parents.

Dr. Edward Baum and Chicago Bears' owner George Halas

Jimmy Murray's account of Charlie Marino's visit to Philadelphia and their subsequent collaboration with George Halas and the Chicago Bears begins on page 206 and recounts a very memorable visit to Lincoln Park.

PITTSBURGH STEELERS
- Art Rooney, Owner

Shady Avenue, Shadyside (opened July 10, 1979)

The Pittsburgh Steelers made it happen

Joe Gordon, Public Relations Director for the Pittsburgh Steelers, attended the first meeting hosted by Jim Murray General Manager of the Philadelphia Eagles to bring the Steelers on board to help open a Pittsburgh House. The Steelers have been part of the mission since that first meeting. Joe Gordon, a founding Board Member, remained on the Board until the 2000s

Once the House was approved, Joe Gordon got several of the Steelers to help renovate it including Andy Russell, **Jack Lambert** (shown above with crowbar in hand) and **Tony Dungy** (shown below).

When this original House was in the process of being purchased, several neighbors were fighting it. Several of the founding members had to present in front of City Council to get approval to open the House. It is said that Art Rooney Sr. showed up in support of the House and the rest is history!

CINCINNATI BENGALS

- Paul Brown, Owner

Above is a photo of the original Cincinnati house, opened in 1982.

Cincinnati's Ronald McDonald House is grateful for the longstanding support provided by the Cincinnati Bengals. One of our favorite times each year is when the rookie players visit our House. Our families love to see the "gentle giants" get down on the floor and color or play. They'll do whatever it takes to make a child smile. After a long day at the hospital, it's one of the best things that can happen to a child staying at the House!

When Bengals rookies arrive at the Ronald McDonald House, they may at first be taken aback by the sight of children who are battling severe illnesses, but those emotions are soon washed away by the tender, trusting souls of children who are thrilled to have these "stars" in their midst...young men who have fought for the opportunity to experience fame and fortune are humbled and raised in spirits by these young souls...a *young rookie may find His House and a cause that brings him pride and happiness...the joy on these faces shows what you find INSIDE a Ronald McDonald House whether its exterior is grand or humble*

Our History — In 1978, a group of concerned parents, known as the Children's Oncology Parent Endeavor, met with the administration at Cincinnati Children's Hospital Medical Center to discuss the living conditions of the families whose children were hospitalized. From this group's initial meeting with Cincinnati Children's, a grassroots effort was born.

November 1982 — Cincinnati's first Children's Family House opened its doors. There were 21 rooms plus a manager's suite. Quickly, the need began to outgrow the capacity of the existing house.

November 2001 — A new Ronald McDonald House opened directly adjacent to Cincinnati Children's Hospital. The new House had 48 bedrooms, including 26 long -term suites. The House included family rooms, a common dining room, laundry facilities, playrooms, an exercise room and on-site parking.

A lot has happened since 2001 — The House expanded to 78 bedrooms in 2009, but is still full every night of the year. There is always a wait list to stay here. To support the families who need it most, the House is expanding yet again.

In January 2020, the House will expand to 177 rooms, making it the largest Ronald McDonald House in the world!

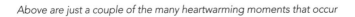

Above are just a couple of the many heartwarming moments that occur

when the Bengals rookies are in the house!

CAROLINA PANTHERS

- DAVID TEPPER, OWNER

1613 E. MOREHEAD STREET, CHARLOTTE, NC 28207

Jimmy & Dianne Murray, Ronald, Dr. Edward Baum & his wife, Ann
(this photo was Taken at the Grand Opening on May 6, 2011)

In June of 2006, the first board of directors was formed for the **Ronald McDonald House of Charlotte.** On October 1, 2006, at a Carolina Panthers game, it was announced that Charlotte would join the hundreds of cities around the world in taking the extra step to care for the families of sick children by building the first Ronald McDonald House in Charlotte. On January 27, 2010 we broke ground and in May 2011 our doors opened to serve 28 families. Our safe and caring "home-away-from-home" is conveniently located just minutes from both Hemby Children's Hospital and Levine Children's Hospital, keeping families together at the most critical times.

When Coach Ron Rivera became the head coach of the Carolina Panthers, Ron and his wife, Stephanie, were committed to philanthropy in Charlotte. Their commitment was made not only individually but on behalf of the Carolina Panthers. In February 2013, Coach and Stephanie Rivera announced their partnership with the Ronald McDonald House of Charlotte.

Coach Ron Rivera and Carsyn Pendley

Angela & Steve Nellis, Ron Rivera, Bruce & Michelle Moser

On the first Saturday of June, the Ronald McDonald House of Charlotte is the beneficiary of Coach Rivera's *Bowl-A-Palooza*. The community purchases bowling lanes and each lane has a Panther player or coach as their 5th bowler. It is a family-friendly, fun-filled Saturday of bowling with the Panthers! Everyone in attendance has a wonderful time while raising money for the Ronald McDonald House of Charlotte so we can continue to provide our families with a "home-away-from-home."

WASHINGTON REDSKINS

- EDWARD BENNETT WILLIAMS, OWNER

Opening of the Washington Ronald McDonald House

QUINCY STREET, NE
WASHINGTON, DC

The original Ronald McDonald House® of Washington, DC (RMH) on Quincy Street Northeast opened its doors in June of 1980, and was the sixteenth House to open nationwide in the six years since the program began. Thanks to the support of several organizations in the community, over the next 18 years, RMH became Ronald McDonald House Charities® of Greater Washington, D.C. (1995) and programs were expanded to include a Ronald McDonald Family Room® at Children's National Medical Center (1994) and a second Ronald McDonald House® in Northern Virginia on the campus of Inova Fairfax Hospital (1998).

One of these critical supporters was the Washington Redskins. For many years, players, coaches, wives, and The Hogettes hosted the "Rally 'Round the Redskins" event to raise money for Ronald McDonald House Charities® of Greater

Washington, D.C. (RMHCDC). Since then, RMHCDC has continued to grow by building a new Ronald McDonald House of Washington, DC, located around the corner from the first House, on 14th Street Northeast. RMHCDC has also added two additional Ronald McDonald Family Rooms to complement our partner hospitals' family-centered approach to patient care, and two

Ronald McDonald Care Mobiles®, which provide free primary health care and health education to under-insured children through more than 4,500 patient visits each year. In 2017, more than 7,785 children were served across these programs. So much of that is made possible thanks to the support of our community, including our Washington-area sports teams.

Washington Redskin, Morgan Moses, visited the Ronald McDonald Family Room with teammates to brighten the day of sick children being treated at Children's National Medical Center.

MINNESOTA VIKINGS
- Zygi, Mark & Leonard Wilf, Owners

Oak Street, Minneapolis, MN

Our first house, in 1979 — a work in progress!

Ronald McDonald House Charities, Upper Midwest (RMHC-UM) began serving families with seriously ill children on October 20, 1979. A small and determined group of parents, physicians, friends and McDonald's owner operators worked together to purchase and renovate a former boarding house near the University of Minnesota's east bank campus. On opening day, the House had room for just eight families.

Over the past 39+ years, the organization has grown considerably. We're now called Ronald McDonald House Charities, Upper Midwest and we've expanded from a single house with limited space to four locations across the Twin Cities, each of which features private overnight rooms, comfortable lounges, large kitchens, complimentary "Cooks for Kids" meals served by volunteer groups seven days a week, laundry facilities, extensive family-focused programming and more.

Ronald McDonald House – Oak Street: Our original house is now a multi-building structure that's home to 48 families every night. With one of the longest average stays of any RMHC chapter in the world, RMH-Oak Street features an on-site K-12 school to help siblings and out-patient children stay on-track academically during their months-long stays with us.

Ronald McDonald House, Children's Hospital, Minneapolis: This very busy facility located on the 3rd floor of the Children's Hospital in south Minneapolis opened in November 2010 and features 15 overnight rooms and 100-125 guests for dinner every night.

Ronald McDonald Family Room inside Gillette Children's Specialty Healthcare, St. Paul: The Family Room at Gillette opened in July 2011 to serve the needs of the pediatric trauma and disability community. It features four overnight rooms, laundry facilities, a busy Cooks for Kids meal calendar, and more.

Vikings' Chad Greenway and RMH kids at a playground dedication

Ronald McDonald Family Room inside Children's Hospital, St. Paul: Our newest facility opened in 2015 to better serve the east metro, including western Wisconsin. Like the Family Room at Gillette, it features four overnight rooms, a Cooks for Kids kitchen, etc.

In 2017, RMHC-UM served 5,466 families and provided $5.6 million worth of lodging, meals, and family-focused programming with the help of more than 5,400 volunteers who worked 61,284 hours. We enjoy close relationships with our hospital partners (University of Minnesota Masonic Children's Hospital, Children's Minnesota and Gillette Children's Specialty Healthcare) and continue to work with them to provide new and expanded programming that supports the whole family, including siblings, extended family members and other adult caregivers.

In addition, we have benefited from the support of local major league teams, including the Minnesota Vikings. Since 2009, the Vikings have generously donated tickets, suite packages, and autographed apparel, balls and equipment to our special event auctions, arranged for player visits to our facilities, and served in advisory roles on our board committees. Currently, we are closely connected to a high-profile player as well as a very popular retired player who have created youth-focused foundations to support organizations such as RMHC-UM and our hospital partners.

Vikings' Kyle Rudolph and RMH mom

ATLANTA FALCONS
- Arthur M. Blank, Owner

Atlanta's First Ronald McDonald House in 1979.

A group of volunteers joined Atlanta area McDonald's restaurant owners to create Atlanta's first Ronald McDonald House (RMH) which opened on March 11, 1979 at 792 Houston Mill Road near Children's Healthcare of Atlanta at Egleston. It was the fourth Ronald McDonald House in the world.

Originally capable of accommodating 9 families, the House was expanded in 1982 to add 3 bedrooms. In 1988, the Bovis/Brunning Company, a home builder, donated a house which was placed on the property, increasing the number of bedrooms to 17.

Because of the increased demand for its services, the Board accepted the challenge in 1994 to add a second House at 5420 Peachtree Dunwoody Road near Children's Healthcare of Atlanta at Scottish Rite. Through the efforts of many dedicated people and organizations, the 10,000 square-foot, 10-bedroom House opened debt-free. A renovation in 1999 funded by Porsche Cars North America, Inc. provided the House with an expanded dining area and 11 new bedrooms.

Between 2004 and 2005, the two Atlanta Houses turned away over 800 families in need of a "home away from home." Therefore, in 2005, Atlanta RMHC embarked on its first major capital campaign to help meet the growing needs of families now and in the future. Referred to as Phase One, the $16.2 million capital campaign funded the expansion at the location near Children's at Egleston, and for the first time, allowed the Atlanta Houses to provide immune-suppressed children with a place to stay with their families near the hospital for extended periods of time. The LEED-certified House opened in June 2008.

Over time, families were being turned away at an increasing rate, and although this House served 286 families in 2012, it had to turn away 254. That agonizing number was proof enough that a larger facility was needed near Scottish Rite to provide a warm, inviting home for families. The Atlanta RMHC Board of Directors embarked on a Phase Two to build, equip, and furnish a new 31-bedroom, three-story House to replace the 11-bedroom facility. The new silver LEED-certified[1] House on Peachtree Dunwoody Road opened in December 2015.

Falcons' players feed the children

Since opening the first Atlanta House in 1979, Atlanta RMHC has served more than 50,000 families of sick and injured children by keeping them close to each other and the specialized medical care they need to battle life-threatening illnesses or injuries. Our city's NFL franchise, the Atlanta Falcons have lent a helping hand to the families in numerous and significant ways over the years. During holidays like Halloween and Christmas, players visit and help serve meals and host parties for our children. One special Christmas, player Levine Toilolo and his wife Stephanie took all of the families on a shopping spree at Target, where they were allowed to purchase Christ-

mas gifts for their children and themselves and Levine and Stephanie paid the final bill! On another occasion, a player decided to donate all of his game tickets to families so that they could take a break from their hospital routine. The entire Atlanta Falcons organization has traditionally donated signed memorabilia and Falcons experiences to both the Atlanta RMHC Golf Classic and the Hearts & Hands Gala to benefit Atlanta RMHC each year. The Falcons owner, Arthur

Grady Jarrett & Ben Garland spend time with the chil-

M. Blank, is personally supportive of the Atlanta RMHC's mission and has provided generous event sponsorships and grant support through his Arthur M. Blank Family Foundation.

---

[1] Leadership in Energy and Environmental Design (LEED) is one of the most popular green building certification programs used worldwide.

NEW ORLEANS SAINTS
- Gayle Benson, Owner

The New Orleans RMH in 1981 as renovations began.

4403 Canal Street
New Orleans, LA

The New Orleans Ronald McDonald House opened December 10, 1983, and was the 53rd Ronald McDonald House in the country.

After the first Ronald McDonald House opened in 1974 in Philadelphia with the help of the Philadelphia Eagles and the McDonald's Corporation, other NFL teams became potent catalysts in the building of more and more houses in the teams' cities.

As the word of Ronald McDonald Houses spread, more parents' groups were formed and more Houses opened. The New Orleans Ronald McDonald House opened December 10, 1983 with the help of the New Orleans Saints.

The New Orleans House, like many of the others, began with a parents' group. They founded Children's Oncology Services of Louisiana (COSLA), a non-profit organization that initially owned and operated the House. COSLA purchased and renovated a run-down rooming house on Canal Street in the Mid-City neighborhood. It opened on December 10, 1983. The House is a beautiful, homey, 15-bedroom house with a huge kitchen and dining room, two laundry areas, a play room, and two living rooms. RMH SLA provides rooms, support, and comfort to over 500 families a year. In 2018, the New Orleans House is celebrating its 35th anniversary.

RMH took on 8 feet of water in 2005's Hurricane Katrina. This picture was taken at the house Grand Re-opening in August, 2006. Former Saint Archie Manning was the special guest for the event.

Ronald McDonald introduces the great Archie Manning

The photo to the right was taken in December, 2016 when the Saints hosted a dinner and "Meet-and-Greet" at RMH during the holidays.

New Orleans players shown here are (from left to right): Landon Turner, Tim Hightower & Brandon Coleman. Players are with RMH moms Danielle Partin & Mickenzie Reed.

JACKSONVILLE JAGUARS
- SHAHID KHAN, OWNER

THE ORIGINAL RONALD MCDONALD HOUSE OF JACKSONVILLE, JEFFERSON STREET

Jacksonville opened a 10-bedroom Ronald McDonald House across from University Hospital (now UF Health Proton Therapy Institute) in November 1988. As pediatric health care providers became more concentrated on the Southbank of Jacksonville, the need for a House with close proximity to those facilities developed. Thus our new 20-bedroom House opened in the historic San Marco community in November 2001. Our new location is centrally located near each of our five healthcare partners: Wolfson Children's Hospital, Nemours Children's Specialty Care, UF Health Proton Therapy Institute, UF Health Jacksonville and Brooks Rehabilitation. To meet the growing need of our House, we completed another expansion in 2004 adding 10 bedrooms.

In 2016, we expanded our House from 30 to 53 bedrooms to better accommodate more families of critically ill children. The $14.5 million expansion also increased common area spaces including kitchens, a large dining room, laundry facilities, play areas, a fitness room, theater room, a youth academic enrichment program called the *Kidzone Learning Center* and a peaceful rooftop garden which are extremely important to making our House feel like a "home away from home." These areas help to foster the emotional connection between families, helping us to go far beyond meeting our families' basic needs.

Ronald McDonald Family Room at Wolfson Children's Hospital
In 1993, our Ronald McDonald Family Room opened on the 5th Floor of Wolfson Children's Hospital. After being moved to the 3rd floor outside of the Pe-

diatric Intensive Care Unit, our Family Room was renovated in 2008. Following a three-month renovation project that began in November 2016, The Ronald McDonald Family Room saw upgrades and expansions to both the interior and exterior that included a rooftop garden complete with a beautiful mosaic.

Ronald McDonald House of Jacksonville & The Jacksonville Jaguars

In addition to overwhelming support from the community, Ronald McDonald House of Jacksonville has enjoyed an amazing partnership with the Jacksonville Jaguars. Since becoming Jacksonville's hometown NFL team, the Jaguars has been a long standing supporter of Ronald McDonald House of Jacksonville. Staff and players regularly visit our House, volunteering to cook meals in our kitchen, and engage in fun activities with our children and their families. They also provide game tickets and unforgettable experiences that our children and their families can enjoy. Our organization has also benefitted from having the Philadelphia Eagles visit our House as well. During the weekend of the February 6, 2005 Super Bowl hosted in

Jaguars' players visit the children

Jacksonville in which the New England Patriots faced the Philadelphia Eagles, the Eagles visited our House to play games, take photos with their mascot, "Swoop" as well as provide signed gear.

Original owners of the Jacksonville Jaguars, Wayne and Delores Barr Weaver, have served on our Advisory Board and have been dedicated financial supporters of our mission. We are very proud of our home team and cannot wait to see the Jacksonville Jaguars make it to the Super Bowl this year! Go Jags!

Jaguars' QB Blake Bortles helps in the kitchen

CLEVELAND BROWNS

- Arthur Bertram "Art" Modell[1], Owner

The original Ronald McDonald House of Cleveland

In February, 1978, pediatric oncologist Samuel Gross of Rainbow Babies and Children's Hospital met with a group of parents whose children he was treating to discuss the concept of the Ronald McDonald House. Dr. Gross learned about this concept through discussions he had with the founders of the original House in Philadelphia and a second House that had opened in Chicago. By that November, those and other key parents had organized into a working nucleus and found a potential property.

The group presented their project plan to McDonald's owners in Northeast Ohio, who gave them unanimous backing and a $150,000 pledge. Shortly thereafter, the parents formally incorporated a non-profit organization, Children's Oncology Services of Northeastern Ohio, secured a mortgage and credit line, and took title to College Motel.

In February of 1979, the Cleveland Browns pledged their support for the Ronald McDonald House project. All-pro defensive safety Thom Darden was named the first official spokesman for the Ronald McDonald House campaign, to be

---

[1] Modell was a key figure in helping promote the NFL and was initially popular in Cleveland for his active role in the community and his efforts to improve the team. However, he made controversial actions during his ownership, which included the firing of Paul Brown, the franchise's first coach and namesake. In 1995, Modell faced widespread scorn in Cleveland when he attempted to relocate the Browns to Baltimore (he did leave with all contracted players). The team is now owned by James "Jimmy" Arthur Haslam III

kicked off by a "Shamrock Shake" promotion at Mc-Donalds throughout Northeast Ohio. Thom made many appearances at McDonald's throughout the promotion and at other events to raise awareness and funds for the Ronald McDonald House.

The ribbon was cut on the Ronald McDonald House of Cleveland on September 25, 1979 with rooms to

All-Pro Thom Darden working the McDonald's drive thru to raise money for Ronald McDonald House of Cleveland during a Shamrock Shake Promotion

Thom Darden works the McDonald's counter to raise money for the Ronald McDonald House of Cleveland

host up to 25 families per night. By the early 1990s, stays at the House were in such demand that a new 37-family House was built on a 4-acre parcel of land on University Circle, our current location. In 2013, again faced with lengthy waiting lists, the House was fully renovated and a new wing was added, increasing the House to its current capacity of 55 families.

In the above photo: Ray Kroc, the Founder of McDonalds watches as Thom Darden and Ronald McDonald help to cut the ribbon with and welcome the first visitor to the House, People like Thom Darden make this country great!

BUFFALO BILLS
- RALPH WILSON[1], OWNER & FOUNDER

BUILT IN 1895, THE GRACIOUS STRUCTURE AT 780 WEST FERRY STREET
HAS BEEN THE RONALD MCDONALD HOUSE OF BUFFALO SINCE 1983

Ronald McDonald House Charities of Western New York

Our cornerstone, the Buffalo Ronald McDonald House, opened in 1983 with the single focus of "Keeping families close" by providing lodging and emotional support for families of children receiving medical treatment in Buffalo. The Ronald McDonald House was built on the simple idea that nothing else should matter when a family is focused on the health of their child – not where they can afford to stay, where they will get their next meal or where they will lay their head at night to rest.

Since that time, more than 18,000 families from Western New York and Northwestern Pennsylvania, the country and the world, have benefited from the comfort provided by our House. Children heal better when surrounded by the comforts of home and family. The Buffalo Ronald McDonald House keeps families close when they need each other the most.

---

[1] On September 9, 2014, it was announced that Terrence Pegula had placed the winning binding bid to purchase the National Football League's Buffalo Bills, a team that was placed up for sale after the death of the original owner and team founder, Ralph Wilson. Pegula was a favorite among most local Bills fans and local politicians to buy the team due to his commitment to the Western New York area and local connections. Terrence and his wife Kim are now co-owners of the Buffalo Bills of the NFL and Buffalo Sabres of the NHL.

Locally, "Sports for Good" is strong in Western New York. Through the years the various professional sports teams, players and their families have been very generous in volunteering at our house, donating goods and services, including game tickets for our families, and assisting with fundraising efforts.

We so appreciate the Buffalo Bills...and their Women's Association. Their "Cooks for Kids" participation and generous Wishlist donations are wonderful examples of this team's support for our families.

IN THE PICTURES ABOVE, CLOCKWISE FROM TOP-LEFT: Phil Hansen, defensive end for Buffalo Bills, autographs a football for Ronald McDonald House guest; our Buffalo Bills Women's Association with their very generous Wishlist and gift card donation; Phil and Dianna Hansen made the first major donation to build a new kitchen at the Ronald McDonald House; kids enjoy a Bills game with complimentary tickets..."Let's Go Bills!"; Mario Williams of the Buffalo Bills donates an XBox 1 and an autographed helmet.

CHAPTER 19

What's it all about, Alfie?

I am closing this effort to catalogue my life. I've tried very hard to capture and share some of the events that occurred throughout my priviliged life in sports. Most people only dream of landing a job with a professional sports team. I landed several, every one of them by accident. It is difficult to look back on 80 years and capture the memories completely, much harder than I imagined. I did my best recalling some of the very best things that happened. Life is funny. Just when I seem to be getting a handle on things, I wake up in the mornings, and I've become an old timer reminiscing about days gone by. I didn't think that would happen to me. Writing this book was a difficult exercise for me for many reasons. First, I'm a story-teller. I've been telling thousands of stories at thousand of banquets for the last 50 years. What should I include, what should I leave out? Do I talk about this? Do I talk about that? What is worthy of the reader's time and interest? Within my mind, I debated and argued. I've met thousands of fascinating people and I have been influenced by so many great people that I'm afraid to slight anyone by a careless omission. So let me deal with that right now. For all of you, who I may have forgotten (because I'm old and forgetful), I'm sorry! There, I apologize. I mean it. I'm sorry. I know I left some important people out. I know there are some great stories that I just plain forgot. Please, let me off the hook!

છ

Throughout my life, I often had the feeling that I was watching myself from the stands. Much of my life I recall as an out-of-body experience. As I look on, I am in every part of every story and every story is fun and exciting. Even the bad moments weren't so bad. I've been blessed to see the world from multiple vantage points. When I was starting out, I saw the world from the eyes of an average to below-average student. Next at Villanova I looked at the world as the eager Baseball Manager and then the effervescent Sports Information Director. Then I stumbled into Minor League Baseball. And ultimately, I got to my dream job, General Manager of an NFL franchise. Still, that wasn't the end of the road. Finally, I became the dedicated servant to the idea of the Ronald McDonald House. There were lots of steps along the way and a bird's eye view of life's highs and lows.

છ

All in all, I've been given the great gift of perspective. And, my Irish nature makes me sit back and take notice of the importance of the small things that we either miss or take for granted. In my quiet moments I reflect on extraordinary, growing from the ordinary.

Take professional football, for example. On the surface, it is a silly kid's game. Further analysis reveals that football is life itself. On any given Sunday in America, football affects millions of people in hundreds of ways. The players put their physical well-being on the line every time they step on the field. A player can be severely injured and lose his livelihood in a split second. Coaches also live moment to moment and their futures hang in the balance of the game being played. Fans, who have every conceivable human problem, push those problems aside for a couple of hours, and live for the outcome of every play and every game. A billion-dollar industry evolved from moving a funny shaped ball over a hundred yards. When you think about it, it's a little insane. Yet, every Sunday from September to the Super Bowl, millions of Americans live and die with their favorite team. Companies can measure profit or loss from the outcome of a football game. Productivity in a typical enterprise can swing up or down from the single act of a 150-pound kicker winning a game in the last seconds of overtime.

I got to see it all. I was there for the explosion. Football emerged from baseball's shadow to dominate the culture as our national pastime. I watched how it was put together. The planning, the mechanisms of success developed by Pete Rozelle and continued today by Roger Goodell. It is no small children's game. What it is, is a textbook on organizing people from all walks of life and moving that organization to where? Who knows? It just keeps getting bigger and bigger until what? People tire of men running into one another? We find something that better entertains us? The medical

community persuades the nation that the game is just too dangerous to support? One thing is definite. Football is big business and
it will continue as big business until for some unforeseen reason,
it is no longer good business. What has fascinated me throughout
my journey in sports is the human element in all of it. Power plays,
jealousies, good guys and bad guys. That was my job in sports, to
navigate the difficult terrain of human behavior within sports organizations. At each stop along the way, my talent was keeping
everyone together, hopefully moving forward for the better. I was
the Pope in charge of shepherding all of the collective interest and
keeping fragile coalitions together for everyone's benefit. The net
result of a General Manager's work can be seen in countless ways.
The fan in the stands (who is your real boss) cheers when his team
wins and he and his kids cry if their team loses. I was the altar boy,
the cheerleader, the hostage negotiator, who at each stage tried to
get all the pieces working together so that family on Sunday left
the stadium smiling. It was a complex task. But in the end, all that
we're looking for is joy. If you think about, all that we want as humans is a few moments of joy. When we are all pulling the oars together we get joy.

I'm not the most articulate fellow when it comes to spouting a
worldview or a working philosophy, but I have witnessed enough
human suffering and compassion to have developed one. If any of
us take our time, live long enough, learn the important values from
all of the important influences in our lives, chances are that will
get a perspective, an overview, an understanding soul. I was a dirty

faced kid from Brooklyn Street, without a lot of smarts or fancy degrees but my training exceeded anything I may have received in school. Loving parents, relatives, teachers, co-workers gave me a leg up on this thing called life. I can't put a number on it but I'd say I've batted a thousand when it comes to the best life has to offer. I've met the most extraordinary people in my life but for the most part, these extraordinary folks were simple and ordinary. The strength and faith of the scores of parents I've known through my RMH experiences have left me humbled and in awe of the power of the human spirit. Back to my philosophy. I've often compared life to the old game "Pick Up Sticks." When you move one little thing, all kinds of things can happen, both good and bad. I made one call to an ad agency about some milkshakes and God led me to the McMiracle. The Ronald McDonald Houses touch more than 20,000 people per night, which translates into more than 7 million per year. One family–one mom–one dad–one child–provided the strictest attention in a time of need. It doesn't make a life-threatening illness any easier but it makes life better when you know you don't suffer alone. The Ronald McDonald Houses make life better, and sometimes easier to understand and handle. No, we won't get all of our answers but remember, everything is connected and everything happens for a reason. I haven't got any answers but I can tell you in closing that your efforts to make the world better, make *you* better, and as Anne Frank said so succinctly,

"No one has ever become poor because of giving."

—Jim

Index

(entries in **boldface** signify photographs)